EXAMINING
Food
& Nutrition

JENNY RIDGWELL

Heinemann

Heinemann Educational Publishers
Halley Court, Jordan Hill, Oxford OX2 8EJ
a division of Reed Educational & Professional Publishing Ltd

MELBOURNE AUCKLAND FLORENCE PRAGUE
MADRID ATHENS SINGAPORE TOKYO
CHICAGO SÃO PAULO PORTSMOUTH NH (USA)
MEXICO IBADAN GABORONE JOHANNESBURG KAMPALA
NAIROBI

First published 1996

99 98 97
10 9 8 7 6 5 4 3

British Library Cataloguing in Publication Data
A catalogue record for this book is available from the British
Library

ISBN 0 435 42058 5

Designed and typeset by Gecko Ltd, Bicester, Oxon
Illustrated by Dave Mostyn, Martin Saunders and Gecko Ltd.
Cover illustration by Kiran Ahmad
Printed and bound in Spain by Mateu Cromo

Acknowledgements

The author would like to thank the following for supplying and
checking information:
the Advertising Standards Authority; Nick Boldison Smith; the
Department of Health; the Food and Drink Federation; Maura
Gibbons; Brenda Jamieson, J. Sainsbury plc; Kelloggs; Juliette
Kellow BSc SRD, Nutritionist; Leatherhead Food Research
Association; Alan Long; the Ministry of Agriculture Fisheries
and Food; Mary Nestor; SMAP; Becky Stanley; Unilever
Research; Annette Yates.

The publishers would like to thank the following for permission
to reproduce copyright material:
Advertising Standards Authority Ltd, for the logo on p. 175;
The Federation of Bakers, for the extract from The Sliced Bread
Diet on p. 69; Bender & Bender, Food Tables, Oxford University
Press, for the tables pp. 29, 46, by permission of Oxford
University Press; Chartered Institute of Environmental Health,
for the certificate on p. 157; Co-operative Retail Services, for
the label on p. 118; Crown copyright is reproduced with the
permission of the Controller of HMSO, for the extracts on pp.
8–9, 170, for graph on p. 12, for the charts on pp. 28, 35, 170,
for the tables on pp. 83, 89, 96, 98, 102, 105, 108, 171; Food
and Drink Federation, Food for our Future – Food and Biotechnology,
for extracts used as a basis for pp. 118–19; The Food Hygiene
Handbook, Highfield Publications, 'Vue Pointe', Spinney Hill,
Sprotborough, Doncaster DN5 7LY, by courtesy of Dr. D.
Roberts, Food Hygiene Laboratory, Central Public Health
Laboratory, Colindale, for the extract on p. 143 and for the
charts on p. 147; Flo Hadley, HMI, Office for Standards in
Education, for the extract on p. 4; © Health Education
Authority, for the extracts on pp. 10, 88, 96, 102, 105, 108, for
the table on p. 11, for the chart on p. 66, reproduced with

permission; Health Which? December 1992, for the extract on
p. 62 and Which? October 1991 for the table on p. 107, 2
Marylebone Road, London NW1 4DF; Kellogg's for product
packaging on which labels are based, pp. 13, 34, 36; Klinge
Chemicals, East Kilbride, for the label on p. 43: LoSalt is a
trademark of Klinge Foods Ltd; Marlow Food Ltd, for the
Quorn labels on p. 74–5; MD Foods plc, for the Lactolite label
on p. 63; Midland Examining Group, for the extracts on
pp. 186–7; National Dairy Council, for tables on pp. 45, 51,
101 and for material on p. 101; National Heart Forum for
extracts from School Meals Assessment Pack, 1995 – available
from SMAP, P.O. Box 7, London W5 2GQ, price £43.50 including
postage and packing, please make cheques payable to BSS –
on pp. 47, 80, 81; Northern Examinations and Assessment
Board, for the extracts on pp. 4, 187; Panasonic UK Ltd, for
the chart on p. 129; Peters, Fraser and Dunlop Ltd, for
material taken from Healthy Eating on a Plate, published by
Vermillion (1995) reprinted by permission of the Peters, Fraser
& Dunlop Group Ltd, on p. 109; Royal Society of Chemistry,
for data from 'The Composition of Foods', 5th edition (plus
supplements), reproduced with permission of the Royal Society
of Chemistry and Controller of HMSO, for the tables on pp. 90,
100; J. Sainsbury plc, Living Today, 'Food Hygiene', for the quiz
on p. 148; 'Packaging' for the chart on p. 165; St. Ivel Ltd, for
the labels on pp. 26–7; Tesco Stores Ltd for the tables on
p. 26, for the label on p. 79, for the symbol on p. 168; The
Vegetarian Society, Vegetarian Issues, for the table on p. 76;
Whole Earth Food Ltd, for the label on p. 91.

The publishers would like to thank the following for permission
to use photographs:
Action Plus pp. 46, 56; Steve Baxter/The Picture Library p.133;
Anthony Blake Photo Library p. 141, 151 (left); Martin Brigdale
p. 106; British Diabetic Association p. 60; British Gas p. 123;
Dr Jeremy Burgess/Science Photo Library p. 140 (bottom right
and top right); J. Allen Cash pp. 83, 105, 107, 169, 171 (both);
James Clevett p. 156; Chris Crofton/Reed International Books
p. 95; A. B. Dowsett/Science Photo Library p. 140 (bottom left);
Laurie Evans/Reed International Books pp. 130, 146, 178; Food
and Drink Federation p. 65; Richard Francis/Action Plus p. 6;
Melanie Friend/Format p. 59 (bottom), 136 (left); Peter Gould
pp. 108, 120, 128, 136 (right), 138, 149, 153, 154, 164, 165;
Melvin Grey/Reed International Books p. 104; Glyn Kirk/Action-
Plus p.55; Graham Kirk/Reed International Books p. 94; Frances
Lang p. 166; Paul McCullagh/Holt Studios p. 150 (bottom);
Meat and Livestock Commission p. 41; Merehurst/The Anthony
Blake Photo Library p. 40; Maggie Murray/Format p. 59 (top);
Ian O'Leary/Reed International Press p. 127; Ulrika Preuss/
Format p. 19; Jenny Ridgwell pp. 7, 77, 124, 151 (right); Peter
Sanders p. 76; Charlie Stebbings/Reed International Books
p. 126; Clive Streeter/Reed International Books pp. 67, 102; Van
den Bergh Foods p. 150 (top); John Walmesley p. 176.

The publishers have made every effort to trace copyright
holders. However, if any material has been incorrectly
acknowledged, we would be pleased to correct this at the
earliest opportunity.

Contents

Introduction

Home Economics: Food and Nutrition

This book focuses on the requirements made by a range of syllabuses for GCSE Home Economics: Food and Nutrition.

Home Economics involves an understanding of diet, health, food choices and food processing. It also involves knowing how to manage resources and to develop relevant, appropriate and transferable skills to meet human needs.

Definitions - Home Economics

'The food curriculum in Home Economics focuses on the production of food for immediate consumption and on the nutritional, social, economic, cultural and aesthetic requirements of people who eat it.'
Source - Flo Hadley HMI, 1995

The aims of Food and Nutrition syllabuses

- To increase students' knowledge and understanding of human needs and the interdependence of individuals and groups and the influence of social, cultural and economic factors.
- To enable students to respond effectively to rapid technological change and the use of information technology and the growth of scientific knowledge and understanding.
- To foster in students a critical and analytical approach to decision-making and problem-solving.
- To develop the knowledge and skills required for the effective organization and management of resources.

Source - NEAB Home Economics: Food and Nutrition

The written examination

The written examination will assess your ability to:
- recall and apply knowledge and understanding specified in the syllabus
- plan and carry out investigations and tasks in which you:
  - identify questions, examine evidence and issues and hypothesize
  - select and use a range of home economics skills competently
  - gather, record, collate, interpret and evaluate evidence.

The questions at the end of each topic in this book are intended to help you to practise all the skills.

Syllabus content: Home Economics: Food and Nutrition

Syllabuses for home economics may be broken down into the following components.

Nutrition and health

- function and role of nutrients
- nutritional value and the role of main food commodities
- dietary reference values

Food choice

- factors affecting food choices
- balanced diets
- nutritional needs for groups
- energy and food

Food preparation and processing

- cooked methods
- effects of preparation/processing of food and nutrients
- the role of additives

Deterioration, safety and preservation of food

- preservation
- deterioration

Marketing, advertising and consumer education

- marketing and advertising
- consumer legislation

These areas have all been covered by this book, which provides up-to-date information on the latest issues concerning nutrition, labelling and food hygiene regulations.

What are Home Economics skills?

These are some of the Home Economics skills identified by the GCSE examining boards:
- **planning** – preparing a plan of action for making food products

- **organization** – being able to organize resources efficiently
- **execution** – being able to execute a variety of food preparation and cooking skills.

Other skills you need to develop include:
- **investigational skills** – factual recall, comprehension, interpretation of knowledge and instructions, analysis, discrimination, user testing on performance and comparative performance, observations, recording of observations, the selection of relevant information from observations required by a given problem, decision-making, evaluation
- **measurement** accurate measurement and estimation of area, shape, size, capacity, quantity, amount, weight, time, distance, temperature
- **communication** – the ability to read, interpret information, follow and give instructions, to learn new words, to understand technical terms and be able to appreciate the importance of accuracy
- **management** – the effective management and organization of time, money, energy, effort, materials, equipment and tools, human aptitudes and interests according to stated criteria for a given situation
- **psycho-motor** – manipulation of materials, shape and form and the effective use of tools and equipment in order to produce desired results
- **technological** – according to availability and development
- **specific** – making, manipulation and cooking of food mixtures; planning, preparation and serving of foods and dishes for individuals and family groups as part of a healthy diet, taking into account the domestic facilities, financial resources, lifestyles and the contribution of food to self and family images.

Coursework

Coursework is designed to assess your ability to apply **knowledge and understanding** in relation to the subject content. Syllabuses require you to carry out **investigations** and **tasks** in which you ask questions, examine issues, predict and hypothesize, gather, record, collate, interpret and evaluate evidence. All Food and Nutrition syllabuses require you to do some coursework as part of your course.

How to use this book for coursework

Many of the investigations suggested in this book can be extended and used for GCSE coursework and investigations. The data shown on charts and graphs, if appropriate, can be used as evidence for coursework and investigations. For example, if the coursework is based on looking at the demand for vegetarian meals, the research presented for the section on Vegetarians can be **examined as issues** and **evaluated as evidence** to support ideas.

Questions in the text

The **questions** asked for each topic relate to the text, and progress in level of difficulty. In some topics, there is something **To do**, which will take more time than the questions. In some sections, there are **investigations**. For many of these investigations, you will need to do some original research by visiting shops and supermarkets, using catalogues, looking at restaurant menus, asking people for their views on different topics and making collections of food labels which can provide a wide source of useful information.

Keeping up to date with food issues

Information about food is always changing and you could collect dated cuttings from newspapers and magazines to help keep your knowledge on food issues such as labelling and hygiene regulations as up to date as possible. At the end of the book, on page 185, there are some useful addresses which you can use to obtain further information on food topics.

As you will see from the references given, information about nutrition in foods can be drawn from many different sources.

Food issues change rapidly, so some of the text in the book may soon become out of date. Check with other references for the latest information.

1 Why do we need food?

*E*very living animal needs food – food is essential to keep us alive and in good health. Chamber's Dictionary describes food as 'that which, being digested, nourishes the body'. Eating food is usually enjoyable and a meal is a social occasion to share with friends and family.

We need food:

- to provide us with energy to keep us active and maintain body functions such as breathing
- to keep us healthy and help fight disease
- for growth and repair of body tissues
- to stop us feeling hungry
- to keep us happy – many people find eating a pleasurable and enjoyable experience.

■ Food provides us with energy for activities

Food and nutrients

All food provides us with **nutrients**, which are essential to keep us alive and healthy. The nutrients that we need include protein, carbohydrate, fat, vitamins and minerals. In addition, dietary fibre (NSP) and water are needed to keep the body working properly, but these are not nutrients. Foods which supply a variety of nutrients are called **nutritious foods**. Some foods are rich sources of particular nutrients, for example, milk is a rich source of calcium, and oranges are a rich source of vitamin C.

Nutrients have different roles to play in the way the body functions.

- Carbohydrates and fats are **energy-rich** and supply the body with energy.
- Proteins are **body-building** and help with growth and repair.
- Vitamins and minerals have many different roles, but in general they are **protective** and help to keep us healthy.

What is a diet?

The type of food that we eat or drink is called our **diet**. Everyone follows a diet, whatever they eat. Some people may say that they follow a poor diet or a healthy diet. People sometimes think that a diet only refers to a slimming diet, when they try to reduce the amount of food they eat in order to lose weight, but this is not correct.

Some people may also follow special diets for specific medical reasons such as diabetes or coeliac disease.

What is a balanced diet?

A **balanced diet** provides all the necessary nutrients in the appropriate proportions and quantities to meet our needs. One way to follow a balanced diet is to make sure we eat a variety of foods which supply a range of nutrients. Carbohydrates in the form of starchy foods such as bread, pasta, cereals and potatoes should be a major part of a balanced diet. We should also aim to eat at least five portions of fruit or vegetables each day.

■ Eating can be a pleasurable experience

Dietary needs

Dietary needs vary from person to person, depending on age, sex and level of activity and lifestyle. Our needs change as our lifestyle changes. If we take lots of exercise, we need to eat more energy-rich foods; if we sit around all day taking little exercise, we need to eat less food. Women who are pregnant or breastfeeding need to make sure their diet provides adequate nutrients for the baby.

How much to eat

If we eat more food than we require for our energy needs the extra energy supplied by the food will be stored as fat. Then our weight will increase and we could eventually become **obese**. Obesity is a problem in the UK since some people are taking less exercise and eating too much fatty, sugary food. Overweight is linked to other illnesses including heart disease and high blood pressure.

Some people eat too little food to meet their needs. **Anorexia nervosa** is an eating disorder associated with teenage girls who refuse to eat and suffer severe weight loss. Some elderly people suffer from **under-nutrition** because they eat too little food to meet their needs. This may be because they are not well enough to cook for themselves or have lost interest in eating. Under-nutrition can lead to health problems such as **anaemia** or **weak bones**.

Do we need food supplements?

Most people in the UK eat sufficient food to meet their needs. In general, if a balanced diet is followed, there is no need to take food supplements such as vitamin and mineral tablets. In fact, there is a danger of having too much of some vitamins through supplements because they can be stored in the body. e.g. vitamins A and D.

Not everyone can afford to eat enough food to meet their dietary needs. In developing countries – such as parts of Africa – wars, drought and pests can affect crop and food production. People may suffer from poor health because their diet is not properly balanced. **Starvation** is caused by not eating enough food to meet energy and nutrient needs. People who are starving become thin and weak and find it difficult to work and move around.

Malnutrition

Malnutrition is imperfect nutrition. Malnutrition may be caused by not eating enough food to meet dietary needs, but is also caused by over-eating which can lead to obesity.

Questions

1 Why do we need food? Think of your own reasons to add to the ideas on these pages.
2 What is meant by the following terms?
   a nutrients   b diet   c a balanced diet
   d malnutrition

Over the years there have been many campaigns to help us improve our eating habits and lifestyles. A few of them are described below.

The Health of the Nation

The Government white paper, 'The Health of the Nation', published in 1992 and updated in 1993, recognizes that the nation's eating and drinking habits affect many aspects of health and disease. It commits the Government to promote health and reduce coronary heart disease and obesity by improving the national diet. 'The Health of the Nation' sets targets for health and nutrition.

Targets for coronary heart disease and stroke include:

- **by the year 2000** to:
  - reduce heart disease and stroke death rates in people under 65 by at least 40 per cent.

Targets for obesity include:

- **by the year 2005** to:
  - reduce the number of people aged 16 to 64 who are obese by at least a quarter for men and at least a third for women.

Targets for diet and nutrition include:

- reduce the average intake of food energy from total fat by at least 12 per cent and from saturates by at least 35 per cent.

Healthy Eating Guidelines from MAFF (Ministry of Agriculture, Fisheries and Food)

Healthy eating often means making only small changes in the meals we already eat, eating a little more of some items and a little less of others.

This is the MAFF checklist for a balanced diet.

The eight guidelines

- Enjoy your food.
- Eat a variety of different foods.
- Eat the right amount to stay at a healthy weight.
- Eat plenty of foods rich in starch and fibre.
- Don't eat too much fat.
- Don't eat sugary foods too often.
- Look after the vitamins and minerals in your foods.
- If you drink alcohol, keep within sensible limits.

Dietary guidelines

In the UK we have had recommendations for dietary guidelines, with specific standards set, for over 30 years.

The **Committee on Medical Aspects of Food Policy (COMA)** produced a report in 1991 called **'Dietary Reference Values for Food Energy and Nutrients for the UK'** which updated dietary requirements and replaced **recommended daily amounts (RDAs)** with **dietary reference values (DRVs)**. These were set to show the amount of food energy and nutrients needed by groups of healthy people of different ages. Details of the report are shown on page 12.

The COMA report recognizes that some people have average needs, some lower-than-average and others high requirements. Dietary reference values cover a range of intakes for most nutrients and are useful for assessing the adequacy of the diets of groups of people.

What has changed over the years?

The recommended figures for 1969 and 1979 were designed to avoid the risk of under-nutrition. People's lifestyles have changed since then. They are taking less exercise and so need less energy from their food in order to maintain a suitable body weight for their height and avoid becoming overweight.

— Question

What is 'The Health of the Nation' white paper about? Give an example of one of its targets.

— To do

Plan a day's meals, snacks and drinks for a family of four. Show how your choice meets some of the eight guidelines for the MAFF checklist for a balanced diet. For example, have you chosen a variety of foods in the day's meals?

EIGHT GUIDELINES FOR A HEALTHY DIET

ENJOY YOUR FOOD

EAT A VARIETY OF DIFFERENT FOODS

EAT THE RIGHT AMOUNT TO BE A HEALTHY WEIGHT
Try to stick to a healthy weight for your height
Keeping physically active helps

EAT PLENTY OF FOODS RICH IN STARCH & FIBRE
All bread, potatoes, rice, pasta and noodles contain
STARCH with only HALF the calories of fat
FIBRE to keep you regular
Essential VITAMINS & MINERALS

DON'T EAT TOO MUCH FAT
Cutting down helps prevent weight gain and decreases your
risk of heart disease

DON'T EAT SUGARY FOODS TOO OFTEN
To help prevent tooth decay,
try to eat them only at mealtimes

LOOK AFTER THE VITAMINS & MINERALS
IN YOUR FOOD
Eat plenty of vegetables and fruit. Store and cook foods carefully so the
vitamins and minerals essential to good health are not lost

IF YOU DRINK, KEEP WITHIN SENSIBLE LIMITS
If you are pregnant, it's best for your baby
if you do not drink alcohol at all

MAFF Ministry of
Agriculture
Fisheries
and Food

Further copies of this poster
(PB1183) and a booklet on
'Healthy Eating' (PB0550)
are available from:
Food Sense, London SE99 7TT
Telephone 081-694 8862

■ Healthy Eating Guidelines (MAFF)

3 The Balance of Good Health

In 1994 the National Food Guide, **'The Balance of Good Health'**, was published. It is based on the Government's (MAFF) eight guidelines for a healthy diet. 'The Balance of Good Health' is based upon *five* commonly accepted food groups which are:

- **bread**, **other cereals** and **potatoes**
- **fruit** and **vegetables**
- **milk** and **dairy foods**
- **meat**, **fish** and alternatives
- **fatty** and **sugary** foods.

The key message of 'The Balance of Good Health' is that there should be a balance of foods which should be consumed to achieve a good healthy diet. This balance should be achieved over several days or a week and is not essential for every meal.

This picture below shows the foods which encourage the balance of good health.

The chart on the opposite page shows the food groups and choices which can be made.

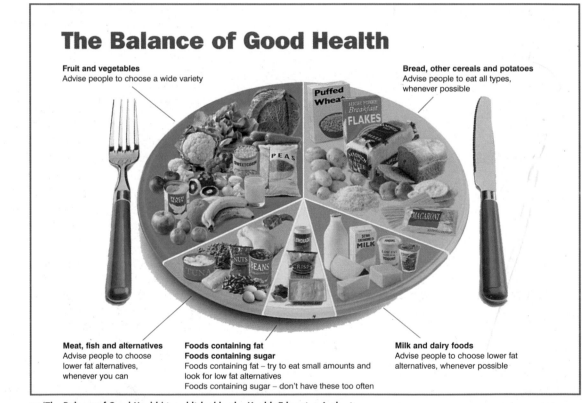

The Balance of Good Health

Fruit and vegetables
Advise people to choose a wide variety

Bread, other cereals and potatoes
Advise people to eat all types, whenever possible

Meat, fish and alternatives
Advise people to choose lower fat alternatives, whenever you can

Foods containing fat
Foods containing sugar
Foods containing fat – try to eat small amounts and look for low fat alternatives
Foods containing sugar – don't have these too often

Milk and dairy foods
Advise people to choose lower fat alternatives, whenever possible

■ 'The Balance of Good Health' is published by the Health Education Authority

— To do

Plan a day's meals, snacks and drinks for yourself. Show how your choice includes foods from the five food groups. For example, make sure you have some fruits and vegetables during the day. You may find the chart useful.

Food groups	Food choices	Which food group the choice fits
bread, cereals and potatoes		
fruit and vegetables		
milk and dairy foods		
meat, fish and alternatives		
fatty and sugary foods		

Food groups and choices

Five food groups	Bread, other cereals and potatoes	Fruit and vegetables	Milk and dairy foods	Meat, fish and alternatives	Fatty and sugary foods
Types of foods	All types of bread rolls, chapati, crumpets, crackers, rice cakes, naan. All types of grain e.g. oats, barley, rye, bulgar wheat. 'Other cereals' means things like breakfast cereals, pasta, rice, noodles. (Beans and lentils can be eaten as part of this group.)	Fresh, frozen and canned fruit and vegetables and dried fruit. Fruit juice. (Beans and lentils can be eaten as part of this group.)	Milk, cheese, yogurt and fromage frais. (This group does not contain butter, eggs and cream.)	Meat, poultry, fish, eggs, nuts, seeds, beans and lentils. Meat includes bacon and salami, meat products such as sausages, beefburgers. Beans such as canned baked beans are in this group. Fish includes frozen and canned fish, fish fingers and fish cakes.	Margarine, low-fat spread, butter, ghee, cooking oils, oily salad dressing, cream, chocolate, crisps, biscuits, cake, ice-cream, rich sauces, sweets and sugar. Fizzy soft drinks. Puddings
Main nutrients	Carbohydrate (starch), fibre, some calcium and iron, B-group vitamins.	Vitamin C, carotenes, iron, calcium, folate, fibre and some carbohydrate.	Calcium, protein, B-group vitamins especially B12, vitamins A and D.	Iron, protein, B-group vitamins, especially B12, zinc and magnesium.	Some vitamins and essential fatty acids but also a lot of fat, sugar and salt.
How much to choose	Eat lots.	Eat lots. Try to have five servings every day.	Eat moderate amounts and choose lower-fat versions whenever you can.	Eat moderate amounts and choose lower-fat versions whenever you can.	Eat fatty and sugary foods sparingly – that is infrequently or in small amounts.
What types to choose	Try to eat wholemeal, wholegrain, brown or high-fibre versions where possible. Try to avoid having them fried too often (e.g. chips), adding too much fat (e.g. thickly spread butter), adding rich sauces and dressings such as mayonnaise.	Eat a wide variety of fruit and vegetables. Try to avoid adding fat and rich sauces to vegetables, adding sugar and syrupy dressings to fruit (e.g. adding chocolate sauce to banana).	Lower-fat versions include semi-skimmed or skimmed milk, low-fat yogurts or fromage frais and lower-fat cheeses. Check the fat content by looking at the labels – compare and choose the lowest.	Lower-fat versions include meat with the fat cut off, poultry without the skin and fish without batter. Cook these foods without added fat. Beans and lentils are good alternatives to meat as they are very low in fat and high in fibre.	Some foods from this group will probably be eaten every day, but should be kept to small amounts, such as margarine, low-fat spreads. Other foods in this group may be eaten occasionally, but should not replace foods from the four main groups.

Source – 'The Balance of Good Health', Health Education Authority

Questions

Use the food chart above to answer these questions.

1 List the five food groups. For each group:
   a give two food examples
   b list the main nutrients
   c explain how to make healthy choices
   d explain which foods should be avoided.

2 For which of the food groups should we:
   a eat lots?   b eat only small amounts?

Give reasons for your answers.

The **Committee on Medical Aspects of Food Policy** (**COMA**) produced a report in 1991 called '**Dietary Reference Values for Food Energy and Nutrients for the UK**' which updated dietary requirements.

Dietary requirements

Our energy and nutrient requirements vary according to our age, sex, body size and levels of activity. Since everyone is different, it is very difficult to be specific about individual energy and nutrient requirements. Scientists have estimated the requirements for groups of people with similar characteristics such as age, sex and levels of physical activity.

The terminology

Dietary reference values (DRVs)

Dietary reference values are for healthy people, and cover a range of consumption levels for energy and most nutrients. They are calculated according to a population or a sub-group of a population. The DRVs include **reference nutrient intakes** (**RNIs**), **estimated average requirements** (**EARs**) and **lower reference nutrient intakes** (**LRNIs**).

Reference nutrient intake (RNI)

The RNI is the amount of a nutrient sufficient for nearly everyone (about 97 per cent of the population), even those with high needs. This level of intake is considered to be higher than most people need.

Estimated average requirement (EAR)

This is an estimate of the average need for food energy or a nutrient. The EAR is not the recommended intake for an individual but is the estimate of the **average** need for a large group of people. Some people will need more, some people less.

Lower reference nutrient intake (LRNI)

This amount of a nutrient is enough for only a small number of people (about three per cent of the population) who have low needs.

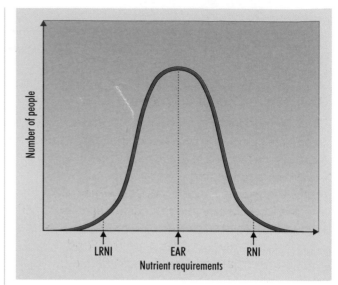

■ How the dietary reference values relate to each other

Source – *Report on Health and Social Subjects 41*, HMSO

Safe intake

When there is insufficient evidence to estimate requirements for a nutrient, the term **safe intake** is used. This level is judged to be enough for almost everyone's needs without causing undesirable effects.

Energy and nutrients	Dietary recommendations
Energy	EARs for energy vary with age, sex and level of activity, for example, for adult males 10 600 kJ each day adult females 8100 kJ each day
Protein	RNI is 55.5 g for men, 45 g for women
Total fat	No more than 35 % of food energy.
Saturates	No more than 11% of food energy.
Carbohydrates of which starch sugars (NME – non milk extrinsic sugars)	50% of food energy 39% of food energy 11 % of food energy
Dietary fibre	12–24 grams for adults
Vitamins	Each has its own dietary recommendation.
Minerals	Each has its own dietary recommendation.

Dietary recommendations

The table at the bottom of page 12 shows the daily dietary recommendations for energy and nutrients.

Recommended daily amounts (RDAs)

'Recommended daily amounts' (RDAs) was the system used for nutritional requirements before the new dietary reference values (DRVs) were introduced. Recommended daily amounts represent the amount of nutrients which are enough for almost everyone, including people with high needs. They will probably continue to be used on nutrition labels for food until the Food Labelling Regulations of 1984 are changed.

━ *Fact* ━

Dietary reference values (DRVs) for nutrients were introduced in 1991.

The RDAs on food labels have absolutely nothing to do with the old RDAs which were used as guidelines for nutrients before the introduction of DRVs. The RDAs on food labels are specially devised recommendations for certain nutrients, based on EC directives, suitable for all of Europe.

━ *Question* ━

Explain the following terms.
a DRVs
b RNIs
c EARs

BRAN FLAKES

A serving of 30 g of Bran Flakes cereal provides at least 25% of the recommended daily allowance (RDA) of the vitamins thiamin, riboflavin, niacin, folic acid, vitamins B_6, B_{12}, C and D; and the mineral iron.

INGREDIENTS

BRAN ENRICHED WHEAT, SUGAR, HONEY, SALT, MALT FLAVOURING, VITAMIN C, IRON, NIACIN, VITAMIN B_6, RIBOFLAVIN(B_2), THIAMIN (B_1), FOLIC ACID, VITAMIN D, VITAMIN B_{12}.

NUTRITION INFORMATION

		Typical value per 100g	per 30g Serving with 125ml of semi-skimmed milk
ENERGY	kJ	1350	650*
	kcal	320	60
PROTEIN	g	11	8
CARBOHYDRATE	g	64	26
(of which sugars)	g	(24)	(14)
(starch)	g	(40)	(12)
FAT	g	2.0	2.5*
(of which saturates)	g	(0.4)	(1.5)
FIBRE	g	16	5
SODIUM	g	0.9	0.3
VITAMINS		(%RDA)	(%RDA)
VITAMIN D	µg	4.2 (85)	1.3 (25)
VITAMIN C	mg	50 (85)	16.3 (25)
THIAMIN(B1)	mg	1.2 (85)	0.4 (30)
RIBOFLAVIN(B2)	mg	1.3 (85)	0.6 (40)
NIACIN	mg	15 (85)	4.6 (25)
VITAMIN B6	mg	1.7 (85)	0.6 (30)
FOLIC ACID	µg	167 (85)	60 (30)
VITAMIN B12	µg	0.85 (85)	0.75 (75)
IRON	mg	11.7 (85)	3.6 (25)

*For whole milk increase energy by 100kJ (25kcal) and fat by 3g.
*For skimmed milk reduce energy by 70kJ (20kcal) and fat by 2g.
Contribution provided by 125ml of semi-skimmed milk -
250kJ(60kcal) of energy 4g of protein, 6g of carbohydrates (sugars), 2g of fat.

750g

 RDAs are used on some labels for vitamins and minerals.

Digestion

*F*ood must be digested so that the **nutrients** in the food can be absorbed into the bloodstream and used for energy, growth and body functioning.

What happens to nutrients and dietary fibre (NSP) during digestion?

- **Proteins** are changed to **amino acids**.
- **Carbohydrates** are changed to **monosaccharides** i.e. **glucose**, **fructose** and **galactose**.
- **Fats** are changed to **fatty acids** and **glycerol**.
- **Minerals** and **vitamins** pass into the blood stream unchanged.
- **Dietary fibre** (NSP) cannot be digested and passes out of the body in the faeces.

The table below shows what happens to different nutrients during digestion.

Important terms	
Term	**Definition**
Disaccharide	Double sugars made up of two monosaccharide units.
Monosaccharide	The simplest form of carbohydrate molecules.
Enzyme	Proteins which speed up a chemical reaction but are not used up during the process.
Peristalsis	Muscular movement of digestive system.
Emulsify	Help fat and oil become an emulsion, where one of the substances is dispersed in very fine droplets suspended in the other substance.

Digestive organ	What happens there
Mouth	Food is chewed into small pieces and mixed with saliva. The **enzyme**, salivary amylase breaks down starch to maltose and dextrin.
Oesophagus	Food is pushed down the oesophagus towards the stomach by the action of peristalsis – the muscular movement in the oesophagus. During this time, salivary amylase continues to digest the starch molecules.
Stomach	Food is churned in the stomach and mixed with gastric juice. This contains mucus, hydrochloric acid and the enzyme pepsin. Mucus moistens the food. Hydrochloric acid lowers the pH and increases acidity which destroys bacteria and provides the conditions needed for the pepsin to work. Pepsin starts to break down protein into peptides. Babies and young children also produce the enzyme rennin which coagulates casein, one of the milk proteins.
Small intestine	Food passes into the small intestine where digestion is completed and nutrients are absorbed into the bloodstream. Bile made by the liver emulsifies fats into small particles so that it can be digested. Pancreatic juice contains enzymes that change emulsified fat into fatty acids and glycerols, starch into maltose and dextrin and proteins into peptides and amino acids. Enzymes in the intestinal juice produced in the small intestine complete digestion by changing: – peptides into amino acids by proteinase enzymes – any remaining fat into fatty acids and glycerol by lipase enzymes – disaccharides (double sugars) such as maltose, sucrose and lactose into the monosaccharides (single sugars) glucose, fructose and galactose by amylase enzymes.

Absorption of nutrients

After digestion, the nutrients pass through the walls of the small intestine into the bloodstream. With the exception of fatty acids and glycerol, the nutrients are then carried to the liver (via the hepatic portal vein). The liver controls their distribution around the body. After absorption, fatty acids and glycerol recombine and are transported (in the form of triglycerides) to the liver via the lymphatic system. The fat-soluble vitamins are also transported in this way. Undigested food, which contains dietary fibre and bacteria, passes into the large intestine (colon) where water is absorbed. The remaining residue, the faeces, is stored in the rectum and is passed out of the body through the anus.

Questions

Describe how the following snacks would be digested.
1 beans on buttered toast – **nutrients**: protein, carbohydrate and fat, dietary fibre, minerals and vitamins
2 fresh fruit salad – **nutrients**: carbohydrate, water, dietary fibre, minerals and vitamins

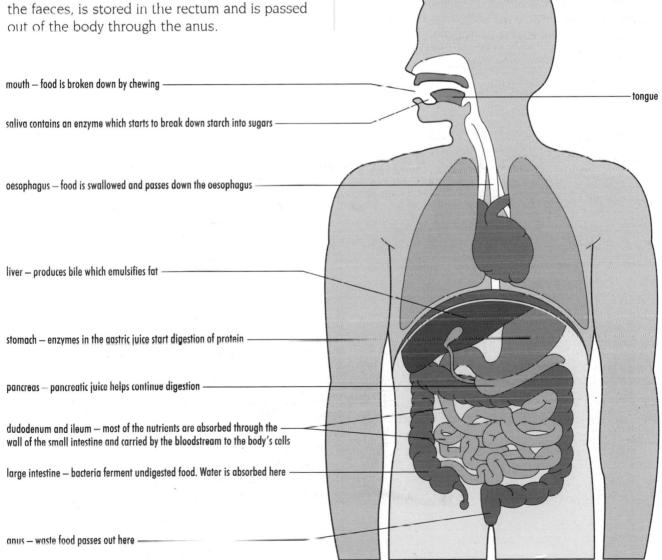

mouth – food is broken down by chewing

tongue

saliva contains an enzyme which starts to break down starch into sugars

oesophagus – food is swallowed and passes down the oesophagus

liver – produces bile which emulsifies fat

stomach – enzymes in the gastric juice start digestion of protein

pancreas – pancreatic juice helps continue digestion

dudodenum and ileum – most of the nutrients are absorbed through the wall of the small intestine and carried by the bloodstream to the body's cells

large intestine – bacteria ferment undigested food. Water is absorbed here

anus – waste food passes out here

■ The digestive system

6 People's food needs

*E*veryone has different nutritional needs. These needs change as we grow older. At different times we have special nutritional needs. For example, when teenagers are growing rapidly, their calcium requirements increase because they need to build strong bones.

Age

As a baby grows, it needs increasing amounts of nutritious food to help build its body and keep it healthy. Adolescents and young adults have high energy needs and high nutritional needs because they are growing rapidly and are often very active. Older people need slightly less energy from food than they did in their middle years as their metabolism is slowing down. It is therefore very important that the foods they do eat are nutritious.

Male and female

Males tend to need more energy from food than females do. This is because men are usually bigger than women and have more muscle tissue.

Physical activity

People who take lots of exercise, or have physically demanding jobs, have greater energy needs than inactive people and those with jobs where they sit down all day.

Special needs

Pregnancy

Pregnant women may need to increase their intake of foods, especially during the last three months of pregnancy, to help keep themselves and their developing babies healthy. This is because requirements for energy and some nutrients increase. Pregnant women, and women planning pregnancy, should also take folic acid supplements every day.

Breastfeeding

When women are breastfeeding they need to make sure their diet contains foods which are good sources of energy, protein, calcium, phosphorus, magnesium and zinc as well as B-group vitamins and vitamins A, C and D. This is so they produce good quality breast milk.

Energy needs

We all need energy from food to keep us alive and active. People have different energy needs depending on their age, level of activity and body size.

Why do we need energy?

We need energy for almost everything we do. We need energy:
- to make our muscles move and carry out physical activities

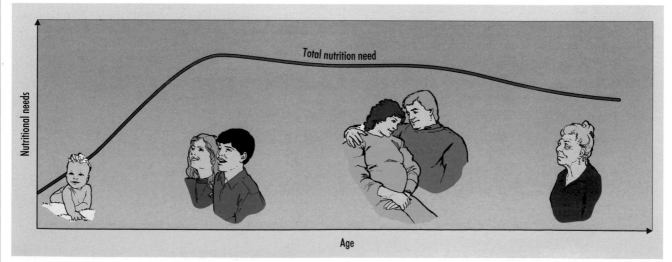

Nutritional needs / Total nutrition need / Age

■ From birth to old age, people have different nutritional needs

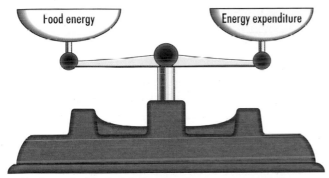

■ Ideally, our food intake is balanced against our energy expenditure

- to maintain our normal body temperature
- to carry out the body's functions such as heartbeat, breathing and metabolism
- for tissue growth and repair.

Energy balance

If we eat more food than we need, the excess energy is stored as fat. If we obtain less energy than we need from the food we eat, and use up more energy by taking exercise, the fat stores in the body are used as fuel and we get thinner. To maintain a constant weight we need to balance the energy taken in as food with the energy used up during activity.

Energy measurement

Energy is measured in **kilojoules (kJ)** and **kilocalories (kcal)**. Nutritionists and dietitians tend to use kilocalories when they are planning diets for people. Food labels show the kilojoule and kilocalorie energy value of the food product.
1 kcal = 1000 calories = 4.184 kJ (usually taken as 4.2)
1 MJ (megajoule) = 1000 kilojoules

Energy value of nutrients		
	kcal per g	kJ per g
Protein	4	17
Carbohydrate	3.75	16
Fat	9	38
Alcohol	7	29

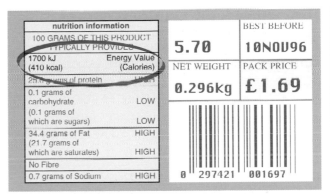

■ This food label shows the energy value of the food

Energy from food

The energy value of food comes mainly from its fat, protein and carbohydrate (starch and sugar) content. Fat supplies almost twice as much energy as the same weight of protein or carbohydrate. As a basic guide, 1 gram of fat provides 9 kcal, carbohydrate provides 3.7 kcal per gram, protein provides 4 kcal per gram and alcohol provides 7 kcal per gram.

Basal metabolic rate (BMR)

The amount of energy a person needs depends upon their **basal metabolic rate** (**BMR**) and their level of activity. The BMR is the amount of energy we need when the body is completely at rest and not moving about. This energy is needed to keep our body functioning and is used for breathing, keeping the heart beating and other body processes.

Men usually have a higher BMR than women and elderly people have a lower BMR than young people. The BMR accounts for about two-thirds of a person's daily energy needs.

— Questions

1 Why do our needs for food change with age and other special situations?
2 Why do we need energy from food? How does the energy value of different nutrients vary?
3 What is meant by energy balance? What happens if we eat too much food to meet our needs?
4 What is meant by BMR?

7 Energy

How does food produce energy?

The energy-producing nutrients in food are **carbohydrates**, **fats** and **protein**. (Alcohol also produces energy.) Carbohydrates and fat are the nutrients mainly used for energy. Protein is only used as an energy source if the diet provides inadequate amounts of energy. Food is processed by the body to release energy.

Carbohydrates

During digestion, carbohydrates are broken down into glucose which is then absorbed into the bloodstream. This glucose can then be used for energy. If extra energy is not needed immediately, glucose can be stored in the liver and muscles as glycogen. This store of glycogen can instantly be reconverted to glucose for the body to use when extra energy is needed. When glycogen stores are full, glucose can be converted into fatty acids and stored in the fat tissue.

Fats

Once fatty acids have been absorbed, they are rebuilt into triglycerides. When triglycerides reach tissues which require energy, fatty acids are released and are used by the cells to produce energy. Fats are also stored in the body in the adipose tissue, for use when extra energy is needed.

Proteins

Proteins tend not to be used for energy, but if energy intakes are low, such as during starvation or when a person follows a very low-calorie diet, amino acids can be used to produce energy.

How much energy do we need?

The amount of energy we need varies with age, gender and the amount of activity we carry out. The table at the top of column 2 shows the estimated average requirements (EAR) for energy.

The EARs are based upon how active people are at the present time. These figures are lower than those recommended in previous reports because people are becoming less active and taking less exercise.

The pie-chart on the right shows where we get our energy from in the food we eat.

The EARS for energy				
Age	EAR (kJ per day)		EAR (kcal per day)	
	Male	Female	Male	Female
0–3 months	2280	2160	545	515
1–3 years	5150	4860	1230	1165
4–6 years	7160	6460	1715	1545
7–10 years	8240	7280	1970	1740
11–14 years	9270	7920	2220	1845
15–18 years	11510	8830	2755	2110
19–50 years	10600	8100	2550	1940
51–59 years	10600	8000	2550	1900
60–64 years	9930	7990	2380	1900
65–74 years	9710	7960	2330	1900
75+	8770	7610	2100	1810

Source – DRV report (1991), Department of Health

Energy for activity

The picture opposite shows two different activities with different energy needs – the more vigorous the activity, the higher the energy requirement.

The table on page 19 shows the amounts of energy used by a man to do various activities.

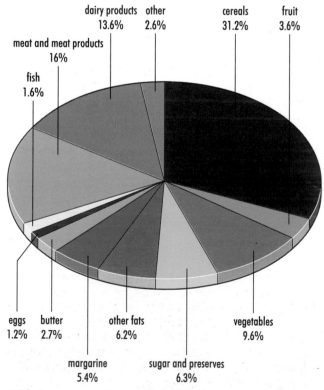

■ Where we get our energy – from the food we eat

■ Some people will have a greater energy requirement than others

How much energy do we use for different activities?	
Activity	**Average energy expenditure (kcal per min)**
Sitting	1.4
Walking slowly	3
Walking quickly	5
Light work	2.5–4.9
Tennis, dancing, jogging, cycling	5.0–7.4
Cross country running, football, fast swimming	> 7.5

Questions

1 How does the body release energy from food?
2 Use the chart on page 18 showing EARs for energy to answer these questions.
   a Explain what happens to our energy requirements as we get older.
   b What is the difference between male and female energy requirements?

To do

Make a collection of food labels and compare the energy value of different foods for a 100-gram serving. Compare the energy value of lower fat versions of similar products, for example mayonnaise. You could fill in a table like the one shown on the right. Which types of food have **a**) the highest energy value, **b**) the lowest energy value? Write a report on your findings.

Food product	Energy value (per 100 g)
Cheese and tomato pizza	286 kcal/1204 kJ

Protein

What are proteins?

Proteins are made up of long chains of building blocks called **amino acids**. These amino acids are made of the elements carbon, oxygen, hydrogen, nitrogen and sometimes sulphur and phosphorus. For our bodies to function properly we need the correct balance of amino acids. There are 20 amino acids which make up proteins. Our bodies can make *eleven* amino acids (non-essential or dispensible amino acids) but we need to obtain the other *nine* (essential or indispensible amino acids) from our diet.

Dietary recommendations for protein

The table below shows the different requirements for protein. Note that females need less protein than males, and protein requirements change with age. In the UK we are unlikely to suffer from a lack of protein in our diet.

The functions of protein

Every cell in the body contains some protein. Protein is needed for **growth** and **repair** of body tissue and muscles and blood cells. An adequate supply of protein is easily achieved by eating a varied diet. Excess protein is converted into glucose in the liver and used as a source of energy.

Foods which provide protein

- **Protein sources from animal origin** – meat, fish, poultry, eggs, milk, milk products such as cheese and yogurt. These foods contain all of the essential amino acids.
- **Protein sources from plants** – peas, beans, lentils, cereals such as rice and wheat, flour, pasta, nuts and seeds. These foods tend to lack one or more of the essential amino acids. However, there is an exception – soya beans contain all of them.

Complementary proteins

Vegetable foods which are good sources of protein usually lack one or more of the essential amino acids needed by humans, so proteins from a single vegetable food are said to have a **low biological value** (**LBV**). For example, wheat and rice proteins are low in the amino acid lysine. Mixtures of proteins from plant foods taken together can **complement** each other by supplying the full range of amino acids needed by humans. The assortment of amino acids needed by the human body can be obtained by eating a mixture of protein foods.

Examples of complementary protein meals include:
- beans on toast
- rice and peas
- rice or chapatis and dhal
- vegetable chilli (kidney beans) and rice.

Animal proteins from meat, fish, milk, cheese and eggs supply all the essential amino acids and are said to have a **high biological value** (**HBV**).

Questions

1. Why does the body need protein?
2. What happens if we eat too much protein-rich food?
3. What are 'high biological value' and 'low biological value' proteins?
4. Explain how and why you would combine protein foods to complement one another.
5. Look at the table for reference nutrient intakes for protein (left). Explain why people of different age groups might need different amounts of protein. Why do pregnant and lactating women need more protein?

COMA reference nutrient intakes (RNIs) for protein		
Age	Male	Female
	(grams per day)	
11–14 yr	42.1g	41.21g
15–18 yr	55.2g	45 g
19–49 yr	55.5g	45 g
50+ yr	53.3g	46.51 g
Pregnant women		extra 6 g
Lactating women		extra 11 g

Source – DRV report (1991), Department of Health

Examples of the protein content of some foods

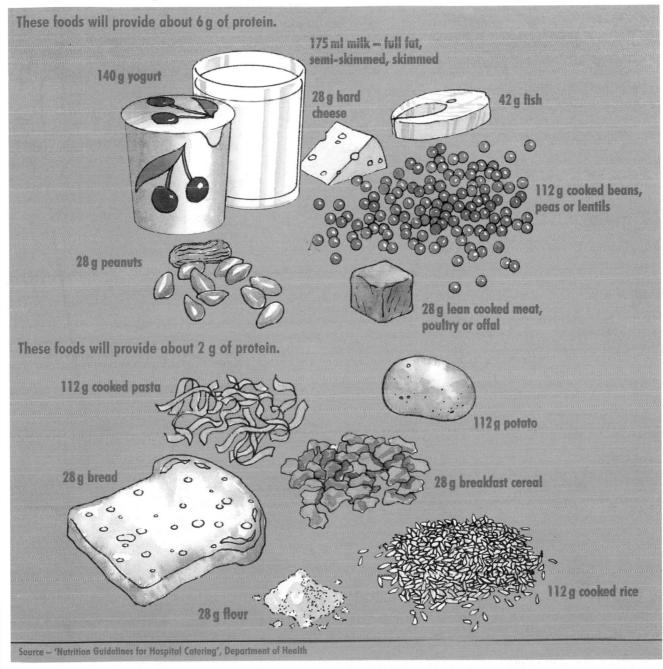

These foods will provide about 6 g of protein.

140 g yogurt

175 ml milk – full fat, semi-skimmed, skimmed

28 g hard cheese

42 g fish

112 g cooked beans, peas or lentils

28 g peanuts

28 g lean cooked meat, poultry or offal

These foods will provide about 2 g of protein.

112 g cooked pasta

112 g potato

28 g bread

28 g breakfast cereal

112 g cooked rice

28 g flour

Source – 'Nutrition Guidelines for Hospital Catering', Department of Health

— Fact

Protein is needed for growth and repair of body tissues.

Protein is made up of amino acids.

Good sources of protein include meat, fish, eggs, cheese, beans and cereals.

— To do

Plan a meal that will provide 18 g of protein. Use food tables or a nutritional analysis computer program to show evidence for your choice.

What are fats?

Fats are made up of the elements **carbon**, **hydrogen** and **oxygen**. In the study of nutrition, 'fats' include both fats and oils. The hardness of a fat depends upon its chemical composition. As a general guide, at room temperature fats are solid and oils are liquid. Most fats contain a mixture of saturated, mono-unsaturated and polyunsaturated fatty acids including trans-fatty acids.

The functions of fat

- It supplies us with a concentrated source of energy.
- It is needed for the structure of all body cells.
- It provides us with vitamins A and D.
- Body fat is stored under the skin and helps to keep us warm.
- It provides us with essential fatty acids.
- Fat is stored around the major organs where it helps to protect them from damage.

Composition of fats

The correct name for a fat is a triglyceride. These are formed from one **glycerol** molecule and three **fatty acids**. There are different types of fatty acids.
- **Saturated fatty acids** – all of the carbon atoms in the fatty acid molecules are linked by single bonds.

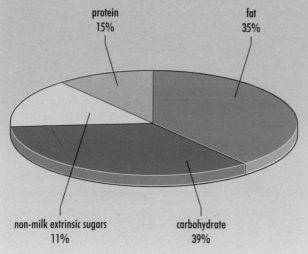

Fat should supply no more than 35% of our food energy

- **Unsaturated fatty acids** – two or more of the carbon atoms are linked by a double bond. Mono-unsaturates contain one double bond. Polyunsaturates contain more than one double bond.

Cholesterol

Cholesterol is found in our blood and in the food we eat. Our bodies make cholesterol as it is a part of all body cells and hormones. Cholesterol is made in the liver using the fat we eat, especially the saturated fatty acids (saturates). High blood cholesterol is thought to be one of the risk factors in the development of heart disease. There are many risk factors for heart disease, including being overweight, taking too little exercise, smoking and drinking alcohol. Saturated fatty acids from the food we eat are important factors which affect blood cholesterol levels. Cholesterol in food has very little effect on blood cholesterol levels. To reduce blood cholesterol levels, we need to cut down on the total amount of fat eaten, especially saturates.

Fat and coronary heart disease (CHD)

Coronary heart disease (CHD) is a major cause of death in the UK and accounted for about a quarter of the deaths in England in 1991. The reduction of the risk of coronary heart disease was a key issue in the report, 'The Health of the Nation'. Smoking, raised blood pressure and raised levels of blood cholesterol all contribute to coronary heart disease. A change in lifestyle and eating habits can help to reduce the risk of death from heart disease and strokes.

The major risk factors which increase the chances of developing coronary heart disease are:
- cigarette smoking
- raised blood cholesterol levels
- high-fat diet
- high blood pressure
- lack of physical exercise
- obesity
- a family history of heart disease
- stress
- being male
- increasing age.

One important way for anyone to reduce the risk of coronary heart disease is to improve their diet by *reducing the amount of fatty foods they eat and increasing the amount of fibre-rich starchy foods they eat.*

— Fact

Fat supplies us with a concentrated source of energy.

Fat should supply no more than 35 per cent of our food energy.

We need to cut down our fat intake by not eating so many fried foods and fatty snacks.

— Fact

How much is a lot?

According to MAFF guidelines, use this rule of thumb for a complete main meal or 100 g snack.

'A lot' = these amounts or more:

10 g of sugars   3 g of fibres
20 g of fats   0.5 g of sodium
5 g of saturates

— Questions

1 Why do we need fat in our diet?
2 Why should we cut down on the amount of saturated fatty acids that we eat?
3 In a complete meal, how much fat is 'a lot'?

Pies, sausages and chips are high in fat. Eat them infrequently

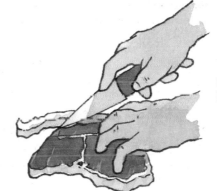

Remove fat from meat before cooking

Choose a lower fat cheese to reduce the fat content

Choose a low fat spread or use less of a full fat spread

Snack foods can be high in fat — eat them in moderation

■ Tips for reducing fat in the diet

23

Dietary recommendations for fat

The COMA report in 1991 and the white paper, 'The Health of the Nation', recommended that no more than 35 per cent of our food energy should come from fat in food. Saturated fatty acids should provide no more than eleven per cent of food energy. In the UK we currently obtain about 41 per cent of our food energy from fat and sixteen per cent from saturates, so we need to cut down on the amount of fatty foods we eat.

Hidden fat in food

The fat in many food products cannot be seen – it is hidden in foods such as cakes, pastries, pies and rich sauces used for pasta. Some processed foods contain large amounts of **hydrogenated fat**. Hydrogenation is the process where hydrogen atoms are added to fats and oils during processing to improve texture, flavour and keeping properties. During this process, some of the unsaturated fatty acids become saturated.

One way to check the fat content of a food product is to read the nutritional information on the label.

Which fats should we choose?

Eating too many fatty foods which are high in saturated fatty acids has been linked with developing heart disease. In the UK most people eat foods which contain too many saturated fatty acids. Foods which are high in saturated fatty acids include butter, lard, ghee, full-fat dairy foods and fatty meats and meat products such as pork pies and sausages. Processed foods such as cakes, biscuits, puddings, crisps and chocolate are also rich sources of saturates. Hard margarine, used for cakes and biscuits, and some vegetable oils contain hydrogenated fat.

How to cut down on fat intake

- Eat fewer fatty foods such as chips and fatty meat products such as sausages and pork pies.
- Try cooking without adding fat – use a non-stick pan to fry things without adding fat.
- Cut down on fried foods – grill, boil or bake foods instead.
- Try not to add extra fat during cooking.
- Remove all visible fat from cuts of meat and bacon and poultry before cooking – the skin on chicken is quite fatty.
- Cut down on fatty snack foods such as cakes, crisps, doughnuts, biscuits and chocolate.
- Use lower-fat spreads instead of butter and margarine – or just eat less of them.
- Buy reduced-fat cheese, or use a little less of a strong-flavoured cheese.
- Use semi-skimmed or skimmed milk instead of whole milk.

Reducing the fat content

The chart on page 25 shows the fat content per 100 grams of different foods. The amount of fat in our diets can be reduced by choosing lower-fat versions of products such as cheese and milk.

— Fact

Fats are made up of different fatty acids.

We should cut down on the amount of both total fat and saturated fatty acids that we obtain from food.

Fat can be hidden in food products such as sausages and pies.

Nutrition information

| | Typical composition when cooked | |
	per 100 g	per 1/4 pizza
Energy	255 kcal	260 kcal
	1071 kJ	1092 kJ
Protein	13.1 g	13.36 g
Carbohydrate	29.7 g	30.29 g
Fat	10.6 g	10.81 g

■ This pizza food label gives information on fat content

Typical fat content (per 100 g) of a range of foods

Tesco brand products	Typical fat content (grams (g) per 100 g)		
	total fat	saturates	polyunsaturates
Cheddar cheese	34.4	22.7	1.1
Half-fat cheese	15	9.9	0.5
Cottage cheese	3.9	2.6	0.1
Double cream	48	31.7	1.5
Natural yogurt	1.2	0.8	trace
Vanilla ice cream	6.5	3.5	0.2
Whole milk	3.9	2.6	0.1
Half-fat milk	1.6	1.1	trace
Virtually fat-free milk	0.1	0.1	trace
Lard	100	41.6	14.2
Olive oil	100	13.0	15.0
Mayonnaise	80.7	12.6	50.9
Reduced-calorie mayonnaise	33.8	4.7	16.7
Butter	81.7	54.0	2.6
Half-fat spread	40.5	7.3	18.0
Very low-fat spread	20.0	3.6	4.0

Source – Tesco *Healthy Eating* guide

Note: The sum of saturates and polyunsaturates does not add up to the total fat content of the foods because the table does not show mono-unsaturates. Also, fat is not totally made up of fatty acids.

Questions

1 Why should we eat less fat?
2 Describe four ways we can reduce the amount of fat in our diet.
3 Look at the chart above which shows the fat content of different foods. To cut down on fat intake, which product would you choose in each of the following categories?
   a a cheese
   b something to go with a dessert
   c a type of milk
   d a dressing for salad
   e a spread to use on bread
   Give reasons for each of your choices.

4 Which three foods in the chart above contain:
   a the highest amount of saturates
   b the lowest amount of saturates?
   What advice would you give someone on choosing to reduce the amount of saturated fat in their diet?

Designing fats and spreads

The food industry is constantly developing products which are lower in fat and saturated fatty acids. Nutrition labels often show the total fat content, and how much of it is saturated, polyunsaturated and mono-unsaturated.

GOLD LOW FAT SPREAD

INGREDIENTS: WATER; VEGETABLE OIL; RECONSTITUTED SKIMMED MILK; HYDROGENATED VEGETABLE OIL; RECONSTITUTED BUTTERMILK; MILK PROTEIN; STARCH; SALT(1.5%); EMULSIFIERS – E471(FROM VEGETABLE OIL), E476; ACIDITY REGULATORS - SODIUM LACTATE, SODIUM CITRATE, E339; STABILISER – POTASSIUM ALGINATE; PRESERVATIVE- POTASSIUM SORBATE; FLAVOURING; VITAMINS A & D; COLOUR – BETA CAROTENE

SUITABLE FOR VEGETARIANS

500g

NUTRITION INFORMATION 100g PROVIDES

ENERGY	377 kcal/1554 kJ
PROTEIN	3.0 g
CARBOHYDRATE	3.5 g
of which sugars	1.5 g
FAT	39.0 g
of which saturates	10.6 g
FIBRE	trace
SODIUM	0.7 g

5031 7264

GOLD UNSALTED LOW FAT SPREAD

INGREDIENTS: WATER; VEGETABLE OIL; RECONSTITUTED SKIMMED MILK; HYDROGENATED VEGETABLE OIL; MILK PROTEIN; RECONSTITUTED BUTTERMILK; STARCH; EMULSIFIERS – E471(FROM VEGETABLE OIL), E476; ACIDITY REGULATORS – SODIUM LACTATE, SODIUM CITRATE, E339; PRESERVATIVE- POTASSIUM SORBATE; FLAVOURING; VITAMINS A & D; COLOUR – BETA CAROTENE

SUITABLE FOR VEGETARIANS

500g

NUTRITION INFORMATION 100 g PROVIDES

ENERGY	387 kcal/1595 kJ
PROTEIN	6.0 g
CARBOHYDRATE	3.0 g
of which sugars	1.6 g
FAT	39.0 g
of which saturates	10.6 g
FIBRE	NIL
SODIUM	0.3 g

UTTERLY BUTTERLY VEGETABLE OIL SPREAD WITH BUTTERMILK

INGREDIENTS: VEGETABLE OIL; RECONSTITUTED BUTTERMILK(28%); HYDROGENATED VEGETABLE OIL; EMULSIFIERS – E471; SALT(1.7%); SOYA LECITHIN; LACTIC ACID; FLAVOURING; VITAMINS A&D; COLOUR – BETA CAROTENE

NUTRITION INFORMATION 100 g PROVIDES

ENERGY	2594 kJ / 630 kcal
PROTEIN	0.9 g
CARBOHYDRATE	1.5 g
of which sugars	1.5 g
FAT	69.0 g
of which saturates	10.6 g
of which mono-unsaturates	32.2 g
of which polyunsaturates	13.5 g
FIBRE	nil
SODIUM	0.7 g

500g e

SUITABLE FOR VEGETARIANS

5 000373 702315 >

MONO RAPESEED OIL SPREAD

INGREDIENTS: RAPESEED OIL; HYDROGENATED VEGETABLE OIL; WATER; SALT (1.3%); EMULSIFIERS – E471, SOYA LECITHIN; LACTIC ACID; FLAVOURING; VITAMINS A & D; COLOUR – BETA CAROTENE

SUITABLE FOR VEGETARIANS

500g

NUTRITION INFORMATION 100 g PROVIDES

ENERGY	675 kcal
	2775 kJ
PROTEIN	nil
CARBOHYDRATE	nil
of which sugars	nil
FAT	75.0 g
of which saturates	11.5 g
of which mono-unsaturates	35.0 g
of which polyunsaturates	14.7 g
FIBRE	nil
SODIUM	0.5 g

5 000373 702292

GOLD LOWEST VERY LOW FAT SPREAD

INGREDIENTS: RECONSTITUTED SKIMMED MILK; WATER; VEGETABLE OIL; RECONSTITUTED BUTTERMILK; HYDROGENATED VEGETABLE OIL; MILK PROTEIN; STARCH; SALT(1.2%); EMULSIFIERS – E471 (FROM VEGETABLE OIL), E476; ACIDITY REGULATORS – SODIUM LACTATE, SODIUM CITRATE, E339; STABILISER – POTASSIUM ALGINATE; PRESERVATIVE– POTASSIUM SORBATE; FLAVOURING; VITAMINS A & D; COLOUR – BETA CAROTENE

SUITABLE FOR VEGETARIANS

500g

NUTRITION INFORMATION 100 g PROVIDES

ENERGY	264 kcal/1090 kJ
PROTEIN	6.0 g
CARBOHYDRATE	3.7 g
of which sugars	1.7 g
FAT	25.0 g
of which saturates	6.5 g
FIBRE	trace
SODIUM	0.7 g

Can help slimming only as part of a controlled diet

5021 6185

Nutrition information

Nutrition information (per 100 g)					
	Waitrose Dairy Butter	*Gold Light*	*Utterly Butterly*	*Gold Extra Light*	*St Ivel Mono*
Energy	3031 kJ/737 kcal	1554 kJ/377 kcal	2594 kJ/ 630 kcal	1090 kJ/264 kcal	2775 kJ/ 675 kcal
Fat	81.7 g	39 g	69 g	25 g	75 g
of which saturates	54.0 g	10.6 g	10.6 g	6.5 g	11.5 g
mono-unsaturates	19.8 g	n/a	32.2 g	n/a	35 g
polyunsaturates	2.6	n/a	13.5 g	n/a	14.7 g
cholesterol	230 mg	n/a	n/a	n/a	n/a
Sodium	0.8 g	0.7 g	n/a	0.7 g	0.5 g

Note: n/a = information not available

▬ *Questions* ▬

1 Look at the labels on these pages. Which fats would you choose:
   a for a lower fat content
   b for a lower saturates content?

2 Use the nutrition information chart above to answer these questions.
   a Sort the fats in order of fat content, listing the highest fat content first.
   b Which fats contain (i) the most saturates (ii) the least saturates?

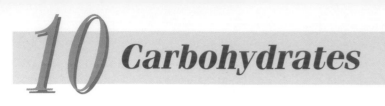

10 Carbohydrates

What are carbohydrates?

There are two types of carbohydrate:
- **starches** which are found in bread, pasta, rice, potatoes, pulses and breakfast cereals.
- **sugars** which give food its sweet taste and are found in fruits, soft drinks, table sugar, sweets and cakes.

Dietary recommendations for carbohydrates

The COMA report on dietary reference values suggested that we should increase the amount of foods rich in starch and dietary fibre but reduce the sugary foods in our diet.

At present about 45 per cent of our food energy intake comes from carbohydrates and the recommendations suggest we increase it to at least 50 per cent of our food energy intake. Of that, 39 *per cent should be provided by starch and milk sugars and intrinsic sugars (sugars found naturally in the cell structure of foods such as fruits and vegetables) and 11 per cent by non-milk extrinsic sugars (sugars not found within the cell structure of food)*.

(a) Sugars

soft drinks 8%
chocolate and other confectionery 16%
cereal products 13%
fruit and fruit products 12%
other foods 5.5%
dairy 13%
sugars and preserves 27%
vegetables 5.5%

(b) Starches

vegetables (including potatoes) 21.0%
other foods 2.5%
cereal products 73.5%
meat and meat products 3%

■ Carbohydrates in our diet

Source – MAFF

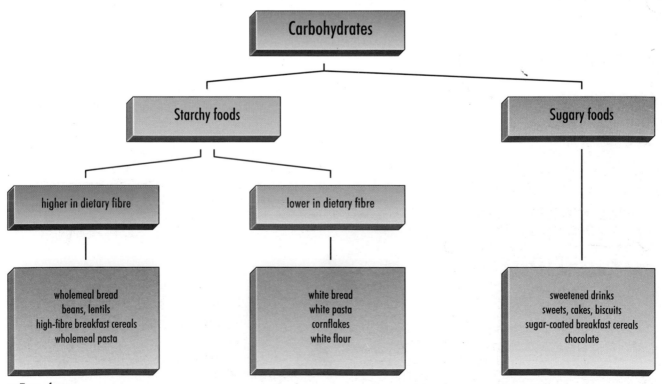

- Carbohydrates
  - Starchy foods
    - higher in dietary fibre
      - wholemeal bread
        beans, lentils
        high-fibre breakfast cereals
        wholemeal pasta
    - lower in dietary fibre
      - white bread
        white pasta
        cornflakes
        white flour
  - Sugary foods
    - sweetened drinks
      sweets, cakes, biscuits
      sugar-coated breakfast cereals
      chocolate

■ Types of sugar

Dietary reference values (DRVs) for sugars and starches

- Non-milk extrinsic sugars   11 per cent of energy
- Starches   39 per cent of energy

The functions of carbohydrates

Carbohydrates contain three elements – **carbon**, **hydrogen** and **oxygen**. Carbohydrates are mainly used to provide **energy**. During digestion carbohydrates are changed into **glucose** which is used for energy. Excess intakes of glucose can be converted into fatty acids and stored as body fat.

Weight for weight, carbohydrates provide almost the same amount of energy as proteins, but less than half the energy value of fat (see the table on page 17).

Sugars include **glucose**, **fructose** (found in fruit), **maltose** and **lactose** (found in milk). Sugars such as glucose can be digested quickly and provide instant energy when it is needed.

Starches are made from more complex molecules than sugars, and are called **complex carbohydrates**.

Starch is a **polysaccharide** made up of glucose units. Starch is partly digested in the mouth and changed in the small intestine to glucose.

The total carbohydrate content in 100 g of food	
	Carbohydrate (per 100 g)
Cornflakes	82 g
White flour	77.5 g
Chapatis made with fat	50 g
Boiled potatoes	20 g
Boiled rice	30 g
White bread	50 g
Sugar	100 g

Source – *Food Tables*, Bender and Bender

What are the advantages of eating more starchy foods?

There is scientific evidence that a diet high in complex carbohydrates – starchy foods – is very healthy and helps to keep blood sugar levels constant.

Starchy foods such as potatoes, bread and pasta provide other nutrients as well as starch. For example, bread is a good source of protein, B-group vitamins and minerals such as calcium and iron.

If we eat more starchy foods this can help to cut down on the amount of fatty foods we include in our diet. Starchy foods help to fill us up and so we are less likely to eat high-fat snacks such as doughnuts and crisps.

Important sources of starchy foods include pasta, rice, bread, breakfast cereals, potatoes and pulses.

— Fact

There are two types of carbohydrate – **starches** and **sugars**.
Carbohydrates are mainly used to provide **energy**.
We should **increase** the amount of starchy, fibre-rich foods we eat.

— To do

The chart on the left shows the amounts of carbohydrate in 100 grams of different foods. We are advised to eat more starchy foods, and reduce the amount of sugary foods. Use detailed food tables, food packet labels or a nutritional analysis computer program to find out the starch and sugar content of the foods shown on the chart. Which of the foods are good sources of starch, and which foods contain some sugar? What types of sugar do they contain? Comment on your findings.

— Questions

1 What is the function of carbohydrate in the diet?
2 What are the dietary recommendations for carbohydrate?
3 What are the advantages of eating more starchy foods?

29

Sugars

Dietary recommendations for sugar

The COMA report suggests that we should cut down on the amount of **non-milk extrinsic sugar** (**NME**) that we eat to eleven per cent of our total food energy intake. This type of sugar is found in table sugar, sweets, sugary drinks, cakes and biscuits and is also added to many processed foods.

In 1992, the average intake of this type of sugar was 490 grams a week – 13.4 per cent of total daily energy intake, so we need to cut down quite a bit on the amount of sugary foods we eat.

Types of sugars

Simple sugars include **monosaccharides** and **disaccharides**. Examples of monosaccharides include **glucose** and **fructose**. Glucose is the main component of disaccharides such as sucrose and of starch. Fructose is a sugar found in fruit.

Disaccharides are 'double sugars' formed from two monosaccharide units joined together. Examples of disaccharides include **sucrose** (table sugar), **lactose** (found in milk) and **maltose**.

Hidden sugar in food

Food manufacturers add sugar to many food products during processing. These **extrinsic** sugars are said to provide **empty calories** which means they provide energy but have very little nutritional value. Sugar is added to a whole range of food products including soups, pasta sauces, canned vegetables and breakfast cereals. This added sugar is called **hidden sugar** because we may not realize that it is included in the foods.

The food label must list the added ingredients and sugar may be in the form of sucrose, glucose, dextrose, fructose, glucose syrup, invert sugar or malto-dextrin.

■ Food labels show added sugar

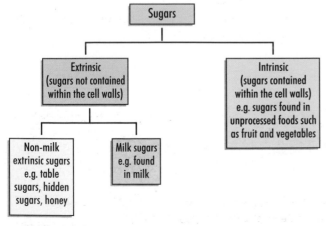

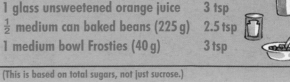

Sugars in foods

1 can cola	7 tsp
1 carton fruit yogurt	5 tsp
1 chocolate digestive biscuit	1 tsp
1 scoop ice-cream	2.5 tsp
1 tbs tomato ketchup	1.5 tsp
1 glass unsweetened orange juice	3 tsp
½ medium can baked beans (225 g)	2.5 tsp
1 medium bowl Frosties (40 g)	3 tsp

(This is based on total sugars, not just sucrose.)

■ Classification of sugars

The teeth

In recent years children have been getting less **tooth decay (dental caries)** which is thought to be due to the use of fluoridated toothpaste and the addition of fluoride to some water supplies.

Sugar and tooth decay

Research shows that all types of sugar can encourage tooth decay. Sucrose (table sugar) is the most likely to cause decay, with glucose, fructose (fruit sugar) and maltose being slightly less damaging.

Dental plaque is a sticky film that clings to teeth and contains **bacteria**. These bacteria use the sugar in food for their energy, and produce acid which can attack the tooth enamel and cause dental caries (tooth decay). Every time sugary food is eaten, the acid produced attacks the teeth, increasing the chance of a cavity developing.

The amount of tooth decay we get depends on a number of factors:
- the strength of our tooth enamel, which is linked to our state of health and genetic factors
- the amount and frequency of sugary foods eaten
- how well we look after our teeth.

How often sugary foods and drinks are consumed is far more important than the actual quantity of sugar consumed, in terms of the development of tooth decay. If sugary foods and drinks are frequently consumed, the teeth may be exposed to acid attacks almost continuously. It takes about 20–30 minutes for the pH of the mouth to return to a less acidic level after sugary foods have been eaten. This means that if one sweet is eaten every 30 minutes during the day, the teeth will be exposed to an acidic environment for most of that time.

It is less damaging to teeth to eat sugary foods at mealtimes, than between meals. After a meal the mouth produces saliva. The saliva washes away food from the teeth and helps to neutralize acid which causes tooth decay. It is thought that if foods such as peanuts and cheese are eaten after a meal, this can help to balance the effects of acid produced by bacterial plaque. Sugar-free chewing gum also increases saliva production.

Ways to prevent tooth decay

- Cut down on the amount of sugary foods, snacks and drinks eaten – reduce your intake of sweets, biscuits and sugary drinks.
- Cut down on snacking on sugary foods and drinks in between meals – the frequency of eating sugary foods is linked to the incidence of tooth decay.
- The oral retentiveness (stickiness) of the sugary food matters. Cut down on foods which stay in the mouth for a long time such as sticky, chewy foods like toffee and some sugary breakfast cereals.
- Brush the teeth at least twice a day using fluoride toothpaste and visit the dentist regularly.
- Babies and toddlers should not be given drinks sweetened with honey or sugar.

═ Questions ═

1. What are the COMA recommendations for sugar intake?
2. What is meant by NME?
3. How can we cut down on the amount of sugary food that we eat?

═ To do ═

Look at some food labels. Make a list of those food products which contain added sugar. Look at the 'Nutrition information' section for this information. Give the

Food	Sugar (in 100 g)	Added sugars shown on label
cheese and tomato pizza	3.6 g	sugar, caramel

names of sugars which are added to these foods. Look at the 'Ingredients' section for this information. You can use a chart like the one shown to fill in your results. Comment on your findings.

12 Vitamins

Vitamins and minerals are called **micro-nutrients** since they are needed in smaller quantities than the **macro-nutrients** – protein, carbohydrate and fat. Vitamins are essential for life because we need them for good health and for growth.

The charts on these pages list the important vitamins, how they are used by the body, good sources of each vitamin, what happens if there is a deficiency in intake, and the requirements for adults.

Groups of vitamins

There are two groups of vitamins – **water-soluble** and **fat-soluble** vitamins.

Water-soluble vitamins

The water-soluble vitamins dissolve in water, and tend to be excreted every day in urine. This means that foods rich in these vitamins need to be eaten regularly. Water-soluble vitamins cannot be stored in the body. They include vitamin C and the B-group vitamins (thiamin, riboflavin, niacin, folic acid, B6, B12, biotin and pantothenic acid).

Water-soluble vitamins can be lost in the cooking water when fruits and vegetables are boiled and during processing.

Fat-soluble vitamins

Fat-soluble vitamins can usually be stored in the body, in the liver. They include vitamins A, D, E and K. Vitamin A is important for night vision and helps to maintain skin and other tissues. Vitamin D works with calcium to develop and maintain strong, healthy bones. Vitamin E appears to be important in preventing heart disease. Vitamin K is needed for blood-clotting.

Questions

1 What is the difference between water-soluble and fat-soluble vitamins?
2 What advice would you give someone who wanted to start taking vitamin tablets on a regular basis?

Fat-soluble vitamins

Vitamin	Use by the body	Good sources	Deficiency	Requirements in adults
Vitamin A – retinol	Good for night vision, healthy skin and tissue.	Animal origin – liver, oily fish, whole milk, butter, margarine, cheese, eggs.	Long-term deficiency may lead to night blindness. Excess may lead to liver and bone damage.	RNI for men 700 µg a day. RNI for women 600 µg a day.
Beta-carotene	Beta-carotene is an antioxidant vitamin which might protect against cancer.	Vegetable origin – carrots, green vegetables, orange and red fruit and vegetables.		
Vitamin D	Works with calcium to form healthy bones and teeth.	Mostly available by exposure to sun. Found in margarine, oily fish, liver.	Deficiency in children can cause rickets. Excessively high intakes associated with hypercalcaemia in children.	There is no RNI set for adults.
Vitamin E	Good for healthy skin. May help to protect against heart disease. Essential for reproduction in some animals.	Eggs, nuts, seeds, cereal products, vegetable oils.	Deficiency rare.	No RNIs but safe intakes have been set at more than 4 mg a day for men and more than 3 mg a day for women.
Vitamin K	Involved with clotting of blood.	Green vegetables, pulses, friut, cereals, meat, liver. Also made by bacteria in the large intestine.	Deficiency rare – normally enough in a balanced diet.	No RNIs but safe intake is 1 µg/kg body weight a day.

Section 1 *Food and nutrition*

Water-soluble vitamins

Vitamin	Use by the body	Good sources	Deficiency	Requirements in adults
Thiamin (B1)	Helps the release of energy from nutrients in every cell in the body.	Fortified breakfast cereals, meat, liver, milk and milk products, eggs and vegetables, including potatoes.	Shortage slows growth and development. Mild deficiency causes tiredness and depression. Severe deficiency causes beriberi.	RNI for men 1.0 mg a day. RNI for women 0.8 mg a day. Increase during pregnancy and lactation.
Riboflavin (B2)	Needed for healthy skin. Helps release energy to cells and in the body's use of carbohydrates.	Fortified breakfast cereals, milk and milk products, meat, liver kidney, eggs, green vegetables.	Shortage slows growth and development. May cause skin and eye problems.	RNI for men 1.3 mg a day. RNI for women 1.1 mg a day. Increase during pregnancy and lactation.
Niacin	Involved in the energy producing reactions in the cells. Helps the nervous system and healthy skin.	Meat, especially offal, cereals, potatoes, bread.	Severe deficiency causes pellagra. Symptoms include diarrhoea, dementia and dermatitis. Very high doses may cause liver damage.	RNI for men 17.0 mg a day. RNI for women 13.0 mg a day. Increase during pregnancy and lactation.
Pyridoxine (B6)	Needed for the metabolism of protein. Helps formation of red blood cells and correct functioning of the nervous system.	Liver, kidney, fish, wheatgerm, poultry, leafy vegetables, potatoes, cereals.	Rare, but deficiency in infants can cause convulsions. High intakes have been linked with poor function of sensory nerves.	RNI for men 1.4 mg a day. RNI for women 1.2 mg a day.
B12	Helps prevent certain forms of anaemia. Helps cells to divide. Protects nervous system. May be deficient in a strict vegetarian or vegan diet.	All animal foods – liver, fish, meat, cheese, milk, eggs. Fortified breakfast cereals.	Deficiency can lead to pernicious anaemia and neurological problems.	RNI for men and women 1.5 μg a day.
Folic acid	Deficiency in the early stages of pregnancy is associated with neural tube defects. Needed for red cell production.	Fortified breakfast cereals, some breads, nuts and pulses.	Mild deficiency leads to tiredness. A deficiency can cause megaloblastic anaemia. Needed in pregnancy to help prevent neural tube defects.	RNI for men and women 200 μg a day. More needed during pregnancy and lactation. Woman planning pregnancy, or in the first 12 weeks, should supplement their diet with 0.4 mg per day.
Vitamin C (ascorbic acid)	Maintains body's connective tissue, important for wound healing. Helps iron absorption. Has antioxidant properties.	Fruits and vegetables, especially citrus fruits including oranges and lemons.	Deficiency may cause scurvy.	RNI for men and women 40 mg a day.

Anti-oxidant vitamins

Vitamin C, found in fruits and vegetables, vitamin E, in vegetable oils, and beta-carotenes found in red and orange fruits and vegetables, are **anti-oxidant** vitamins. A diet rich in anti-oxidant vitamins is thought to help reduce the risk of heart disease and cancer.

The World Health Organization (WHO) advises that we should 'Eat a pound of vegetables a day'. This is the equivalent of five portions of fruits and vegetables. Foods high in anti-oxidant vitamins include carrots, broccoli, cabbage, tomatoes, blackcurrants, vegetable oils and citrus fruits.

Fortification of foods with vitamins

Some foods are fortified with vitamins which are manufactured. These are identical in structure to the vitamins found naturally in food and behave in the body in the same way.

Dietary recommendations for vitamins

The COMA report gives the **reference nutrient intake** (**RNI**) which is the amount of nutrient which is enough – or nearly enough – for most people. The charts on pages 32–3 show the dietary recommendations for vitamins for adults.

B-group vitamins

The B-group vitamins have three main roles.
- They help in the conversion of food to energy.
- They are needed for nerve, brain and muscle function.
- They are needed for red blood cells.

— *Fact* —

Vitamins are essential for life.

They are needed in small amounts to keep us in good health.

Fresh fruits and vegetables, nuts and seeds are good sources of anti-oxidant vitamins.

Kellogg's®
COCO POPS® ™
THE BEST FOR YOU

INGREDIENTS

RICE, SUGAR, COCOA, SALT, WHEY POWDER, MALT FLAVOURING, FLAVOURING, NIACIN, IRON, VITAMIN B$_6$, RIBOFLAVIN (B$_2$), THIAMIN (B$_1$), FOLIC ACID, VITAMIN B$_{12}$.

NUTRITIONAL INFORMATION

		Typical value per 100g	Per 30g serving with 125ml of Semi-Skimmed Milk
ENERGY	kJ	1600	750 *
	kcal	380	170
PROTEIN	g	5	6
CARBOHYDRATE	g	87	32
(of which sugars)	g	(39)	(18)
(starch)	g	(48)	(14)
FAT	g	0.8	2.5 *
(of which saturates)	g	(0.3)	(1.5)
FIBRE	g	1.0	0.3
SODIUM	g	0.9	0.3
VITAMINS		(%RDA)	(%RDA)
THIAMIN (B$_1$)	mg	1.2 (85)	0.4 (30)
RIBOFLAVIN (B$_2$)	mg	1.3 (85)	0.6 (40)
NIACIN	mg	15 (85)	4.6 (25)
VITAMIN B$_6$	mg	1.7 (85)	0.6 (30)
FOLIC ACID	µg	167 (85)	60 (30)
VITAMIN B$_{12}$	µg	0.85 (85)	0.75 (75)
IRON	mg	7.9 (55)	2.4 (17)

* For whole milk increase energy by 100kJ (25kcal) and fat by 3g.
* For skimmed milk reduce energy by 70kJ (20kcal) and fat by 2g.
Contribution provided by 125ml of semi-skimmed milk:-
250kJ (60kcal) of energy, 4g of protein, 6g of carbohydrates (sugars), 2g of fat.

■ Vitamin information on a box of breakfast cereal

The B-group vitamins are water-soluble so they cannot be stored in the body, and they need to be eaten daily. Foods which are good sources of B-group vitamins include wholemeal cereals, yeast, meat and leafy vegetables.

Vitamin C (ascorbic acid)

Vitamin C is needed to form the connective tissues of the body and it may help to protect against some illnesses and infections. Good sources of vitamin C include blackcurrants, oranges, citrus fruits and green, leafy vegetables. As vitamin C cannot be stored by the body, a daily dietary supply is needed. Vitamin C is easily destroyed during cooking so fruits and vegetables should be cooked quickly in a little water and not kept warm for long periods of time. A deficiency of vitamin C can lead to scurvy but this is very rare in the UK today.

The pie chart from the National Food Survey (right) shows the foods which make up our vitamin C intakes.

Vitamin A

There are two forms of vitamin A – **retinol** and **beta-carotene**.

Retinol is the main form of vitamin A found in animal foods such as milk, cheese, butter and oily fish. By law margarine must be fortified with vitamin A.

Beta-carotene is found in green vegetables and red and orange fruits, especially carrots, tomatoes and apricots. Beta-carotene is converted in the body to retinol in the small intestine.

Vitamin A is important for growth and vision in dim light. A deficiency can result in night blindness. Beta-carotene may help protect against cancer and heart disease. Retinol is stored in the liver, so a deficiency of vitamin A is rare. Excessive intakes using supplements can have harmful effects.

Vitamin D

Vitamin D is important for the absorption of calcium. Vitamin D is obtained mainly by the action of sunlight on the skin. For people who are housebound or who do not expose their skin to sunlight, a good dietary supply of vitamin D, found in oily fish, fortified margarine and fortified cereals,

is essential. Vitamin D supplements may also be needed. Vitamin D deficiency can result in rickets where the bones soften and bend out of shape due to inadequate calcium levels.

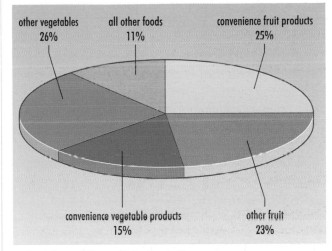

other vegetables 26% all other foods 11% convenience fruit products 25%

convenience vegetable products 15% other fruit 23%

■ **Foods from which we obtain vitamin C**
Source – National Food Survey

— *To do* —

Make a collection of food labels and list the foods which are fortified with vitamins. You could use a chart like the one shown.

Food product	Vitamins added
banana bubbles	B6, riboflavin, thiamin, folic acid, B12

— *Questions* —

1. Explain why each of the following vitamins is important in the diet and which foods are good sources.
   a vitamin A   b B-group vitamins
   c vitamin C   d vitamin D
2. What vitamins and minerals have been added to the breakfast cereal shown on the label (opposite), and what is their function?

13 Minerals

Minerals, like vitamins, are called **micro-nutrients** – nutrients which are needed in very small quantities. Different minerals are used in the human body to help form bones, skin and tissue and are necessary for many body processes. Each mineral has a specific function, as shown in the chart opposite. By eating a variety of foods we should be able to obtain enough minerals to meet our needs. The two minerals most often lacking in the diet are **calcium** and **iron**.

Nineteen minerals are needed by the body. The main ones are calcium, phosphorus, potassium, sodium, chlorides and magnesium. Other minerals such as iron, zinc, copper and fluorides are needed in smaller amounts and are called **trace elements**.

A poor intake of minerals can lead to health problems. Calcium is needed for strong bones and teeth. If the diet provides too little calcium, the bones may not become as strong as they could be. This can lead to the development of **osteoporosis** (brittle bones) in adults. This disease affects one in four women over the age of 65. Calcium is one of the minerals which is only found in a few foods such as milk, cheese and fortified flour.

Foods fortified with minerals

Some foods have minerals added to them. These foods include breakfast cereals fortified with iron, and white flour which is fortified with calcium.

Investigation

Carry out some research about mineral supplements. What are your views about mineral supplements?

Questions

1 What is the importance of minerals in our diet?
2 Using food tables or a nutritional analysis computer program, choose three minerals and find four foods which are good sources of each mineral.

500g e

BRAN FLAKES

FORTIFIED WITH VITAMINS AND IRON

Wheat flakes enriched with 30% bran

■ Breakfast cereals are often fortified with vitamins and iron

Some of the main minerals needed to maintain a healthy body

Minerals	Use by the body	Sources	Deficiency	Requirements for adults
Calcium	Important for bones and teeth, muscle contraction, blood clotting and enzyme secretion.	Milk, cheese, yogurt, white bread, fish in which the bones are eaten, e.g. sardines, green leafy vegetables, nuts, seeds, dried fruit, oranges.	Too little calcium results in stunted growth and rickets.	RNI for adults 700 mg a day. Increase during lactation.
Phosphorus	Important for development of bones and teeth.	Nearly all foods contain phosphorus – particularly milk, cereal products, cheese, meat, bread.	People are rarely deficient in this mineral.	RNI for adults 550 mg a day. Increase during lactation.
Magnesium	Involved in bone mineralization and transmission of nerve impulses. Needed for activity of some enzymes.	Found in a variety of foods such as cereals, bread, meat, potatoes, fruits and vegetables and milk.	People are rarely deficient in this mineral, but deficiency symptoms are tiredness and depression.	RNI for men 300 mg a day. RNI for women 270 mg a day.
Potassium	Helps control the balance of fluids in the body. Also essential for muscle and nerve function.	Found in a range of foods including milk, fruits and vegetables, meat.	May cause weakness and confusion.	RNI for adults 3500 mg a day.
Zinc	Needed for enzyme function and wound healing. Also needed for normal growth.	Found in milk, cheese, yogurt and whole-grain cereals, meat.	Deficiency is rare but may cause poor growth in children.	RNI for men 9.5 mg a day. RNI for women 7 mg a day. Increase during lactation.
Sodium	Maintains fluid balance. Excess sodium has been linked to raised blood pressure.	Table salt, salty snacks and meats, canned foods, take-away meals.	Deficiency in sodium is unlikely.	RNI for adults 1600 mg a day.
Iron	Forms part of the red blood cell protein, haemoglobin, which carries oxygen around the body. Iron deficiency is fairly common in young women as requirements are high due to loss of blood in periods (menstruation) and dietary intakes are often poor.	Meat, liver, kidneys, some breakfast cereals, fortified bread, green leafy vegetables, dried fruit, pulses.	Iron-deficiency anaemia may occur, with symptoms of weakness and tiredness.	RNI for men 8.7 mg a day. RNI for women 14.8 mg a day.
Iodine	Essential part of the thyroid hormones which help to regulate growth and metabolic rate.	Fish, shellfish, milk and milk products, fruit, vegetables, cereals.	A deficiency causes enlargement of the thyroid gland and causes goitre.	RNI for adults 140 μg a day.
Fluoride	Involved in the formation of bones and teeth. Helps to make them resistant to decay.	Fluoride toothpaste, drinking water and seafood.	A deficiency is rare. Excessive amounts of fluoride can cause mottling of teeth.	No official recommendation.

Calcium

The functions of calcium

Calcium helps to form bones and teeth and it is one of the most important minerals needed by the human body. The adult body contains more than a kilogram of calcium, most of which is found in the skeleton. Calcium is also needed for blood-clotting, muscle contraction and enzyme secretion.

How much calcium do we need?

The RNI for calcium is 700 mg a day for adults. Teenagers need more – 1000 mg a day for boys and 800 mg for girls. Women who are breastfeeding need almost twice as much calcium in their diet to help with their milk supply for their baby.

When young children are growing, their calcium needs are high in relation to their body size because their bones are growing rapidly. At around 18 years the bones have stopped growing in length, but they become heavier until peak bone mass is reached at about 30 years.

The teenage years are especially important as most calcium is thought to be deposited in the bone bank during this time.

Deficiency in calcium

If we do not eat enough calcium in our food to maintain the blood calcium level, then some is used from our bones. A poor intake of calcium from the diet means that less calcium is deposited in the bones and this, in turn, results in a lower bone mass and a weaker skeleton.

Reference nutrient intake for calcium	
Age	RNI (mg per day)
0–12 months	525
1–3 yr	350
4–6 yr	450
7–10 yr	550
11–18 yr	1000 male
	800 female
19+	700
Lactating women	> 550

Osteoporosis

Osteoporosis is the condition of weakening and thinning of the bones. It is most common in elderly people, especially women. The bones fracture and break easily. Evidence seems to show that a diet with a good supply of calcium, particularly during childhood and the teenage years, together with regular exercise, may help to protect against osteoporosis. Avoiding smoking and drinking excessive amounts of alcohol are also important.

Good sources of calcium

Milk and dairy foods such as cheese and yogurt are important sources of calcium in the British diet. This calcium is more easily absorbed by the body than calcium found in other foods. Calcium is added to white flour, so white bread is a good source of calcium, as are green, leafy vegetables, nuts, seeds, dried fruit, and fish in which the bones are eaten, such as sardines.

Calcium and other foods

Cereals contain substances called **phytates**, and spinach contains substances called **oxalates**. If they are present in the diet in large quantities, both these substances can hinder the absorption of calcium from foods. Elderly people are advised to avoid eating raw bran as the phytate present in the bran can block important mineral absorption. Phytates and oxalates can also hinder the absorption of other nutrients such as zinc.

Calcium and vitamin D

Vitamin D is needed, together with calcium and phosphorus, to help build and maintain strong bones and teeth. Most people get sufficient vitamin D from sunlight, but some people who do not go out very often, such as the elderly, or people who keep their skin covered, such as traditional Asian families, need to make sure they eat foods which are good sources of vitamin D. These include oily fish, eggs and fortified breakfast cereals and margarine.

Vitamin D supplements may be needed. There are no dietary guidelines for vitamin D for children over the age of four years, or adults, but for pregnant and breastfeeding women, and adults over the age of 65 years, the RNI is $10\,\mu g$ daily. The RNI for babies under six months old is $8.5\,\mu g$ daily and for children between six months and four years old it is $7\,\mu g$ daily.

— To do

Plan a day's menus and show which foods you have included to provide calcium and some vitamin D.

— Fact

Calcium helps form bones and teeth.
It works with vitamin D and phosphorus.
Good sources of calcium include milk, cheese and yogurt.

— Questions

1 What is the function of calcium in our bodies?
2 How does our calcium requirement change with age?

milk (115 mg per 100 g)

nuts (78 mg per 100 g)

yogurt (190 mg per 100 g)

dried fruit (e.g. apricots: 15 mg per 100 g)

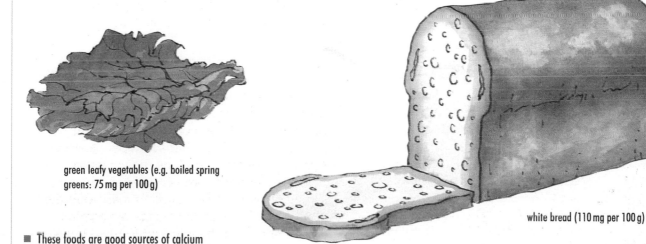

green leafy vegetables (e.g. boiled spring greens: 75 mg per 100 g)

white bread (110 mg per 100 g)

■ These foods are good sources of calcium

Iron

*A*naemia, caused by lack of iron in the diet, is one of the most common nutritional problems world-wide. Women and children are at greatest risk of developing iron deficiency anaemia. Most cases of anaemia can be prevented by following a healthy diet, eating plenty of iron-rich foods. Supplements are not recommended unless iron deficiency anaemia actually occurs. Evidence suggests that if iron supplements are given to young children who have adequate iron stores, growth may be delayed.

Why do we need iron?

Iron is needed to form part of haemoglobin, which gives red blood cells their colour. These cells carry oxygen in the blood to body cells. Iron deficiency anaemia is caused by a shortage of iron. Inadequate amounts of haemoglobin are formed and so the blood is unable to carry sufficient oxygen to the cells and the body becomes easily tired.

How much iron do we need?

Girls and women lose blood during their monthly periods and this iron loss needs to be replaced. Teenage girls and women of child-bearing age need more iron than men of the same age. The chart below shows the daily reference nutrient intake (RNI) for iron. The body stores iron in the liver so it is not essential to meet the requirements each day. However, it is important that this average requirement *is* maintained over the space of two or three days.

Good sources of iron

The best sources of iron are found in offal such as liver and kidney. Other good sources of iron include red meat, oily fish, poultry, and game, fortified bread, green leafy vegetables such as broccoli and spinach, pulses such as beans and lentils, dried fruit and fortified breakfast cereals. In the UK some foods, such as breakfast cereals and bread, are fortified with iron.

Iron obtained from meat is more easily absorbed than iron from plant foods. About 45–60 per cent of the iron in meat is found in the form of

How much iron do we need?		
Age (years)	Average daily requirement (mg)	
	Male	Female
11–18	11.3	14.8
19–50	8.7	14.8
50+	8.7	8.7

haem iron which is easily absorbed and used by the body. Iron in cereals and vegetables is **non-haem iron** and this is not so easily absorbed. Vitamin C increases the amount of non-haem iron absorbed so foods containing iron from plant sources should be eaten with foods rich in vitamin C, such as oranges and green vegetables preferably at the same meal.

— *Fact* —

Iron is needed to help form red blood cells.
A deficiency of iron can lead to anaemia.
Iron is found in meat, liver and kidneys.
Vitamin C helps increase iron absorption from non-haem sources.

— *Did you know?* —

Researchers found that the iron content of cook-chill Balti curries increased once they were heated in a Balti wok. If food is cooked in the small cast iron wok, a little iron enters the food in a form which is readily absorbed by the body.

■ **A Balti wok**

Vegetarians need to make sure they obtain an adequate iron supply from foods such as bread, cereals, pulses and vegetables.

Blocking iron absorption

Iron absorption is reduced by the presence of tannins found in tea and coffee, phytates found in unrefined cereals such as raw bran, and phospho-protein in eggs. To ensure that iron absorption from non-haem sources is maximized, large quantities of foods containing tannins and phytates should not be eaten at the same meals as iron-rich foods, e.g. avoid drinking tea with iron-rich foods.

━ To do ━

Plan a day's menus for a teenage girl who is a vegetarian. Show how you have included iron-rich foods and foods which are good sources of vitamin C.

━ Questions ━

1 What is the function of iron in our bodies?
2 Which foods are good sources of iron?

■ Sources of iron (haem iron sources on the left of the picture, non-haem iron sources on the right)

16 *Sodium and salt*

The most common form of sodium in the diet is salt (sodium chloride). Sodium is needed to control body fluids. The COMA report on cardiovascular disease, published in 1994, recommended that people of all ages should cut down on their salt intake. The average intake of salt in the UK is 9 g. The advice is to reduce this by one-third to 6 g a day.

Salt and blood pressure

Raised blood pressure is one of the risk factors associated with heart disease and strokes. Many people in western countries have relatively high blood pressure. Even a small reduction in average blood pressure of the population could help to reduce the incidence of heart disease and strokes. Dietary and lifestyle factors contribute to the increase in blood pressure in western countries and levels increase with age. Dietary and lifestyle factors which may raise blood pressure include high dietary salt intakes, high alcohol consumption, low exercise levels and increased body weight. All of these factors need to be tackled in order to lower average blood pressure levels.

Salt and health

- High intake of salt over a long period of time may be linked with high blood pressure.
- The amount of salt eaten in Western populations is high so it could easily be reduced.

In western countries, the typical daily intake of salt is 10 g for men and 8 g for women. Of this intake:
- 15 per cent is added during cooking or at the table
- 10 per cent occurs naturally in food
- 75 per cent is added during processing.

A reduction of 3 g of salt a day would correspond to COMA recommendations.

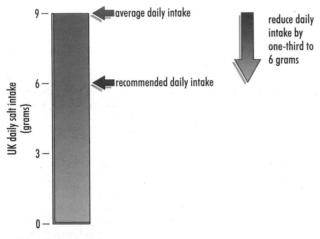

■ The reduction of salt

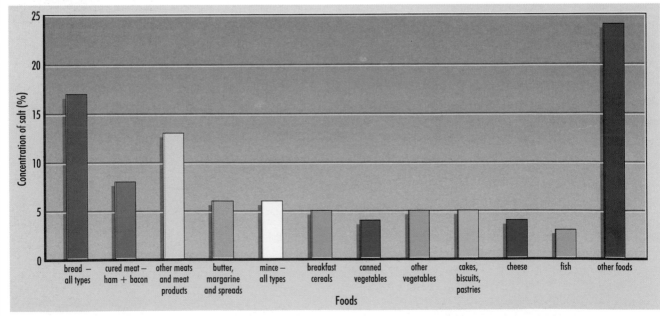

■ The salt content of some foods

The salt in our food	
Food	Amount of salt (g)
2 sausages	3.4
2 large slices bacon	2.5
Ham and cheese sandwich	3.5
Quarter pound cheeseburger	3.7
Small tin baked beans	2.0
Bread medium slice	0.5
1 tsp soy sauce	3.6
1 tsp baking powder	1.3
1 tsp table salt	5
50 g salted nuts	0.5
1 bag ready-salted crisps	1

Source – *Food Magazine, July–September 1995*

Tips

The aim is to reduce salt intake to 6 g a day.

- Read food labels to see if they give the amount of sodium or salt they contain. If not, look for ingredients which contain salt or sodium – sodium chloride, monosodium glutamate, bicarbonate of soda.
- Many ready-to-eat foods are already salted.
- Cook with less salt – use herbs, spices or lemon juice to give flavour instead.
- Cut down on salty snacks such as crisps.
- Use less sauce and pickles, such as tomato ketchup.
- Eat fewer salty meat products such as sausages, beefburgers, canned meats, meat pies.
- Eat fewer take-aways such as pizza and Chinese meals.

The main foods that contribute salt in our diet, according to MAFF's National Food Survey 1994, are shown in the chart at the foot of page 42.

— *Fact*

Most of our sodium comes from salt added to foods during processing..

Sodium is needed to control body fluids.

We should cut down on the amount of salt we eat to help reduce the risk of high blood pressure.

Salt can be hidden in processed food.

■ A label from a reduced-salt alternative

— Questions

1. Why should we try to cut down on the amount of salt in our diet?
2. Which foods contain high amounts of salt?
3. Give some ideas of how to reduce the amount of salt used in cooking.
4. Suggest how you could reduce the salt content of the foods you eat in a typical day.
5. Look at the label for LoSalt. What is the main ingredient in LoSalt? Why do you think this product has been designed?
6. What are the main foods that contribute salt to our diet?

Non-starch polysaccharides

Dietary fibre is now referred to as **non-starch polysaccharide** (**NSP**). It is a non-digestible carbohydrate found in plant food. Why is the term NSP used? The non-digestible part of food is made up of a complex mixture of compounds and scientists could obtain different results for the amount of dietary fibre in food, depending upon which method of analysis they used. The COMA panel decided to use the term 'non-starch polysaccharides' and adopted the analytical method developed by Englyst and Cummings in 1988 for their recommendations on suitable intakes.

The functions of dietary fibre (NSP)

Dietary fibre (NSP) cannot be broken down by the digestive system so it passes through the intestine, absorbing water and increasing in bulk. This process helps to strengthen the muscles of the intestine and push out undigested food.
  Dietary fibre (NSP):
- is needed for the digestive system to function properly
- may help prevent various bowel disorders including constipation, diverticular disease, bowel cancer, appendicitis and haemorrhoids (piles)
- can help people to control their body weight because high-fibre foods are filling.

Types of dietary fibre (NSP)

There are two types of dietary fibre (NSP) – **insoluble** and **soluble** – which have different functions.

Insoluble fibre

Insoluble fibre absorbs water and increases in bulk. This helps the stools become soft and bulky and helps to keep the gut in good working order.
  Foods rich in insoluble fibre include wholemeal bread and flour, whole-grain breakfast cereals and pasta, brown rice and some fruits and vegetables.

Soluble fibre

Soluble fibre is thought to slow down the digestion and absorption of carbohydrates and so

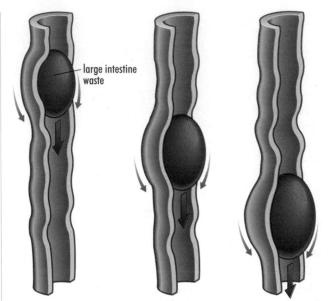

large intestine waste

fibre helps waste to move through the large intestine easily

■ Food waste passing through the intestines

helps to control blood sugar levels which helps to stop us feeling hungry. Soluble fibre may also reduce blood cholesterol levels and this in turn reduces the risk of coronary heart disease. Good sources of soluble fibre include oats, peas, beans, lentils, most types of fruit and vegetables.

Recommendations for dietary fibre (NSP)

COMA recommended that the dietary reference value (DRV) for dietary fibre (NSP) is 18 grams for adults with a range of 12 grams to 24 grams a day. Children may need to eat less because of their smaller body size. Very young children shouldn't eat too many fibre-rich foods, otherwise their diet could be very bulky and filling, which makes it difficult for them to fulfil their energy needs.

Wheat bran

Wheat bran contains a substance called phytate that can bind minerals found in food such as calcium, iron, zinc and copper and make them unavailable for the body to use. Raw bran should therefore be avoided unless recommended by a doctor.

Serving portions of a selection of foods with NSP content		
Food	Serving size (weight)	NSP content (g)
All Bran	1 medium bowl (40 g)	9.8
Weetabix	2 biscuits (40 g)	3.9
Porridge	1 medium bowl (160 g)	1.3
Cornflakes	1 medium bowl (30 g)	0.3
Wholemeal bread	1 medium slice (36 g)	2.1
Brown bread	1 medium slice (36 g)	1.3
White bread	1 medium slice (36 g)	0.5
Wholemeal flour	1 tbsp (30 g)	2.7
White flour	1 tbsp (30 g)	0.9
Whole-wheat pasta	medium portion (230 g)	8.1
White pasta	medium portion (230 g)	2.8
Brown rice	medium portion (180 g)	1.4
White rice	medium portion (180 g)	0.2
Orange	1 medium (160 g)	2.7
Apple	1 medium (100 g)	1.7
Banana	1 medium (100 g)	1.1
Baked potato skin	1 medium (180 g)	4.9
Baked beans	3 tbsp (120 g)	4.4
Frozen peas	2 tbsp (60 g)	3.1
Lentils, boiled	3 tbsp (90 g)	1.7
Tomato	medium (85 g)	0.9

All figures for NSP have been calculated using the Englyst method of analysis.
Source – *Learning about Food and Nutrition*, National Dairy Council

How to eat more dietary fibre

- Eat more wholegrain foods including bread and cereals.
- Eat more fruits and vegetables, pulses and nuts.

— *To do* —

Use the chart on the left, showing the dietary fibre (NSP) content for serving sizes for different foods.

Plan a day's menus for yourself to include some of these foods. The aim is to provide about 18 grams of dietary fibre (NSP). Give examples for breakfast, lunch and evening meal as well as snacks. Try to keep the fat and sugar content within recommended limits.

— *Fact* —

Dietary fibre is important in preventing constipation.

COMA recommends an average fibre intake of 18 g a day. The average person eats about 12 g a day so this means increasing intake by 50 per cent.

Good sources of fibre include wholegrain cereal foods, pulses, nuts, fruits and vegetables.

The advantages of eating foods rich in dietary fibre (NSP)

Cereals, fruits and vegetables which are good sources of dietary fibre (NSP) are low in fat and are good sources of vitamins and minerals. Many fruits and vegetables are good sources of vitamin C and beta-carotene. Wholemeal bread and breakfast cereals contain the B-group vitamins.

Good sources of dietary fibre (NSP)

These include wholemeal flour, wholemeal and high-fibre varieties of bread, whole-grain breakfast cereals, porridge oats, beans, lentils and peas, fresh fruits and vegetables, potatoes in their skins, nuts and seeds and dried fruit.

— *Questions* —

1 Dietary fibre is now called NSP. What is meant by NSP?
2 What is the function of dietary fibre (NSP) in our diet?
3 What are the two types of dietary fibre (NSP) and what foods are good sources of each type?
4 How much dietary fibre (NSP) should adults eat each day? Why should children eat less dietary fibre (NSP) than that recommended for adults?

Water

*N*early 65 per cent of the human body is made up of water and it forms part of all organs, tissues and body fluids. Water is essential for us to live. Experts recommend that we drink about 6–8 watery drinks (e.g. water, fizzy water, sugar-free diluted orange squash) each day. These drinks could be plain water, but could also include unsweetened fruit juices, milk and sugar-free drinks, weak tea and coffee.

Why do we need water?

- Water is a component of many body fluids such as blood which carries nutrients, oxygen and carbon dioxide round the body.
- Nearly all the body processes need water for them to take place e.g. digestion.
- Water helps to regulate body temperature – for example, when we sweat water evaporates from the skin and cools us.
- Water helps to excrete waste products from the body. They are filtered by the kidneys and eliminated in the urine.

■ This marathon runner is taking a welcome water break

How do we lose water?

We lose water from the body in urine, faeces, sweat and exhaled air. Every day we need to replace the water we have lost through our normal body functions. If we take lots of exercise we lose more water, mostly in the form of sweat, so when we do any exercise we should drink plenty of water before, during and afterwards.

There must be a balance between input and output of water, otherwise dehydration occurs and we become unwell.

Food contains water. The chart below shows the percentage of water in certain foods.

Water in food	
Food	**Percentage of water in the food**
Ham	73
Lettuce	96
Milk	87.6
Cheese, Cheddar	37
Yogurt, natural	86
Apples	65
Bananas	70

Source – *Food Tables*, Bender and Bender

— Did you know? —

Water provides us with no energy (kilocalories/kilojoules).

— Investigation —

Investigate the range of bottled waters and soft drinks on sale in supermarkets. Make a list of some of their claims. Why do you think the sales of such drinks are increasing?

—Questions—

1 Why is it important to make sure we drink enough fluids each day?
2 Which types of food contain high percentages of water?

Try this quiz. You may want to write down more than one answer.

1 Foods can be sorted into five groups: fruits and vegetables; breads, potatoes and cereals; meat, fish, poultry and alternatives; dairy products; fats and oils.
A varied diet means eating:
a foods from one group only
b foods from all five groups.

2 Which three food groups contribute most of the fat in our diet?
a fruits and vegetables
b breads, potatoes and cereals
c meat, fish, poultry and alternatives
d dairy products
e fats and oils

3 Which food group contains yam, chapatti, paratha, pitta, farge, rice and pasta?
a fruits and vegetables
b breads, potatoes and cereals
c meat, fish, poultry and alternatives

4 Breads, potatoes and cereals are known as starchy foods. They are a good source of:
a protein
b fibre
c energy.

5 Fruit and vegetables give us fibre and vitamins. We eat different parts of them. Write down two examples of vegetables of which we eat:
a the roots
b the leaves
c the seeds.

6 Meat, fish, chicken, cheese, beans, pulses and nuts all contain.
a sugar
b fibre
c protein.

7 Many of our foods are processed by cooking or mixing them with other foods before we eat them. What did these foods start out as?
a crisps
b yogurt
c jam
d beef sausages

8 Many foods are made by mixing together a range of ingredients and cooking them. Write down:
a two ways in which we add fat to our foods
b one cooking method that can reduce the fat in our foods.

9 If you cook with, or drink, semi-skimmed milk instead of whole milk, would it:
a increase the amount of fat you eat?
b decrease the amount of fat you eat?

10 The two largest ingredients (apart from the fizz) in a can of non-diet cola are:
a fruit
b sugar
c water
d flavourings.

Source – Taken from *School Meals Assessment Pack* published by the National Heart Forum, 1995 (see details on pages 80–1)

Answers

1 A varied diet involves eating foods from all 5 food groups, which, when eaten in combination, supply the right amount of nutrients for a balanced diet.

2 In Britain, the majority of fat in our diets comes from fats and oils; meat, fish, poultry and alternatives; dairy products.

3 These are all examples of the breads, potatoes and cereals group from a variety of countries.

4 Starchy foods are a good source of energy. Some are also fibre rich.

5 Root vegetables include potatoes, carrots, parsnips, swede, mooli; leaf vegetables include spinach, cabbage, leeks, lettuce; seed vegetables include sweetcorn, peas, beans.

6 Meat, fish, chicken, cheese, beans, pulses and nuts all contain protein.

7 Crisps start as potatoes, yogurt as milk, jam as fruit, beef sausages as beef cattle.

8 We add fat by frying, wrapping in pastry, spreading with butter, dressing with mayonnaise, coating or filling with cream. Cooking methods which reduce the fat in foods include removing visible fat before cooking, grilling and baking instead of frying, using less pastry, substituting low-fat alternatives.

9 Using semi-skimmed milk would reduce the amount of fat you eat. Semi-skimmed milk contains less than half the fat of full-cream or whole milk yet retains almost the same taste and cooking properties.

10 The two main ingredients in a can of non-diet cola are water and sugar. Cola also contains flavouring and colours.

Pregnancy

It is important for women who want to become pregnant to follow a healthy diet. The diet before pregnancy can affect the chances of having a successful pregnancy and the health of the baby when it is born.

Energy (kilocalories, kilojoules)

The need for energy increases during the last three months of pregnancy to allow for the rapid growth of the developing baby. However, it is *not* true that pregnant women need to eat for two.

Protein

Protein requirements increase slightly during pregnancy. Pregnant women should try to eat protein-rich foods, such as meat, fish, milk, cheese, eggs (well cooked), yogurt, pulses, nuts, bread and cereals, every day.

Folic acid

Folic acid is one of the B-group vitamins. In recent years, women have been advised to make sure their diet contains adequate supplies of folic acid before and during pregnancy, especially in the first twelve weeks of their pregnancy. Supplements have been found to reduce the risk of a baby being born with a neural tube defect, such as spina bifida, by as much as 70 per cent. Folic acid supplements of 0.4 mg (400 μg) should be taken daily. Good dietary sources of folic acid include fortified breakfast cereals, wholemeal bread, yeast extracts such as Marmite, and green leafy vegetables.

Calcium

Requirements for calcium during pregnancy are the same as for non-pregnant women. This is because the mother's body adapts to absorb calcium more efficiently. However, it is important to make sure intakes are adequate. Sufficient vitamin D should be included in the diet to make sure the calcium is absorbed. Good dietary sources of calcium include milk, yogurt and cheese, fish where the bones can be eaten and green leafy vegetables. White bread is fortified with calcium. Vitamin D is found in butter, margarine, eggs and oily fish. Vitamin D can also be manufactured by the skin when it is exposed to sunlight.

Iron

Pregnant women should include in their diet some iron-rich foods such as red meat, oily fish, fortified bread and breakfast cereal, pulses, dried fruits and nuts. Vitamin C helps iron absorption. Plenty of fresh fruit and vegetables should be eaten with iron-rich foods.

The importance of dietary fibre (NSP)

Eating fibre-rich foods help to prevent pregnant women from suffering from constipation and piles. Good sources of dietary fibre (NSP) include wholemeal bread, whole-grain breakfast cereals, pulses, wholemeal pasta, brown rice, potatoes in

If you are pregnant or thinking of becoming pregnant, you are recommended to increase the amount of folic acid in your diet. This can reduce the risk of spina bifida and similar neural tube defects. The normal recommended daily allowance (RDA) of folic acid is 200 micrograms. Prior to pregnancy and during the first three months of pregnancy, you are recommended to increase that level to 600 micrograms a day. The average serving of this cereal can provide 32 per cent of the RDA in two biscuits (37.5 grams).

■ Pregnant women need to eat a variety of foods for a healthy diet

their skins and fruits and vegetables. Drinking plenty of fluids can also help to prevent constipation.

Foods to avoid during pregnancy

Soft ripened cheeses such as Brie and Camembert may contain listeria bacteria which can be harmful to an unborn baby, so pregnant women should avoid these types. However, other soft cheeses such as cheese spreads, cottage cheese and cream cheese, and hard cheeses such as Cheddar are suitable. Other foods which may contain listeria bacteria include cook-chill meals and paté. Raw eggs may contain salmonella bacteria, so eggs should be thoroughly cooked until both the white and the yolk are solid, to avoid the risk of food poisoning. Foods containing raw egg, such as home-made mayonnaise, should also be avoided. Pregnant women are advised to avoid eating liver and its products such as liver paté as they may contain very large amounts of vitamin A which can be harmful to a developing baby. Pregnant women should avoid taking supplements of vitamin A unless advised to do so by their doctor.

Breastfeeding

After a woman gives birth, her body produces milk for the baby. This is called **lactation**. During lactation, a woman has higher requirements for energy and some nutrients, to produce good quality breast milk, which has to contain enough nourishment to provide for the needs of the growing

child. During breastfeeding a woman should make sure she eats foods which are good sources of protein, calcium, iron, zinc, B-vitamins and vitamins A, C and D. She should also drink plenty of liquid more than normal – to help produce the milk. Much of the extra weight gained during pregnancy is likely to be lost if the mother breastfeeds.

— *Fact* —

Pregnant women need to take care what they eat.

They should choose foods which are good sources of energy and nutrients.

Breast milk provides for the needs of the baby, so the mother must follow a healthy diet.

— *To do* —

1 Plan a healthy day's meals for a pregnant woman. Explain your food choices for each meal.
2 What are the special dietary needs of a woman who is breastfeeding? Give examples of foods which are good sources of the nutrients she needs.

— *Question* —

Explain why folic acid is important in the diet of women who want to become pregnant and those in the first twelve weeks of pregnancy.

21 Babies

Breastfeeding

Experts recommend that babies are breastfed for at least four months as there are real health benefits.

Advantages of breastfeeding

- The milk contains all the energy and essential nutrients babies need in an easily absorbable form.
- Breast milk cannot be prepared incorrectly.
- The milk contains **antibodies** and other factors which help protect babies against infection.
- Breastfed babies are less likely to be overweight.
- Feeding helps bond the mother and child.
- Breast milk is free and convenient.
- Breastfeeding may help to reduce the incidence of allergies.
- Breastfeeding may help the mother to lose excess fat stores gained during pregnancy.

Bottle-feeding

Specially modified infant formulas have been developed for babies so that they can be bottle-fed. The bottles, teats and equipment must be thoroughly sterilized to prevent the baby from becoming ill. Care must be taken when preparing the milk. It is important to follow the instructions on the side of the tin – for example an extra scoop of milk will make the food too concentrated and can lead to dehydration and overfeeding.

Weaning

Babies should not be given solid food until they are four months old. By this time their bodies have developed enough to cope with a more varied diet and this is when solids can be introduced. The changeover from milk to solid food is called **weaning**. During the early stages of weaning, the baby will still get most of the required nutrients from breast or formula milk.

As weaning progresses, solid foods become more important sources of energy and nutrients. Breast milk or infant formula should continue to be given as the main drink until a baby is one year old. After this time, cows' milk can be given as the main milk drink.

Special care during weaning

- Babies under six months should preferably be given gluten-free cereals – **coeliac disease** is triggered by a substance called gluten which is one of the proteins in wheat. Because those children who are likely to suffer from this disorder cannot be identified in advance, gluten should not be introduced to a baby's diet until six months.
- Make sure that weaning foods are sugar-free or low in added sugar.
- Foods used in weaning should not contain added salt.
- Weaning foods should be of a suitable texture.
- First foods should taste bland.
- Babies should never be left unsupervised whilst feeding.
- Do not give nuts to babies as they could choke.

Feeding infants

Infants need to follow a healthy diet so that they grow and stay active and healthy. Infants should be encouraged to eat a variety of foods.

Tips on preparing food for infants

- Foods should contain a wide range of nutrients – for example milk pudding with fruit purée.
- In the early stages of weaning, food needs to be mashed or puréed to a suitable texture so that the baby can eat it easily.
- Give small children foods similar to the rest of the family, but make sure it is free from added salt and low in sugar – for example, carrots can be mashed and mixed with potato.
- Whether to use home-made or ready-prepared baby food is a matter of personal preference. Most people choose to use a mixture of both.

Ready-prepared baby foods

Some parents like to use ready-prepared baby foods as they are easy and quick to use.

The advantages of ready-prepared baby foods

- They are easy and quick to use when in a hurry or out shopping.
- A range of products is available to offer the baby

Nutrients in our drinks						
Nutrient content of drinks per glass (200 ml)	Calories (kcal)	Calcium (mg)	Protein (g)	Vitamin B12 (µg)	Riboflavin (mg)	Vitamin C (mg)
Whole milk	136	238	6.6	0.8	0.36	2
Orange juice	76	24	1.2	0	0.04	100
Cola	78	8	trace	0	0	0
Squash	43	3.2	trace	0	trace	trace

Source – National Dairy Council

a choice of tastes.

- Some baby foods offer a range of nutrients and some have extra vitamins and minerals added.

The disadvantages of ready-prepared baby foods

- They are more expensive than home-made food.
- They may not provide a full range of nutrients. In the later stages of weaning babies may need to eat very large amounts in order to meet their energy and nutrient requirements.
- Children's eating habits start early – is eating ready-made meals a habit to be encouraged?
- Parents do not experiment with their cooking skills and may come to rely too heavily on these products.

— Fact

Breastfeeding is better for babies than bottle-feeding.

Babies can be weaned from the age of four to six months.

Young children need to eat nutritious food for healthy growth and development.

Babies may get so used to the taste and texture of these foods that they become unwilling to eat home-made foods.

What is available?

Food producers make a range of baby foods including breakfast, savouries, desserts and drinks. These foods may be complete meals in jars or cans, dried foods in packets, baby drinks and milks prepared in cartons or in powdered form, designed to meet the baby's needs in later months. Information on the food labels helps parents choose the type of product they want to buy.

— Questions

1 Give your views on the advantages and disadvantages of breastfeeding and bottle-feeding a young baby.
2 What advice would you give a mother about:
   a choosing food for a baby who is being weaned
   b the choice of drinks for her child?
   Use the chart at the top of this page to help.

— Investigation

Visit your local supermarket or chemist and investigate the range of infants' foods for sale. Find out what savoury and sweet foods are available and their cost. At which time of day could the foods be served?

Give a rating for their nutritional value and convenience. You could use a scale of 1–5 where 1 = poor and 5 = excellent. You could fill in a chart like the one shown below. Write a short report on your findings.

Food	Description	Savoury or sweet	Mealtime	Nutritious 1–5	Convenient 1–5	Cost 1–5

Dietary goals

Children should eat a variety of foods to provide a range of nutrients. Their diets should include some starchy, fibre-rich foods such as wholemeal bread, beans and potatoes in their jackets provided energy intakes are achieved. As children approach school age their fat intakes should be in line with the recommendations for adults (no more than 35 per cent of food energy). They should eat more fruits and vegetables and fewer sweets and chocolates.

Why do children need a healthy diet?

- Children need nutritious food for growth and development.
- Good eating habits start in childhood and poor eating habits may be difficult to change in later life.
- Poor diets can lead to health problems in childhood and later in life.
- Children need to cut down on how much sugary food they eat and how often they eat it, to help prevent tooth decay.
- A healthy diet will help children avoid becoming overweight or obese.

Toddlers and young children

Small children (under five) need a balanced diet which provides a range of nutrients.

Tips on feeding small children

- Encourage them to eat foods which are good sources of a wide range of nutrients – e.g. cheese, cereals, fruit, vegetables, eggs, milk, meat, bread.
- Eating should be fun and shared with other family members – don't leave children to eat a meal on their own. Children learn by copying their parents and brothers and sisters.
- Try not to give too many snacks, especially of sweets and crisps which fill children up but have a low nutritional value.
- Chop food into small pieces and make it look attractive.
- Small children usually have small appetites so they may need to be given small portions of food at mealtimes, with snacks between meals.
- Give them a wide variety of foods so that they get used to a range of tastes and textures.
- Limit the amount of sugary and fatty foods they eat.
- Try to encourage them to drink nutritious drinks such as milk or diluted unsweetened fruit juices instead of sweetened, fizzy drinks such as cola. To keep teeth healthy, fruit juices should be limited to mealtimes only.
- Children should become independent at feeding themselves as soon as possible.
- Hard foods such as sticks of carrot and apple help develop strong teeth and gums.
- Let young children help with food preparation.
- Aim to provide three meals, with nutritious snacks between meals, each day.
- Do not include too much fibre-rich food – a diet which is very high in fibre can be very filling, and children would be unable to eat enough food to supply all the energy and nutrients they need for growth.

How can the diets of younger children be improved?

- Make food tasty and fun – get children to help design funny face pizzas and to help with cooking.
- Give children small amounts of food – they can ask for more if they want it.
- Try to get children to eat healthier snacks instead of sugary sweets, cakes, crisps and biscuits. They could try fresh fruit, carrot sticks, cheese and crackers, plain yogurts, wholemeal scones, small sandwiches, toast and smooth peanut butter.
- Get them to help plan a healthy packed lunch box.

■ Children need a healthy diet

Teeth

The first teeth develop in a baby before birth, so children need to learn how to take care of their teeth from an early age.

Some factors that increase the likelihood of tooth decay in young children

- Giving drinks with added sugar, honey or fruit juices in bottles.
- Using feeding bottles or teats for a long time.
- Giving large amounts of sugary foods or drinks.
- Giving sugary foods and drinks frequently throughout the day.
- Poor dental hygiene, i.e. not brushing teeth.

Research has shown that 26 per cent of children aged $1\frac{1}{2} - 3\frac{1}{2}$ who took a sugary drink such as juice or squash with them to bed had tooth decay. This compared with twelve per cent who drank milk and eleven per cent who drank water. Dentists recommend that after teeth have been brushed, children should drink only water.

Milk contains the sugar called lactose, but according to the Department of Health, milk does not cause harm to teeth.

Preventing tooth decay

To help prevent tooth decay

- Avoid giving young children frequent sugary snacks and sweets, especially sticky foods such as toffee and chewy chocolate which stays in the mouth for a long time.

- Never add sugar or honey to milk or other drinks given to young children.
- Do not add sugar or sweet foods such as fruit concentrates or honey to weaning foods or foods for older children.
- Don't leave children to suck at feeding bottles or teats full of drink for long periods of time.
- Encourage good dental hygiene – brushing teeth is important.
- Register with a dentist before problems occur, and have check-ups.

Dentists believe that cheese is a useful snack food as it may help to protect teeth against decay.

— *Fact* —

Small children should eat a variety of foods which supply a range of nutrients.

Children in the UK need to reduce the amount of sugary and salty foods they eat.

Care should be taken with teeth from an early age.

— *Questions* —

1 Why is it important not to give young children sweetened drinks in feeding bottles?
2 Give some ideas to show how you would encourage a toddler to follow a healthy diet.

— *To do* —

Plan a day's meals for a family with a toddler. Draw up a list of the family meals and show what foods the toddler can share and what foods may need extra preparation to make them easy for the toddler to eat. You may include ready-prepared foods in the meals.

Example:

Mealtime	Family meal	Toddlers meal if different	Any special preparation needed
Breakfast	porridge with milk and banana, orange juice and tea	porridge with milk and mashed banana, diluted, unsweetened orange juice	Make sure the porridge is cool enough to eat. Mash the banana. Dilute the orange juice.

23 Older children and adults

Snack foods

By the year 2000 there will be eight million 5–14 year olds in the UK. Many children have their own money to spend on sweets and snacks and a report estimated that children under twelve years old have about £1.40 in weekly pocket money. In 1990, 140 new food and drink products aimed at children were launched in the UK and over half of these were chocolate, sweets and soft drinks. (*Leatherhead Food Research Association*)

Teenagers

Teenagers are growing fast and have higher energy requirements than adults.

| Age (years) | EAR (kcal a day) | |
	Male	Female
11–14	2220	1845
15–18	2755	2110
19–50	2550	1940

Dietary needs

Teenagers have increased requirements for:
- energy
- calcium
- iron.

11–14 years

- Energy requirements increase and protein requirements increase by about 50 per cent.
- **Boys:** need more of all vitamins and minerals.
- **Girls:** need more minerals, especially iron when their periods start.

15–18 years

- **Boys:** energy and protein requirements increase, as well as thiamin, riboflavin, niacin, vitamins C and A and some minerals.
- **Girls:** need more energy, protein, B and C vitamins, and some minerals.

Teenagers often lead busy lives, so their meals and snacks should provide a range of nutrients to meet their dietary needs. If they are taking part in lots of sports, their energy needs will increase and they will need to eat more than other people.

Adults aged 19–50 years

Adults have a lower energy requirement than teenagers, since they have stopped growing and are often less active. Their needs for protein, and most vitamins and minerals remain similar to older teenagers.

Question

Children are eating more and more snack foods. A study in 1990 showed that each week the average eleven year old ate:

four packets of crisps,

six cans of soft drinks,

seven bars of chocolate or sweets,

seven biscuits.

Give examples of healthy snacks which could replace the sweets and chocolates which are popular with children.

Investigation

Carry out a survey to find the typical foods eaten by teenagers during the day. Rate the nutritional value of their food choices. You could use a chart like the one shown below. Use the results of your survey to suggest ways that the teenage diet could be improved.

Food choice	High in fat	High in fibre	High in sugar	High in starch	Healthy choice?	Suitable alternative
crisps	yes	no	no	yes	no	

*A*nyone taking part in regular exercise should eat regularly and choose their food carefully, since this can help improve performance and stamina. Sport is not just for the professionals. Regular exercise is important for good health. It can include aerobics, working out in the gym, running, cycling, swimming, football, netball and walking.

Nutritional advice and dietary requirements will vary according to the sporting activity, but it is important to eat enough foods rich in starchy carbohydrate to maintain the stores of muscle glycogen which are used to provide energy during exercise. We also need to drink enough fluid before, during and after exercise, since fluid is lost in sweat. Water is perfectly suitable for replacing fluid lost as sweat.

Increasing carbohydrates in the diet

Most people, including sportspeople, are encouraged to eat plenty of starchy, carbohydrate-rich foods such as rice, bread, cereals, pasta and potatoes. Experts recommend that at least 50 per cent of food energy in the diet should come from carbohydrates, predominantly from starchy foods. In Britain today, about 45 per cent of our food energy comes from carbohydrates, but a large proportion of this is from sugary foods.

Why do we need to increase carbohydrate intake?

Carbohydrate-rich foods help to build up the glycogen reserves in the muscles which are needed to release energy during long, energetic activity. These glycogen supplies must be replaced after exercise to improve future training.

The table on the right shows the amounts of carbohydrate in 100 grams of typical foods.

■ Food choices are very important for sportspeople

Carbohydrate in 100 g of foods	
Food (100 g)	Carbohydrate (g per 100 g)
Boiled rice	30
Boiled potatoes	20
Boiled pasta	26
White bread	50
Banana	19
Baked beans in tomato sauce	10
Cornflakes	85
Milk	5
Sugar	100

— To do

Plan a day's menu for a sportsperson. Use food tables or a computer program to work out if the menu supplies 50 per cent of the food energy as carbohydrate. Make changes if necessary to meet this requirement.

— Question

What advice about diet would you give to active sportspeople?

The number of older people in the UK is increasing – there are about nine million people aged over 65 in the UK, representing about sixteen per cent of the population, and life expectancy continues to rise. Many older people enjoy active, healthy lives but older people still need to follow a healthy diet and try to take regular exercise.

- A healthy, well-balanced diet can help maintain a suitable weight and fulfil requirements for energy and nutrients.
- A diet with high-fibre starchy foods helps to keep the digestive system healthy.
- Eating fewer foods which are high in total fat and saturated fat can reduce the risk of heart disease.

Changes with age

Many people stay fit and active as they get older, but the natural changes that occur with age may mean that their bodies do not function as efficiently as when they were younger. People are usually less active as they get older and so need less energy from food. If less food is eaten it is possible for the intake of some nutrients to become very low. This can lead to ill health and weakness. It is therefore important that older people eat foods which contain plenty of nourishment such as meat, fish, cheese, milk, eggs, cereals, bread and nuts. Older people tend to suffer more often from ill health and often do not recover as quickly as younger people do following periods of illness.

Poor nutrition in the elderly can lead to a range of problems such as:

- constipation and other digestive disorders
- anaemia
- bone disorders such as osteoporosis, and osteomalacia (the adult form of rickets)
- overweight
- coronary heart disease and stroke
- mouth problems and swallowing difficulties
- depression.

Malnutrition

Malnutrition includes under-nutrition (not eating enough) as well as over-nutrition (eating too much). Far more elderly people are overweight than underweight, but both men and women over 75 years of age are, on average, lighter than men of 35–74 years and women of 45–74 years. Surveys show that underweight elderly people are more likely to suffer from poor health than those who are of a suitable weight for their height.

■ Many people stay fit and active as they get older

Food and exercise

In the report 'Eating well for older people', prepared by a group called **The Caroline Walker Trust**, the expert panel suggests that as well as improvement in the nutritional quality of food other factors need considering.

- Older people should take regular exercise to strengthen and build up bones and muscle.
- Regular dental check-ups should be provided – mouth problems can lead to low food intake.
- Architects designing sheltered accommodation should design areas where residents can sit in sunlight to help improve vitamin D levels. (The action of sunlight on the skin makes vitamin D.)

Special dietary needs of older people

- Foods should supply **a range of nutrients**. Older people need slightly less energy than younger adults, but requirements for nutrients stay the same. Meals and snacks should therefore be nutritious, and should provide a range of nutrients. In general, healthy eating guidelines should be followed – older people should eat less fat, especially saturated fat, less sugar and more starchy fibre-rich foods.
- Make sure there is **adequate intake of fibre and fluid**. This is essential to prevent constipation. Good sources of fibre include wholemeal bread, whole-grain breakfast cereals, pulses, fruits and vegetables. Raw wheat bran should not be added to foods as it contains phytates which may interfere with the absorption of calcium and iron. For people who have difficulty in chewing, fruits and vegetables can be puréed.
- Make sure there is **enough iron in the diet**. To help prevent anaemia, older people should be encouraged to eat iron-rich foods such as red meat, liver, oily fish, fortified breakfast cereals, bread and pulses. Food and drink rich in vitamin C should be included with the meal to increase iron absorption, particularly if the meal does not contain meat.
- Make sure there is enough **calcium and vitamin D** in the diet. Older people should eat foods that are rich sources of calcium, such as milk and cheese to help keep bones healthy. Vitamin D helps in the absorption of calcium, and is formed in the skin by the action of sunlight, so older people should be encouraged to sit in the sunshine, as well as eating foods which are good sources of vitamin D such as oily fish, eggs and fortified margarine.
- **Mouth problems** – many older people have false teeth or only a few of their natural teeth remaining. They may have difficulty chewing certain foods such as meat, fruits and vegetables and this can reduce their intake of important nutrients. Regular dental check-ups can help. It is also important to look after existing teeth by using fluoride toothpaste and eating less sugary foods.
- To help reduce the risk of **coronary heart disease or stroke**, everyone is advised to reduce their fat intake and to eat more fruits and vegetables and fish. This also applies to older people. High salt (sodium) intakes are thought to be one of the risk factors for high blood pressure, but older people do lose their sense of taste, so may be reluctant to cut down on the amount of salt they add to their food. They could be advised to use herbs, spices and lemon juice to flavour food instead.

Fact

People tend to need less energy from food as they get older.

Under-nutrition is more of a problem in the elderly than in younger adults.

Exercise is important in strengthening bones and muscle.

To do

Plan a day's meals for an older person living on their own. Show how you have made a healthy choice, in line with nutritional guidelines.

Question

Why should older people be encouraged to take regular exercise?

As people get older they may not be able to prepare their own food or look after themselves. Many such people rely on the support of friends, relatives or community services to help with the shopping and to prepare meals. Only four per cent of the elderly population live in residential accommodation run either by the private or public sector.

What meals are provided for elderly people?

- Older people can have meals delivered to their homes – Meals on Wheels.
- Lunch clubs or day centres provide meals and snacks.
- Residential homes provide meals throughout the day.

The Caroline Walker Trust recommends that there should be nutritional guidelines for food prepared for older people in residential care and that local authorities should adopt these guidelines for community meals.

Meals delivered to the home

In 1992, 32.9 million meals were served to elderly people in their homes. These meals are important, as they encourage people to remain independent in their own homes for as long as possible.

Nutritional Guidelines for Community Meals for the Elderly

The nutritional guidelines for community meals for older people suggest the following average energy and nutrient content for each meal.

- Each meal should provide more than 33 per cent of the recommended average day's food intake.
- Energy – not less than 40 per cent of the estimated average requirement (EAR).
- Fat – 35 per cent of food energy.
- Starch – 39 per cent of food energy.
- NME (sugar) – 11 per cent of food energy.
- Fibre (NSP) – not less than 33 per cent of DRV (= 6 g).

An example of a community lunch menu for one day	
Food for lunch	*Amount*
Fruit juice	100 ml
Steak and kidney pie	120 g
Mixed vegetables	60 g
Cauliflower	60 g
Mashed potato	100 g
Trifle	120 g
Source – *Eating well for older people*, The Caroline Walker Trust	

- Protein – not less than 33 per cent of RNI.
- There should be an adequate supply of B-group vitamins, folate, vitamins C and A, calcium, iron, sodium and potassium.

What other problems affect elderly people's choice of food?

Shopping may be difficult for elderly people. They may find it difficult to get to the shops. Carrying heavy foods such as potatoes may be a problem. Small quantities of food, bought locally, may be more expensive than at a supermarket and are not always available. However, many food companies are making ready-to-eat meals in single portions which can prevent wastage of ingredients and save time and effort.

Cooking equipment may be heavy or difficult to use. An elderly person may be unable to lift heavy saucepans and undo screw-top packages. Equipment has been designed to help people with these problems. Storage space may also be limited.

Lack of money may prevent elderly people from buying adequate food and from travelling to the shops. Another problem may be loss of appetite which can result from illness, depression or drug therapy.

Cooking skills

Some elderly people may not have the skills to prepare their own meals – local day centres may provide cookery classes to help.

An example of a vegetarian community lunch menu for older Asian people	
Food for lunch	**Amount**
Dahl	200 g
Spinach and potato	150 g
Yogurt raita	125 g
Side salad	n/a
Rice	50 g
Chapati without fat	60 g
Banana	150 g
Source– *Eating well for older people*, The Caroline Walker Trust	

Meals on Wheels

Around the country, the Women's Royal Voluntary Service (WRVS) delivers 15 million Meals on Wheels to housebound people, as well as serving three million meals in lunch clubs. The WRVS works with the local authority and delivers both hot and frozen meals to people's homes. The aim of Meals on Wheels is to make sure that the meal is prepared to a nutritional standard specified by the local authority, and hygiene standards and temperature control must meet legal requirements.

— Investigations —

1 Find out about the types of menu and services offered by your local Meals on Wheels service. How much do the meals cost? What are the constraints on temperature control and the delivery and storage time?

2 Investigate the range of cooking equipment which has been designed to help people with disabilities to cook and prepare food.

— To do —

Look at the charts for the two lunch menus, at the top of these pages. Why is it important to provide meals for people from different ethnic backgrounds? Create two lunch menus of your own which could be served to an older person living on their own. Carry out a nutritional analysis of the two meals using a computer program or food tables. Show how the meals meet nutritional guidelines.

■ Meals on Wheels deliver food to housebound people

— Fact —

Elderly people can have their meals provided for them.
Dietary guidelines have been suggested for these community meals.

— Questions —

1 Describe the range of meals which are provided for elderly people.

2 What problems affect elderly people's choice of food?

3 Why do you think it is important to have nutritional guidelines for community meals? Give three reasons.

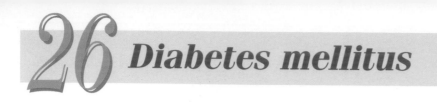

Diabetes mellitus is a condition in which the body is not able to convert, or becomes less efficient at converting, glucose in the blood into energy. As a result, the amount of glucose (sugar) in the blood starts to rise. About 1.4 million people in the UK are known to have diabetes, so it is a fairly common health condition.

Glucose is obtained from the digestion of carbohydrates. Blood glucose levels rise after a meal and **insulin** is released into the blood. Insulin is a hormone produced by the **pancreas**. It controls the level of glucose in the blood and stops it rising too high.

When someone has diabetes, the pancreas does not make, or release enough insulin into the bloodstream to convert the glucose into energy. As a result, the amount of glucose in the blood starts to build up. The body starts to use its fat stores to provide energy and so people with untreated diabetes often lose weight. They may also feel very tired. Once the amount of glucose in the blood reaches a certain level, the excess is excreted by the kidneys into the urine. The urine becomes more concentrated, and so water is prevented from being reabsorbed. As a result, the volume of urine increases which results in a loss of fluid from the body. This in turn causes thirst, so people with undiagnosed or untreated diabetes often pass a lot of urine and are very thirsty.

The two main types of diabetes

Insulin-dependent diabetes mellitus (**IDDM**) or Type 1 diabetes develops when there is a severe lack of insulin available for controlling blood glucose levels. This type of diabetes usually appears in young people and it is treated with insulin injections and by diet. It develops quickly, usually over a period of weeks, but the symptoms are quickly relieved with treatment.

■ People with diabetes need to follow a healthy diet

Non-insulin dependent diabetes mellitus (**NIDDM**) or Type 2 diabetes usually occurs in middle or old age and this is a far more common type of diabetes – about 75 per cent of people with diabetes have this type. With NIDDM usually the body still produces some insulin but not enough for its needs. This type of diabetes is treated by diet alone, by diet and tablets or very occasionally by diet and insulin injections. The symptoms develop quite slowly and are not usually as severe as those seen with insulin-dependent diabetes. Non-insulin dependent diabetes tends to run in families, and often occurs in overweight people.

Symptoms of undiagnosed or poorly controlled diabetes

The main symptoms of diabetes are:
- thirst and a dry mouth
- passing large amounts of urine, especially during the night
- tiredness
- blurred vision
- weight loss.

How is diabetes treated?

Insulin-dependent diabetes

People with insulin-dependent diabetes take daily injections of insulin for the rest of their lives and need to follow a healthy diet. They also carry out regular tests on their blood or urine to measure glucose levels and may adjust the insulin dose and the diet according to the results.

Non-insulin dependent diabetes

People with non-insulin dependent diabetes need to follow a healthy diet and may need to take tablets to keep their blood glucose levels normal.

▬ *Fact* ▬

About 1.4 million people in the UK are known to have diabetes.

People with diabetes do not need a special diet – they should follow normal dietary guidelines.

Healthy eating for people with diabetes

People with diabetes do not need to follow a special diet. They can follow the dietary guidelines for healthy eating which are recommended for everyone. So their diet should be high in starchy, fibre-rich foods and low in sugar and fat.

Tips on healthy eating

- Follow a well-balanced, healthy diet which contains plenty of starchy foods, high in dietary fibre.
- Eat regular meals to keep the blood glucose level normal. Avoid missing meals.
- Eat fewer fatty foods.
- Cut down on sugary foods and drinks.
- Drink alcohol in moderation only.
- Avoid being overweight.
- Avoid special diabetic food and drink products – they are unnecessary.

▬ *Investigation* ▬

Investigate how a person with diabetes plans their food choices over a period of a week. You could write to The British Diabetic Association. Visit a supermarket or large chemist and make a list of the range of diabetic food products for sale. Why are these foods unnecessary?

▬ *Questions* ▬

1 Describe the two types of diabetes and how they can be treated.
2 People with diabetes are advised to follow a healthy diet. What does this mean? Give an example of a healthy meal and explain your choice of foods.

Food intolerance and food allergy

Food intolerance is a reproducible unpleasant reaction to a specific food or food ingredient. **Food allergy** is a form of intolerance in which there is evidence of abnormal immunological reaction.

True food intolerance affects less than two per cent of the population. A food intolerance happens when the body reacts to a certain food or food ingredient. The most common foods that cause reactions are eggs, peanuts, cows' milk, wheat, fish, shellfish, nuts, soya beans and rice. A food allergy is a type of intolerance which involves the body's immune system. In such circumstances, a food protein acts as an **antigen**, causing a reaction whenever the food is eaten.

An intolerance to food may have several different types of cause, for example:

● People may lack certain enzymes which help to digest foods, e.g. people with lactose intolerance lack the enzyme lactase which helps to digest the milk sugar, lactose.
● Large quantities of some foods may act like drugs, i.e. have a pharmacological effect. For example, large amounts of caffeine can cause symptoms like migraine.
● The body's immune system may provoke specific reactions.

How do you know if you have a food intolerance?

If you react in an unusual way to some foods, you could be intolerant to them. If an allergy is suspected, see your GP for referral to a dietitian or for further tests. Other expert help may be needed. A child's diet should not be altered without specific medical advice.

Milk protein allergy

A small number of people experience unpleasant symptoms after consuming foods or drinks which contain cows' milk protein. Milk protein allergy is most common in babies and young children, particularly if other family members suffer with allergies. However, most children 'grow out' of the allergy by the time they go to school. Babies,

children and adults should always be referred to a dietitian for dietary advice.

Milk intolerance

There are two main types of reaction to milk. The first is an allergic reaction to milk protein; the second is an intolerance to the milk sugar, lactose.

── *Fact* ──

Psychological food intolerance is an emotional reaction to food which does not occur if the food is eaten in a hidden form. So people may think they are allergic to something like a food additive, but when it is hidden in a food product and they do not know about it, they do not react.

True food intolerances can produce a wide range of symptoms, from minor irritations to the skin through to vomiting and abdominal cramps. In a recent survey, seven per cent of the survey population claimed to react to food additives. Follow-up investigations showed that only 0.01–0.23 per cent of this population were actually affected.

Fatal Food Allergy

Around one in every twelve children has some sort of allergy to food. Severe, life-threatening allergic reactions to food are rare, but they probably cause more deaths than allergic reactions to insect bites.

Investigators in the US recently collected thirteen examples of severe allergic reactions to food in children, six of whom died. All the children suffered from asthma and nine also had eczema. All were known to be allergic to some foods, often peanuts. In every case the child had eaten food without realizing it contained the dangerous ingredient. The early symptoms were itching around the mouth, a feeling that the lips were swelling and the throat tightening, a blotchy rash, a sick feeling, cramps and vomiting. The interval between the first symptom and death from suffocation was $1\frac{1}{2}$ to 5 hours. The children who survived were given early treatment with anti-allergic drugs.

Parents and teachers should be aware how quickly severe symptoms may develop from food allergy, and be prepared to get medical help immediately.

Source: *Which? Way to Health*, December 1992

Recognized food intolerances and allergies			
Type of intolerance or allergy	Foods to be avoided	Symptoms	What to do
Milk intolerance	Cows' milk.	Wind, cramps, diarrhoea.	Use other milks or soya milk.
Gluten intolerance	Wheat, rye, oats, barley food products.	Children don't grow properly, weight loss.	Use gluten free foods.
Wheat intolerance	Foods made from the whole of the wheat grain.	Asthma, itchy skin, diarrhoea.	Avoid all foods made from wheat.
Peanut allergy	Foods made with peanuts.	Affects breathing, can cause anaphylactic shock	Avoid all foods made with peanuts.
Egg allergy	Foods products made from eggs.	eczema and rash.	Avoid all egg products.
Fish and shellfish allergy	All fish and shellfish.	Nettle rash and anaphylactic shock.	Avoid all fish and shellfish.
Soya allergy	Soya products such as tofu, soy sauce.	Eczema, asthma and diarrhoea.	Avoid soya products.
Certain colourings and preservatives	Food products made with certain colourings and preservatives.	May cause hyperactivity in children.	Avoid food products made with certain colourings and preservatives.

Lactose intolerance

People with lactose intolerance cannot digest the milk sugar, lactose. Symptoms of lactose intolerance include cramps, diarrhoea and wind after eating milky products.

People with lactose intolerance should avoid drinking milk but can eat cheese and yogurt because the lactose has been changed to lactic acid.

Lactolite is cows' milk with the enzyme lactase added. This enzyme digests the milk sugar, lactose, and changes 95 per cent of it to the sugars glucose and galactose. This milk can be drunk by people with lactose intolerance.

▬Questions▬

1 What is meant by
   a food intolerance
   b food allergy?
2 Give examples of intolerance or allergies, the foods which should be avoided and the likely symptoms of the intolerance or allergy.

WHAT IS LACTOLITE?

Lactolite is natural cows' milk with a natural lactase enzyme added, that has reduced over 95% of the lactose content to a more digestible form (glucose and galactose)

Lactose is a naturally occurring sugar found in all cows' milk. Which some people are unable to digest properly.

NUTRITIONAL INFORMATION

Typical values per 100 ml

	LACTOLITE	NORMAL MILK
Energy	284 kJ/68 kcal	284 kJ/68 kcal
Protein	3.2g	3.2g
Carbohydrate	4.8g	4.7g
(of which sugars	4.8g	4.7g)
(of which lactose	less than 0.24g	4.7g)
(of which glucose	2.4g	NIL)
Fat	4.0g	4.0g
(of which saturates	2.5g	2.5g)
Fibre	NIL	NIL
Sodium	0.06g	0.06g

■ Lactolite can be drunk by people with lactose intolerance.

Coeliac disease (gluten intolerance)

People with coeliac disease are unable to eat products made from **wheat**, **barley**, **oats** or **rye** as they are sensitive to **gluten**, the protein found in these cereals. This is because the lining of the small intestine is damaged by gluten. This damage hinders the absorption of nutrients from the small intestine so that weight loss, and eventually malnutrition, occurs. Children who suffer from coeliac disease do not grow properly.

The condition can be treated by removing all foods containing wheat flour, oats, rye or barley from the diet. This means foods such as bread, cereals, pasta, cakes, biscuits, pastry, pies and any foods containing flour made from wheat must be avoided. Food labels must be checked carefully to see if they contain any of the following wheat products:

breadcrumbs, hydrolyzed wheat protein, rusk, wheatbran, wheat binder, wheat flour, wheat germ, wheat germ oil, wheat gluten, raising agent containing wheat starch, wheat starch, wheat thickener, whole-wheat.

Many foods contain gluten and so need to be eliminated from the diet. The only way to control this disease is to follow a **gluten-free diet**. Gluten-free products are available.

Food allergy to soya

If people have a food allergy to soya their body's immune system has a strong reaction to soya and foods made from soya, such as **textured vegetable protein** (**TVP**). The reactions associated with this allergy include eczema, asthma and diarrhoea. Foods which are made from soya include tofu, vegetable oil, hydrolyzed vegetable protein and soya flavourings.

Peanut and nut allergies

Certain foods can cause **anaphylaxis**, with peanuts and other nuts being the most common trigger. Anaphylactic shock is a very serious – potentially fatal – condition that can develop in sensitive people within a few seconds or minutes of eating peanuts. Sufferers of peanut allergy can also be sensitive to other nuts. Research into this allergy is being undertaken since the causes are not properly understood.

Wheat intolerance

Sufferers from wheat intolerance are sensitive to the whole grain of wheat, whereas people with coeliac disease are sensitive to the wheat protein, gluten. Wheat intolerance gives symptoms of asthma, itchy skin and sometimes diarrhoea.

Egg intolerance

Egg intolerance can produce eczema and a rash. Sufferers need to avoid all eggs and egg products.

Fish and shellfish

People who are intolerant to fish may react by getting a nettle rash, but it can lead to anaphylactic shock in some cases.

The Food Intolerance Databank

This databank was set up in 1987 by the Leatherhead Food Research Association, in conjunction with the Food and Drink Federation, the Royal College of Physicians and the British Dietetic Association. Information provided on the food label may not be sufficient to identify potential ingredients that might cause food intolerance so, after much research, a food intolerance databank was set up. This databank lists the names of branded foods declared free from ingredients including certain additives known to cause intolerance. Around 4000 products are listed on the databank. By 1996 a network of databanks should be established throughout Europe. This service is available only to dietitians.

The food ingredients that are known to cause food intolerance in a number of people include milk and milk products, eggs and egg products, wheat and wheat products, soya products, some additives including sulphur dioxide and azo colours.

■ The Food Intolerance Databank in use

— Fact

Up to two per cent of people are believed to be intolerant to everyday foods such as milk, eggs, fish, and wheat.

Lactose and wheat are the main food intolerances.

The Food Intolerance Databank keeps records of 4000 food products which are free from one or more of the ingredients that most commonly give rise to food intolerance.

— Questions

1 Why is it important for some people to know the ingredients in ready-to-eat food products?

2 What are the main foods which cause food intolerance?

3 How would you find out what food products were:
   a free from wheat and rye products
   b free from certain additives?

4 Why is it important to set up a national database to provide information on the ingredients in food products?

— To do

Make a collection of food labels. Identify ingredients on the food label which might cause allergies or food intolerances for certain people. Record your findings on a chart like the one below to show how food producers are tackling this issue. You could write to supermarkets and ask for any information on food advice for allergies. Write a report on your research.

Food product	Ingredients which might cause concern	Allergies which need care

*I*t is not good for our health to be either overweight, or underweight. Obesity is one of the risk factors for heart disease, high blood pressure, diabetes and gallstones. Overweight people may also suffer from problems with their bone joints. In contrast, underweight people may not be eating enough food to supply sufficient nutrients such as vitamins and minerals needed for good health. (See page 68 for how to work out the ideal body weight.)

Obesity

Many people in the UK are overweight. A government report in 1995 predicted that, in Britain, by the year 2005, 25 per cent of women and 18 per cent of men will be obese. Although average energy intakes of the population have decreased over the past few decades, activity levels have also dropped. In other words, people are now taking less exercise than they used to, and this is likely to be one of the reasons for the increase in the number of people who are overweight or obese.

Why do people put on weight?

If we eat food which provides more energy than we need for our normal activities and lifestyle, this extra energy is stored as body fat. For body weight to remain constant, energy intake must equal energy output.

Health problems associated with obesity

- High blood pressure and strokes are twice as likely in obese people.
- The onset of diabetes in adults is five times more common in overweight people.
- Extra weight places undue strain on hips, knees and back and causes joint problems in those areas.
- As well as physical problems, there are psychological problems associated with obesity.

Alarm over huge rise in obesity

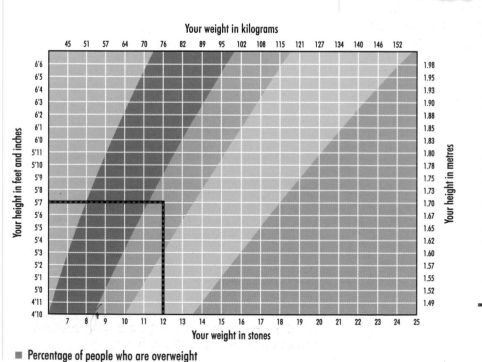

Underweight
Maybe you need to eat a bit more. But go for well-balanced nutritious foods and don't just fill up on fatty and sugary foods. If you are very underweight, see your doctor about it.

OK
You're eating the right quantity of food but you need to be sure that you're getting a healthy balance in your diet.

Overweight
You should try to lose weight.

Fat
You need to lose weight.

Very fat
You urgently need to lose weight. You would do well to see your doctor, who might refer you to a dietician.

------ For example, a person who is 5' 7 tall and weighs 12 stones is overweight.

Percentage of people who are overweight

Source—Health Education Authority

Slimming diets

In a survey, up to 90 per cent of women said they had tried to lose weight by dieting in the last year. Research shows that many people who put themselves on a so-called slimming diet have no medical reason for losing weight, and may not actually be overweight. In western countries slimming has become an obsession, especially among women.

Long-term effective weight loss is not just based upon cutting down the amount we eat. It is also important to take exercise on a daily basis. A combination of healthy diet, together with regular exercise, is the best way to lose weight.

Slimming products and diet programmes

Special food products and dieting programmes have been developed which claim to help people lose weight. There are slimming clubs, formula drinks, low-calorie snacks and meals, biscuits and many different slimming magazines. But the only way to lose weight is to eat foods which provide less energy than the body needs. This means that fat stores are used to provide the extra energy needed.

The best advice for people who want to lose weight is to follow a healthy diet, with plenty of fresh fruit and vegetables, and starchy, fibre-rich foods, and to cut down on fatty and sugary foods as well as alcohol. Fat and alcohol contain about twice as many calories as the equivalent weight of protein or carbohydrate.

■ A healthy diet is important

How to lose weight

Overweight people need to reduce their energy intake and take more exercise (i.e. increase their energy output) if they want to lose weight. These are some of the ways to lose excess body fat.
- Cut down on the amount of food eaten each day.
- Cut down on fatty and sugary foods.
- Take more exercise.
- Eat more starchy, fibre-rich foods, and fruits and vegetables which are low in calories and are good sources of fibre, vitamins and minerals. These foods help to fill you up.
- Cut down on alcohol.

— *Fact*

About 45 per cent of men and 36 per cent of women (aged 16–64) are overweight.

Obesity may cause health problems such as high blood pressure and increases the risk of heart disease.

The best way to lose weight is to reduce the amount of energy obtained from food and take more exercise.

Source: Dietary & Nutritional Survey of British Adults 1990

— *Questions*

1 What is meant by 'obesity'?
2 What health problems are associated with overweight?
3 What advice would you give to someone who wanted to lose weight?

— *Investigation*

The slimming industry is a multi-million pound business in this country. Carry out an investigation into the range of food and drink products which are on sale and targeted at people who want to lose weight. Make a collection of newspaper and magazine articles about losing weight and slimming, as well as food labels which claim to help with dieting. Present your findings and comment on your research. Suggest ways that people can eat healthily without buying specially designed slimming food products.

What is the ideal adult weight?

One way of telling if you are a healthy body weight as an adult is to use the **body mass index (BMI)** equation.

Divide your weight in kilograms by your height in metres, squared. If the answer is less than 20 this shows that you are underweight and in the long term this can be a hazard to health. An answer between 20 and 24.9 is desirable, 25–29.9 is overweight, and over 30 is obese and this is a serious danger to health.

$$\text{Body mass index} = \frac{(\text{weight in kilograms})}{(\text{height in metres})^2}$$

The healthy BMI is in the 20–24.9 band.

Underweight

People who eat less food than they need become underweight and may be subject to health risks since they are not following a diet that provides sufficient nutrients for their needs. Elderly people sometimes suffer from underweight since they may have lost interest in preparing and eating food. Nutritional hazards include anaemia resulting from a lack of iron.

Under-eating during pregnancy

Research has shown that women who follow a poor diet before and during pregnancy may give birth to small babies. Low birth weight has been linked with health problems in later life, such as high blood pressure.

Body image

Many people are concerned about their personal body image, thinking they are too fat or too thin, or the wrong shape and size. A poor body image can lead to health risks and emotional unhappiness with friends and family. Rather than worrying too much about our size and shape, it is far more important to concentrate on keeping our bodies fit and healthy by following a balanced diet and taking plenty of exercise.

Eating disorders

Anorexia nervosa

Anorexia nervosa is a psychological condition sometimes known as the slimming disease. A person suffering from this disease uses food as a way of expressing unhappiness. This is a serious disease which mainly affects teenage girls, although the problem is spreading to younger and older women and to men. Someone suffering from anorexia nervosa becomes obsessional about losing weight and has a distorted view of their own body size. After a time, they become very thin, their lifestyle suffers and in women the periods stop. People suffering from anorexia nervosa often become depressed and may develop other health problems as a result of under-nutrition. Sufferers require long-term specialist help from psychiatrists and dietitians, as well as support from their families and friends.

Bulimia nervosa

Bulimia nervosa is a serious eating disorder in which the sufferer binges and then vomits, often repeatedly, in order to lose or control weight. People suffering from bulimia nervosa are often slightly overweight and they often eat large quantities of food before making themselves sick. Treatment looks at the whole lifestyle of the person. People suffering from bulimia nervosa need special support from doctors, psychiatrists and dietitians.

— To do —

1 Evaluate the 1400 kilocalories a day slimming diet shown opposite. The aim of the diet is to eat six slices of bread a day with plenty of fresh fruits and vegetables. This slimming diet is designed to provide 50 per cent of the total calories from carbohydrates. You could use a computer program or food tables to test this out.

2 Design a menu for a day for someone on a slimming diet which provides up to 1400 calories and which meets dietary guidelines.

An example of a balanced slimming diet – providing 1400 kilocalories per day

Daily allowances to be used with the food choice:

300 ml skimmed milk, 14 g butter or margarine or 25 g low fat spread

DAY 1

BREAKFAST	**LUNCH**	**DINNER**
bowl of branflakes (40 g) with skimmed milk. 2 slices of toast	**Cheese salad** 30 g reduced-fat Edam cheese, chopped cucumber, tomato and a tablespoon of fat-free French dressing. 2 slices of bread	**Bean feast** small can of baked beans (135 g) on 2 slices of brown or white toast, with grilled tomatoes and grilled mushrooms 150 g pot of low-fat yogurt with fresh fruit

SNACKS

piece of fruit, 40 g slice of bun loaf

Source – Federation of Bakers

▬ *Questions* ▬

1 What health problems might occur if people don't eat sufficient food to meet their dietary needs?

2 What is meant by the terms:
   a anorexia nervosa
   b bulimia nervosa?

3 Describe ways that adults try to change their body shape and size. Give your views of one of the ways they might do this, explaining the advantages and disadvantages of this method.

A strict vegetarian avoids products that come from animals that are used for foods, toiletries, clothes and household goods. Other vegetarians may just avoid foods obtained from the slaughter of animals, such as meat, poultry, fish and their products.

Types of vegetarian

- **Semi or demi vegetarians** don't eat red meat but will eat fish and poultry.
- **Lacto-ovo vegetarians** don't eat meat, poultry or fish but will eat dairy products (milk, yogurt, butter, cheese) and eggs.
- **Lacto vegetarians** don't eat meat, poultry, fish or eggs but will eat dairy products.
- **Ovo vegetarians** don't eat meat, poultry, fish, dairy products, but will eat eggs.
- **Vegans** don't eat meat, poultry, fish or animal products including dairy products and eggs.

Examples of the food groups not eaten by vegetarians

- **Meat** e.g. lamb, beef and pork
- **Poultry** e.g. chicken and turkey
- **Fish and seafood** e.g. cod, haddock, plaice, salmon, prawns, crab, mussels
- **Products from slaughtered animals** e.g. gelatine, lard, suet and margarine made from animal products
- **Other foods** including game, rabbit, venison, horse meat and new products such as ostrich

Why do people choose a vegetarian diet?

There are many reasons why people choose to follow a vegetarian diet.

- **Religion** – vegetarianism is the dietary choice for several religions.
- **Health** – some people think that a diet which includes cereals, fruits, vegetables, pulses and nuts, possibly with the addition of milk products and eggs, is healthier than one which contains meat and meat products.
- **Animal welfare** – some people believe that it is wrong to kill animals for food, or they may object to the way animals are reared and kept in intensive farming.
- **Taste** – some people don't like the taste and texture of meat or fish. Allergy or intolerance is not usually a reason.
- **Environmental issues** – people may feel that meat production is expensive compared with cereal and other crop production, and that it is wasteful in resources and pollutes the environment.

Trends in vegetarianism

About 3–4 per cent of adults in the UK are vegetarian and the numbers of vegetarians seem to be increasing. The main reasons may be wider food choices, including interesting vegetarian dishes, people settling in the UK from ethnic groups with a vegetarian food culture, and concerns over animal welfare.

THE VEGETARIAN SOCIETY ⋁

The Vegetarian Society's V symbol guidelines for vegetarian products

1 No animal flesh (meat, fowl, fish or shellfish).

2 No meat or bone stock (in soups, sauces or other dishes).

3 No animal fats (suet, lard, dripping) or ordinary white cooking fats, or ordinary margarine (some contain fish oil) in pastry, frying, for greasing tins or other cooking.

4 No gelatine, aspic, block or jelly crystals for glazing, moulding, or other cooking. Agar agar is an acceptable alternative.

5 No other products with ingredients derived from slaughterhouse by-products (e.g. some E numbers).

6 No battery eggs or intensively produced eggs.

7 No royal jelly.

The graphs on the right show:

A the trend of non-meat eaters and vegetarians and vegans since 1984

B the trend in non-meat eaters by age/sex.

How can you tell if a food product is suitable for a vegetarian?

Many food producers have designed symbols to show that their food product is suitable for vegetarians. Some examples are shown below. The Vegetarian Society's V symbol is used to show that the ingredients are vegetarian and the product has been approved by the Vegetarian Society.

■ Food symbols for vegetarian products

Trends in vegetarianism

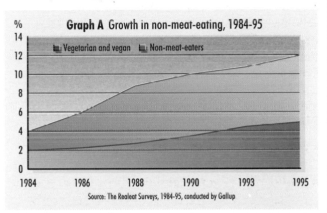

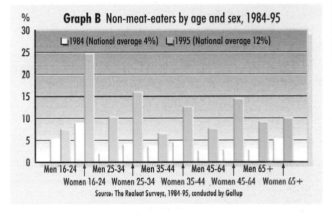

▬ *Questions* ▬

1 Make a list of the different kinds of vegetarian and explain their food choices.

2 What are the reasons why people become vegetarians?

3 Use the graphs to answer the questions.
 Graph A shows the growth in non-meat eating during the period 1984–95.
 a Explain in words what you think is shown in graph A.
 Graph B shows non-meat eaters by age/sex for the period 1984–95.
 b Which is the largest group of non-meat eaters?
 c What is the trend in non-meat eating for people aged 45 and over?

4 If you were designing a range of vegetarian foods, which group would you target for sales and why?

5 Would the following products get the Vegetarian Society's V symbol? Give your reasons.
 a Scones – ingredients: wheat flour, sugar, vegetable margarine, egg, vegetarian whey powder, salt
 b Raspberry flavour jelly – ingredients: sugar, glucose syrup, invert sugar syrup, water, gelatine, citric acid, flavouring
 c Mozzarella cheese – ingredients: pasteurized milk, salt, bacterial culture, microbial rennet
 d Wholewheat bread – ingredients; wholewheat flour, water, yeast, salt, sesame seeds

6 Give two reasons why it is useful to label a product 'suitable for vegetarians'.

7 Write a sentence to explain the following words.
 a bone stock b gelatine c aspic
 d agar agar e E numbers f battery eggs
 g royal jelly
 You may need to use reference books to help.

71

Health and vegetarianism

Studies show that vegetarians as a group may have lower risks of developing heart disease and some cancers if they consume more fruit and vegetables and less fat. More research is being carried out to investigate how the vegetarian lifestyle and diet affect health. Eating more fruits and vegetables and less saturated fat is known to be beneficial to health, but care must be taken in interpreting research information as lifestyle plays an important part in health status.

Adult food energy requirements are easily met by vegetarian and vegan diets. As vegetarians eat lots of fruits and vegetables, which are bulky and lower in energy, their diets are generally lower in fat. Studies show that protein intakes for vegetarians appear sufficient to meet the EAR for protein.

Care is needed when planning a vegetarian diet for people with special nutritional needs, such as growing children, and women with high iron requirement. A bulky vegetarian diet is not suitable for very young, active children.

How does a vegetarian and vegan diet compare with that of omnivores who eat all foods?

Omnivores – those people who eat all foods	Vegetarians – those people who don't eat meat but eat milk and eggs	Vegans – those people who avoid all animal products
Intake of total food energy similar to vegetarians.	Intake of total food energy similar to omnivores.	Intake of total food energy may be less.
Intake of macro-nutrients similar to vegetarians.	Intake of macro-nutrients similar to omnivores.	Intake of macro-nutrients close to DRV for UK.
Dietary fibre intake not as high as vegetarians or vegans.	Higher intakes of dietary fibre since more wholegrain cereals, fruits and vegetables eaten.	Higher intakes of dietary fibre since more wholegrain cereals, pulses, nuts, fruits and vegetables eaten.
Similar fat intake to vegetarians, but diet higher in saturated fatty acids from meat and meat products.	Similar fat intake to omnivores since they eat dairy products and eggs, but their diet is lower in saturated fatty acid and a higher proportion of dietary fat as polyunsaturated fatty acids.	Proportion of energy from fat lower, and less saturated fatty acids since diet is mainly cereals, nuts and vegetables.
Need to increase carbohydrate intake in proportion to other nutrients.	Need to increase carbohydrate intake in proportion to other nutrients.	Higher intake of carbohydrate due to diet rich in cereals and starchy vegetables – 50–55% compared with 40–45% in survey of 2000 adults.
Micro-nutrients in adequate supply.	Micro-nutrients in adequate supply.	Micro-nutrients – calcium, vitamin D and vitamin B12 may be difficult to achieve. Vegans can get additional supplies of micro-nutrients from fortified foods.

■ *Questions* ■

1 Use the chart above to help explain the following.
   a Why do vegetarians have high intakes of dietary fibre?
   b Why is the vegetarian diet likely to be lower in saturated fatty acids?
   c Why do vegans have a high intake of carbohydrate foods?

2 Vitamin B12 is found naturally in animal-source foods. Why do you think vegans are sometimes advised to eat fortified foods or supplements containing B12?

Quorn was developed by Marlow Foods Ltd. It is made from myco-protein (a tiny plant that occurs naturally in soil) and is available in pieces or minced for use in savoury dishes. It is also sold as burgers, sausages and fillets or in ready meals.

per 100g		Quorn	Skinless chicken	Minced beef	Baked potato	Tofu
Energy	(kJ)	355	621	955	581	304
	(kcal)	85	148	229	136	73
Protein	(g)	12.3	24.8	23.1	3.9	8.1
Fat	(g)	3.2	5.4	15.2	0.2	4.2
Carbohydrate	(g)	1.8	0	0	31.7	0.7
Dietary fibre	(g)	4.8	0	0	2.7	0
Cholesterol	(mg)	0	76	83	0	0

Quorn™ is a good source of nutrition. See for yourself how Quorn™ compares...

5 019503 001112

SWEET 'N' SOUR STIR FRY

LOW IN FAT

Quorn is a healthy, tasty food which comes from a natural, tiny plant and has a mild savoury flavour.

Quorn **SWEET 'N' SOUR** Stir Fry is a combination of tender strips of Quorn ready marinated in an authentic sauce, which can be quickly and conveniently cooked to make a tasty, healthy meal.

INSTRUCTIONS - Prepare the following:
1 medium carrot, diagonally sliced
1/2 small red pepper and green pepper, sliced
1 small onion, sliced

1. Heat 1 tablespoon of sunflower oil in a large frying pan or wok.
2. Add the vegetables and stir fry for 3 minutes.
3. Add the contents of the pack and stir fry together with vegetables for a further 4 minutes.
Serve with either rice or noodles.

For more information about Quorn please contact:
THE QUORN KITCHEN, FREEPOST, P.O. BOX 7, BRENTFORD, MIDDLESEX TW8 9BR.

INGREDIENTS

QUORN (Myco-protein, water, egg-white, vegetable flavouring), pineapple juice, white wine vinegar, tomato, vegetables (onion, red peppers), sugar, orange juice, honey, modified starch, soy sauce, ginger, salt.

NO ARTIFICIAL ADDITIVES

NUTRITION INFORMATION	AVERAGE VALUES	
	Per 100g Quorn in Marinade	Per 125g Serving
Energy - kJ	441	551
- kcal	104	130
Protein	6.8g	8.5g
Carbohydrate of which	14.8g	18.5g
- sugars	13.1g	16.4g
Fat of which	1.8g	2.3g
- saturates	0.3g	0.4g
- cholesterol	Nil	Nil
Fibre	2.7g	3.4g
Sodium	0.3g	0.4g

STORAGE INSTRUCTIONS

Keep refrigerated and use by the date shown on the front of pack. Once opened eat within 24 hours.
Can be frozen on day of purchase and kept for up to 3 months.

suitable for vegetarians

Quorn™ and Quorn logo™ are trade marks of Marlow Foods Ltd, 9 Station Road, Marlow, Buckinghamshire SL7 1NG.

PRINTED ON RECYCLED BOARD

Quorn™ is also available MINCED or as PIECES as a versatile and highly nutritious ingredient suitable for a range of tasty, healthy recipes.

QUORN AS AN INGREDIENT - THE FACTS

▼ **LOW FAT**
- Less fat than skinless chicken
▲ **GOOD SOURCE OF PROTEIN**
- Gram per gram as much protein as an egg
▲ **GOOD SOURCE OF FIBRE**
- More fibre than baked potatoes
NO CHOLESTEROL-NO ANIMAL FATS

With only 85kcal per 100g Quorn can help slimming or weight control only as part of a calorie controlled diet.

▬ *Questions* ▬

Use the *Quorn* label to get the information you need to answer these questions.

1 The chart on the label compares the nutritional values of *Quorn*, skinless chicken, minced beef, baked potato and tofu. Which of these foods has:
   a the lowest energy value (in kJ or kcal)
   b the most protein
   c the most carbohydrate
   d the highest amount of dietary fibre
   e the lowest cholesterol?

2 Any nutritional claims made on a label must be supported with nutritional evidence.

   Explain what nutritional evidence supports each of the following statements on the *Quorn* label.
   a low fat – less fat than skinless chicken

   b good source of protein – gram per gram as much protein as an egg
   (**Tip:** you will need nutritional tables for this answer.)
   c good source of fibre – more fibre than baked potatoes
   d no cholesterol.

3 Why do you think *Quorn* can claim to be a healthy food?

4 Use the ingredients list to explain:
   a why this product is suitable for vegetarians but not vegans
   b what *Quorn* is made from.

5 Do you think that *Quorn* is a useful new product to use in recipes? Give your reasons.

Many religions have dietary rules which limit their food choices. The chart below shows the food choices by different religious groups.

Food and festivals

Special foods are served during religious festivals.

- The **Jewish New Year** falls in September or early October. The **Day of Atonement** falls during this time and is the holiest day in the Jewish year. The family eats before the sun sets and then a 24-hour fast begins. After the fast the family comes together for a celebration meal.
- **Ramadan** is the ninth month of the Muslim calendar and lasts for a month. During this time Muslims do not eat or drink from dawn to sunset. At the end of Ramadan there is the festival to break the fast, and three days of special foods and parties.
- **Christmas** is the Christian festival to celebrate the birth of Jesus. Christians serve special foods on **Christmas Eve** and **Christmas Day**.

Religious laws concerning food

Christian

The Christian religion does not forbid eating any foods but, in some denominations, there is a tradition that fish is eaten on Fridays instead of meat.

Muslim

Food must be **halal** (lawful), which means animals are slaughtered according to Muslim law.

■ A halal butcher

Forbidden food includes meat incorrectly slaughtered, pork, fish without scales and shellfish. Alcohol is also forbidden.

Jewish

All food must be **kosher** which means that meat is slaughtered and prepared to strict Jewish laws. Meat from pigs, birds of prey, eels, fish without scales and most shellfish are forbidden. Meat must not be cooked with or eaten in the same meal as dairy products, cheese must be made with vegetable rennet, not animal rennet, and meat must not be cooked with butter. Separate cooking equipment is used for milk and meat.

Hindu

For Hindus the **cow** is sacred and cannot be eaten but other meats are permitted for non-vegetarians. Many Hindus are vegetarians. Alcohol is forbidden.

The food choices of different religious groups						
Religion	Beef	Pork	Other meat	Non-scaly fish or shellfish	Eggs	milk
Muslim	halal	X	halal	X		
Hindu	X	?	?	?	?	
Jew	kosher	X	kosher	X		
Sikh	X					
Buddhist	X	X	X	X (some)		
Seventh Day Adventist	X	X	X	X	?	
Rastafarians	X	X	X	X	X	X

X – foods generally avoided   ? – may be avoided by some members
Source – *Vegetarian Issues*, The Vegetarian Society

■ The altar is filled with foods for celebration at the Roman Catholic festival of the Day of the Dead, in Mexico

Buddhist

Many Buddhists are vegetarians as their religion preaches against killing. However, eating meat is not actually forbidden and they can eat fish.

Sikh

Food restrictions are less strict than those for Hindus and Muslims. All meat except **beef** is permitted. Alcohol is forbidden.

Rastafarian

Most rastafarians will only eat 'I-tal' foods, i.e. foods which are considered to be in the natural or whole state. The degree of dietary restriction depends upon the individual. Some follow vegetarian or vegan diets. Pork, seafood without scales or fins, and stimulants such as coffee and alcohol are forbidden.

— To do

Plan a menu for an airline which had to cater for different dietary needs, including religious groups. Show how your menu is suitable for a range of dietary requirements.

Seventh Day Adventists

Some follow vegetarian diets. Pork and fish without scales or fins are avoided. Stimulants such as alcohol and coffee are avoided.

— Investigation

1 Carry out an investigation into foods sold in supermarkets to find out how they help people with special dietary needs to make food choices.
2 Find out how your school meals service caters for people with a range of food restrictions due to religious beliefs.

— Questions

1 Name two religious groups that follow a vegetarian diet. In each case explain what foods they avoid.
2 These food products may contain forbidden ingredients for vegetarians and different religious groups. For each food product, explain why certain people may need to avoid them.
   a jelly made with gelatine
   b pastry made with lard
   c pork pie
   d ham sandwich

Breakfast

'Breakfast' means 'breaking the fast'. A fast is a time when no food is eaten. Breakfast is the first meal of the day and breaks an overnight fast which could be as long as sixteen hours.

What if you miss breakfast?

Research shows that repeatedly missing breakfast over a long period of time can affect behaviour and performance at school and at work. Skipping breakfast has been associated with low blood sugar and insulin levels in the morning and these low levels may be linked to poor problem-solving abilities later in the morning. Teenagers and younger adults often skip breakfast but may feel hungry in the middle of the morning, so eat fatty and sugary snacks and drinks such as crisps, doughnuts and fizzy drinks.

Some schools are offering breakfast as well as school lunch for their students.

Nutritional value of breakfast

Breakfast should supply 25 per cent of our daily intake of energy and nutrients. The chart on this page shows daily nutritional requirements for an adult. Breakfast should supply a quarter of these requirements.

What do people eat for breakfast?

In Britain 45 per cent of people eat cereals for breakfast and others eat toast and/or a drink or a cooked meal. Five per cent eat nothing at all. A healthy breakfast is an important part of a healthy diet. A bowl of breakfast cereal with milk for breakfast can supply many important nutrients, including vitamins and minerals.

Adult daily nutritional requirements	
Nutrient	*Dietary recommendations RNI a day*
Energy value of food	Varies with age, sex and activity adult male 2550 kcal, female 1940 kcal
Protein	55 g for men, 45 g for women
Fat	No more than 35 per cent of food energy
Carbohydrates of which starch	50 per cent of energy value of food 39 per cent of energy value
Sugars (NME)	11 per cent of energy value
Dietary fibre	18 grams for adults
Vitamins	Requirements vary
Minerals	Requirements vary

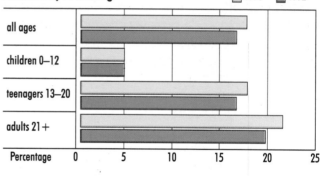

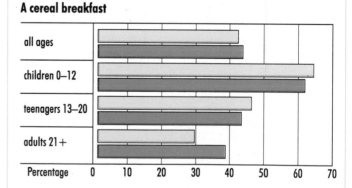

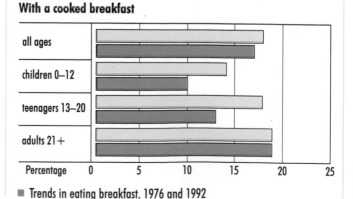

■ Trends in eating breakfast, 1976 and 1992

A survey showed that children who ate breakfast cereals had higher intakes of some vitamins, calcium and iron, but also had less energy in their diet from fat. Breakfasts cereals are high in carbohydrates and may provide dietary fibre, so they form part of a healthy eating plan.

Snack foods

In many countries people eat snacks throughout the day, instead of sitting down to formal meals. In the West, we mark the day according to mealtimes, so we have breakfast, lunch time, tea time and supper time. However, our mealtime habits are changing, and as a nation we are eating more snacks and take-away foods. This may be because more women are going out to work and have less time to prepare

meals. But also many people now have busier lifestyles, e.g. more social activities outside the home, longer distances to travel to work, or they may live alone. It is also partly due to the increase in choice of ready-prepared snack foods.

People are spending more and more on snack foods. Research estimates that we shall spend £2 billion on crisps, nuts and snacks by the year 2000.

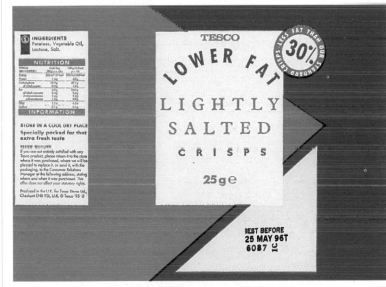

■ There are many reduced fat snack foods now available

— *Investigation* —

Carry out an investigation to find out what foods are served for breakfast. Plan a nutritious breakfast for a teenager. Use food tables or a nutrition analysis computer program to check if your choice meets 25 per cent of daily requirements. Modify your choice if necessary.

— *Questions* —

1 Why is breakfast important?

2 Use the chart on page 78 to work out the nutritional requirements for a breakfast (25 per cent of daily requirements).

3 Look at the graphs showing trends in eating breakfast (page 78). Explain and comment on the evidence.

Look at the label for Tesco lower fat crisps on the left.

4 Do you think there is a demand for this sort of product? Give reasons for your answer.

— *Investigation* —

Investigate the types of snack food on sale that can be eaten instead of a meal. What is the nutritional value of each snack? Record your findings using the headings below. Tick the boxes that you think are appropriate for each food. Draw conclusions from your results about the nutritional value of the snacks we choose to eat.

Snack food	High in starch	High in fat	High in sugar	Healthy	High in fibre	High in vitamins and minerals

33 *School meals*

History of school meals

The school meals service started in 1906, mainly to provide meals for poorly-nourished children at school. The number of pupils eating school meals varies from school to school, but in 1979 nearly two-thirds of pupils in England ate school meals. In 1989 less than half of pupils ate school meals while in Scotland the number is rising.

Nutritional value of school meals

School meals can make an important contribution to the diets of schoolchildren as they provide 30–43 per cent of children's average daily intake.

The Government's report, '**The Diets of British Schoolchildren**', concluded that much of the total intake of energy for young people comes from three foods – chips, cakes and biscuits. The diets of most children are too high in fat and sugar and too low in dietary fibre and some vitamins and minerals.

Who provides school meals?

Since 1988 caterers have provided school meals to a specific contract. This means the local education authority, school or other organization decides the specifications for the school meal service contract. This contract can include the cost, nutritional guidelines and quality of the meals to be provided. Not every school has school meals provided.

Nutritional guidelines for school meals

Since 1980 there have been no compulsory nutritional standards for school meals. However, the contract to the caterers can specify the nutritional content of the meals. This can be monitored by using computer programs to analyse the meal content to see if it meets dietary guidelines.

The School Meals Assessment Pack (SMAP)

This is a computer-based method of assessing the nutritional content of the average meal and other lunch items over at least five school days. Students keep a diary of all the foods and drinks

School Meals Assessment Pack

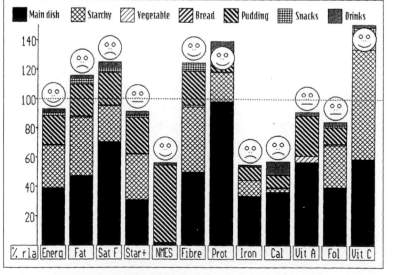

The face symbols indicate how the average meal scored against the recommendation for each nutrient:

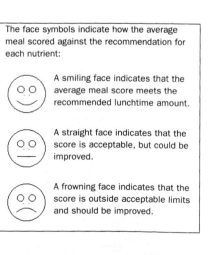

A smiling face indicates that the average meal score meets the recommended lunchtime amount.

A straight face indicates that the score is acceptable, but could be improved.

A frowning face indicates that the score is outside acceptable limits and should be improved.

■ This is a printout from the SMAP program

The School Meals Assessment Pack is available from SMAP, P.O. Box 7, London W5 2GQ

they consume for lunch over five school days. They enter the information to the SMAP computer program, along with information on the ingredients and cooking methods. Then SMAP assesses the choice based on the RLA – **recommended lunch-time amount** – for energy and eleven nutrients.

The pack has been developed by the National Heart Forum and other organizations. The aim of the pack is to help improve the diets of children aged 11–16 years and encourage them to eat more bread and starchy, fibre-rich foods, more fruits and vegetables and less fat, sugar and salty food. The pack is intended for use both in classroom teaching with 11–16 year olds and by people who monitor the choice of school meals, including caterers, school governors, teachers and contract organizers.

Recommended lunch-time amounts (RLA)

The recommended lunch-time amounts used by SMAP are taken from nutritional guidelines for school meals published by **The Caroline Walker Trust** and based upon the Government's dietary recommendations.

◼ *Questions* ◼

1 Do you think that school meals are necessary? Explain your answer.
2 Why do you think it is important to have nutritional guidelines for school meals?

Recommended lunch-time amounts (RLA) for 11–16 year olds

	RLA amounts used in the SMAP computer program		Caroline Walker Trust Nutritional Guidelines for school meals
Energy	634 kcal		30% of the EAR.
Fat *	Not more than 35% of food energy.	Maximum	Not more than 35% of food energy.
Saturated fat *	Not more than 11% of food energy.	Maximum	Not more than 11% of food energy.
Starch	Starch plus intrinsic and milk sugars (i.e. carbohydrate excluding NME sugars), not less than 39% of food energy.	Minimum	–
Carbohydrate	–	Minimum	Carbohydrate including not less than 50% of food energy.
NME sugars *	Not more than 11% of food energy.	Maximum	Not more than 11% of food energy.
Fibre (non starch polysaccharides) **	Not less than 30% of the CRV.	Minimum	Not less than 30% of the CRV.
Protein	Not less than 13 g.	Minimum	Not less than 30% of the RNI.
Iron	Not less than 5.9 mg.	Minimum	Not less than 40% of the RNI.
Calcium	Not less than 350 mg.	Minimum	Not less than 35% of the RNI.
Vitamin A (retinol equivalents)	Not less than 183 μg.	Minimum	Not less than 30% of the RNI.
Folate	Not less than 80 μg.	Minimum	Not less than 40% of the RNI.
Vitamin C	Not less than 13 mg.	Minimum	Not less than 35% of the RNI.
Sodium	Should be reduced in catering practice.	Maximum	Should be reduced in catering practice.

* As there is no absolute requirement for sugars or fats (except essential fatty acids), these values represent a maximum.
** The Dietary Reference Value for non-starch polysaccharide is 18 g for adults, and children should eat proportionately less, based on their lower body size.
Abbreviations: NME = non-milk extrinsic sugar RNI = reference nutrient intake EAR = estimated average requirement CRV = calculated reference value
Source – *School Meals Assesment Pack*, National Heart Forum, 1995

SCHOOL LUNCH MENU

MONDAY

lambburger
fish cake
macaroni cheese
tinned tomatoes

green beans
creamed potatoes
tomato ketchup

Viennese jam tart
chocolate milk shake
custard

TUESDAY

shepherd's pie
turkey burger
veggie burger

peas
spaghetti rings
boiled rice
tomato ketchup

mousse
iced cup cake
fresh fruit
custard

WEDNESDAY

chilli con carne
cheese and tomato pizza
cheese and vegetable finger

Brussels sprouts
diced carrots
creamed potatoes
tomato ketchup

chocolate cake
fruit jelly
fresh fruit
chocolate sauce

THURSDAY

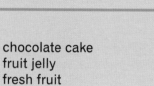

fish fingers
turkey curry
vegetarian ragout

sweetcorn
baked beans
boiled potatoes
tomato ketchup

steamed syrup sponge
raspberry buns
fresh fruit
strawberry flavoured sauce

FRIDAY

turkey burgers
carrot and cheese slice

cabbage
mixed vegetables
chips
tomato ketchup

lemon meringue pie
strawberry yogurt
fresh fruit
custard

— To do

1 Make a lunch choice for each day from the menu provided. Explain whether you have made a healthy choice. How could your choice be improved? What changes, if any, would you make to this menu to make it more appealing to students?

2 Use a computer program or food tables to help analyse the nutritional value of a school meal. Use the chart showing recommended lunchtime amounts (on page 81) to evaluate your choice.

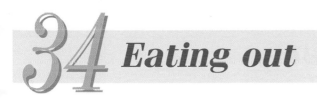

Eating out

*I*n recent years people have been eating out more frequently. Look in your local newspaper and check the number of food choices available in the range of restaurants, snack bars, take-aways and companies that deliver food to your home.

The chart below shows the average number of meals eaten out by each person each week. You can see the increase in the number of meals eaten out over the period of just one year.

Meals eaten out of the home		
Meals	1992	1993
Midday	1.72	1.77
All meals	2.78	2.91
Source — National Food Survey		

— To do

Carry out a survey to find out where people eat out and how often they eat meals prepared out of the home each week. How much do they spend on each meal? What places do they think are value for money? Show your results in a bar chart or pie chart.

Draw conclusions from your survey. What are the trends and fashions in eating out?

Take-away food

Many people can ring for a pizza and have it delivered to their home.

■ Food can be delivered to the home

— Questions

1 What are the reasons for the increase in the number of meals eaten out of the home and take-away meals?

2 How can you make healthy food choices when choosing to eat out or from a take-away menu?

■ Most town centres have a wide variety of food on offer

— Investigation

Investigate the types of take-away food available in your area. Collect newspaper advertisements, menus and fliers to show the range of foods available. What is the range of food you could buy? How much does it cost? Can it be delivered to your home? You could fill in a chart like the one below.

Type of take-away food	Range available	Cost — cheap, average, expensive	Value	Comments
Chinese take-away	Chinese food, pizza	average	good	well presented

What are your views about take-away food and food which can be delivered to your home?

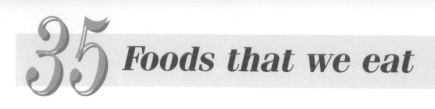

Foods that we eat

*H*ere are some examples of the range of foods we eat. You can find further information on the pages that follow.

Starchy foods – wheat, flour, bread, pasta, breakfast cereals, potatoes, rice,

Fats and oils – butter, margarine, low-fat spreads, cooking oils, olive oil

Fruits and vegetables – apples, oranges, bananas, salads, carrots, broccoli

Meat and meat products, chicken, fish – pork, lamb, beef, chicken, sausages, bacon, fish

Eggs

Milk and milk products such as yogurt

Beans, seeds, lentils, nuts

Sugary foods – sugar, sweets, honey

■ There are a wide variety of foods available to purchase

Nutritional value of foods and food products	
Food	**Nutritional value**
Cereals, bread, potatoes	High in carbohydrate (starch), dietary fibre, calcium, iron, B-group vitamins.
Fats and oils	Fats and vitamins A and D.
Fruits and vegetables	Some carbohydrate, vitamin C, carotene, folate, dietary fibre (NSP).
Meat and fish	Protein, iron, B-group vitamins, especially B12.
Milk and dairy products	Protein, fat, calcium, vitamins A and D.
Beans, seeds and lentils	Protein, fibre, carbohydrate.
Sugary foods	Sugar.

— To do —

Make your own list of five foods which come under each of the following headings.

cereals, bread, potatoes

fats and oils

fruits and vegetables

meat and fish

milk and dairy products

beans, seeds and lentils

sugary foods

Plan a day's meals using foods from each group.

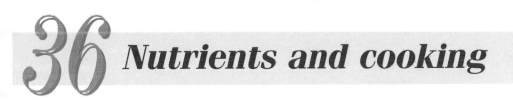

36 Nutrients and cooking

*S*ome nutrients change during cooking, while others remain unchanged. The chart below summarizes the main effects of cooking.

Questions

1 Explain what nutritional changes might occur when you cook the following foods.
  a boiled broccoli   b cheese on toast
  c fried egg
2 Give two examples of how you could adapt your cooking to prevent loss of nutrients.

	Effects of cooking	How is this used in the cooking process?	Nutritional changes
Starch	1 With dry heat, e.g. toasting bread, starch turns to dextrin. 2 Heated with liquid, starch granules soften and swell and absorb water and thicken liquids (gelatinization).	1 To make toast crisp. 2 To thicken soups, sauces and custards.	The carbohydrate value is not lost unless the food is burnt and becomes inedible.
Sugar	When heated, sugar dissolves, changes from white to golden, caramelizes and eventually burns.	Used to make syrups and caramel for caramel custard.	The carbohydrate value is not lost unless the food is burnt and becomes inedible.
Fats – solid	Fats melt to a liquid, bubble and can decompose at high temperatures when they give off smoke and burn. Fats have different melting and decomposition temperatures. Low-fat spreads contain a lot of water and are not usually used in cooking.	Solid fats are used for frying – for example butter is used to fry onions.	Fat is not changed in value during cooking unless it is burnt and becomes inedible.
Protein	Protein denatures (changes) on heating, then coagulates and sets.	Eggs go through various changes as they are fried, boiled or poached, and eventually become solid. Meat hardens and goes brown.	The protein value is not lost in cooking unless the food is burnt and becomes. inedible.
Vitamins – fat-soluble (A and D)	Fat-soluble vitamins are not affected by the cooking process. They are not soluble in water so are not lost when food is cooked in water or soaked.		Fat-soluble vitamins are not lost during cooking.
Vitamins – water-soluble (B and C)	Because these vitamins are water-soluble they dissolve in cooking water. High-temperature cooking such as frying and baking destroys these vitamins.	Vitamin C is easily lost during preparation and cooking of vegetables. Avoid long cooking times and keeping vegetables warm.	Water-soluble vitamins can be lost during cooking. Vitamin C is lost if fruit and vegetables are stored too long.
Dietary fibre (NSP)	Dietary fibre softens when heated with liquid.	Cabbage and other vegetables become soft when boiled in water.	Dietary fibre remains indigestible after cooking.
Minerals	There is little mineral loss during preparation and cooking.		There is little mineral loss during preparation and cooking. The cooking water can be used in the sauce or gravy.

37 Properties of food

Food has many properties which are used in different ways when preparing dishes and meals. The chart below shows some examples.

Properties	Examples
Adding flavour to foods	Salt, pepper, herbs and spices all help to improve the flavour of savoury dishes. Strongly-flavoured foods such as bacon and tomatoes add flavour to sauces. For sweet foods, chocolate, nuts and dried fruits can be added. Sometimes a delicate flavour such as vanilla may be added to an ice-cream.
Adding colour	Food should be attractive and colourful. The appearance of a dish can be improved by adding a garnish, such as parsley to a white sauce, or a cherry on top of a dessert.
Adding textures	Sometimes food is dull so another food can be added to give texture, such as a crunchy salad with a soft pasta dish. Foods such as peas provide colour and texture to a rice dish, and fresh fruit pieces improve the texture of a yogurt or milky dessert.
Thickening	Sauces, soups and stews may need thickening; a variety of flours or starchy vegetables or bread can be used to thicken the sauce or soup.
Bulking	Some foods are used for bulk – they make up the main part and fill out the recipe. Flour is a good bulking agent used in bread and pastry, oats are used as the bulking agent in muesli, and rice is the main food in risotto.
Sweetening	Many foods can be used to sweeten dishes, but the main food used is sugar. Dried fruits which add sweetness include raisins, sultanas and apricots; honey and preserves such as jam can be used to sweeten desserts, and fresh fruits can be added to foods such a muesli for sweetness.
Setting food	Foods such as jellies and cold sauces are set using a variety of ingredients. Gelatine is used to set jelly, cold sauces such as blancmange are set with cornflour and other sauces may be set with other starch products such as flour.
Aerating	Many foods need to be made lighter by adding a gas such as air, carbon dioxide or steam. This can be done by whisking ingredients such as eggs to introduce air, adding raising agents such as yeast to introduce carbon dioxide gas or using liquid such as milk in batter to introduce steam when the product is cooked.
Preserving	Ingredients can help other foods to keep longer. Sugar is needed for jam-making to preserve the fruit, vinegar for pickles to preserve the vegetables and salt for salting fish to increase the keeping time.
Emulsifying	Ingredients such as eggs help other liquids hold together, for example when making mayonnaise.
Shortening	Ingredients such as fats and oils help to shorten a flour mixture such as pastry and make it crisp in texture and crumbly to the palette.
Binding	Some ingredients need binding together, for example in beefburgers, vegetable burgers and pastry. You can use water and eggs to bind things together and other ingredients such as flour will help the ingredients to stick together.

▬ *Questions* ▬

1 For each of the food products listed below, describe the properties of some of the ingredients.

Use some of these key words and phrases to help.

adding flavour   adding colour   adding textures thickening   bulking   sweetening   setting food aerating   preserving   emulsifying   shortening binding

  a Flapjacks made from oat flakes, sugar, golden syrup and butter

  b Dhal made from lentils, spices, garlic, onion and oil

  c Fruit bread made from flour, yeast, sugar, butter, dried fruit, eggs

  d Samosa made from flour, oil, spices, peas, potato, onion

Add other examples of your own and work out the properties and functions of the ingredients.

2 Copy this chart and fill it in with your own examples to show how food ingredients have different properties.

Examples of foods	Property
	Adding flavour to foods
	Adding colour
	Adding textures
	Thickening
	Bulking
	Sweetening
	Setting food
	Aerating
	Preserving
	Emulsifying
	Shortening
	Binding

38 *Starchy foods*

Starchy foods come from grains, cereals, flours and root vegetables and include food products such as bread, pasta, rice, potato snacks and breakfast cereals.

This chart shows nutritional information and advice about starchy foods.

Starchy Foods	
Types of foods	Bread, cereals, breakfast cereals, pasta, potatoes, rice, noodles. Beans and pulses can be eaten as part of this group.
Main nutrients	Carbohydrate (starch). Fibre (NSP), some calcium and iron, B-group vitamins.
How much to choose	Eat lots.
What types to choose	Try to eat wholemeal, wholegrain, brown or high fibre versions where possible. Try to avoid: • having them fried too often e.g. chips • adding too much fat e.g. thickly spread butter • adding rich sauces and dressings such as mayonnaise.

Source – 'The Balance of Good Health', Health Education Authority

Wheat

Wheat is an important cereal in the UK and is used for flour to make bread, cakes, biscuits and snacks. Wheat grain is made up of three important parts:

- **bran:** twelve per cent of the wheat – the outer coat of the wheat which is a good source of dietary fibre (NSP)
- **wheatgerm:** three per cent of the wheat – contains nutritious vitamins and oils
- **endosperm:** 85 per cent of the wheat – the white part of the wheat containing starch and protein.

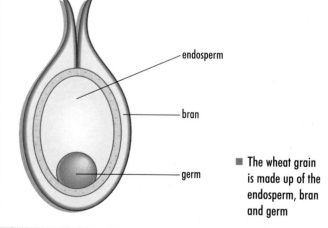

■ The wheat grain is made up of the endosperm, bran and germ

Flour and how it is used	
Types of wheat flour	*Uses*
White flour – 75% of wheat grain plain strong white flour made from hard wheat self raising flour	Used for thickening sauces and pastry. Used for bread-making. Used to help cakes and biscuits rise.
Wholewheat or wholemeal flour 100% flour from the whole grain	More nutritious than white flour and used for breads and pastries.
Stoneground flour 100% flour and whole grain	Good flavour and used for breads and pastries.
Malted wheat flour A brown flour with a nutty flavour from added malted wheat grains	Adds flavour and texture to breads.

— Investigation —

Find out what products can be made from the cereals shown on the chart below, and the ways in which the cereals are processed for sale   for example, oats are made into flakes. Make a copy of the chart to record your findings.

Type of cereal	What products can be made from this cereal?	How is this cereal processed for sale?
Wheat		e.g. flour, flakes, semolina
Oats		e.g. flakes
Maize		e.g. cornflour, polenta
Rye		
Rice		e.g. whole grains, flour
Barley		
Arrowroot		
Millet		

—Questions—

The table below shows the trend in the consumption of bread, cereals and cereal products, per person per week.

Consumption (ounces)	1991	1992	1993
White bread (loaf)	13.71	12.95	13.27
Brown bread	3.64	3.29	3.32
Wholemeal bread	3.67	3.86	3.70
Other breads	5.51	4.33	4.52
Flour	2.84	2.84	2.91
Cakes and pastries	4.15	4.08	4.16
Biscuits	5.18	5.23	5.03
Oatmeal and oat products	0.69	0.53	0.49
Breakfast cereals	4.72	4.66	4.54
Other cereals	7.20	7.61	7.70

Source – National Food Survey

1 Comment on the trends in consumption of bread, cereals and other cereal products shown in the National Food Survey.
2 What are the three main parts of the wheat grain? How is each part used?

39 Bread

Bread is an important food in Britain, but we consume less bread than people in other European countries. Bread is very nutritious since it is a good source of carbohydrate, protein, B-group vitamins, and the minerals calcium and iron.

White breads are made from mainly white flour, brown loaves from a mixture of white flour and bran, and wholemeal bread is made from the whole of the wheat grain. Wholemeal bread contains more fibre that white, but white bread must, by law, contain added vitamins, calcium and iron. In the UK as a whole, we eat over 50 million loaves a week and sliced, white bread makes up nearly 75 per cent of bread sales.

There are regional trends in bread-eating habits. People in Scotland eat more bread rolls than others – 25 per cent above the national average. People in Lancashire consume 19 per cent more wrapped, sliced bread than the national average.

Large-scale bakers produce very many different types of breads, rolls and other baked products, including products made from flour such as scones, crumpets, Danish pastries and buns.

There are more and more kinds of bread on sale, including Italian ciabatta, Middle Eastern pitta bread, rye bread, Indian naan, French baguettes, Irish soda bread and Mexican tortilla.

How is bread made?

Most bread is made from flour, liquid and a raising agent which is usually yeast.

There are many ways to cook the bread. For example, naan is cooked on the sides of the tandoor, a clay oven which can be heated with hot charcoal. Tortillas are traditionally grilled on large, flat iron pans.

■ Some of the types of bread available.

— Investigation —

Investigate the range of breads and baked goods on sale in a local bakers' shop or supermarket.

You could sort the breads into categories:

Types of sliced bread

- Breads with nutritional claims such as 'added fibre'
- Breads from around the world
- Special sweet and savoury breads
- Morning goods – scones, muffins etc.

Write a report on your findings. What is the trend in bread recipes? What new products are on the market? Invent a bread product that you think could appeal to a target group such as teenagers.

The nutritional value of bread and other starchy foods

	Energy	Protein	Carbohydrate	Fat	Fibre	Sodium
White sliced bread (100 g)	926kJ/217 kcal	7.6 g	46.8 g	1.3 g	1.5 g	530 mg
Wholemeal bread (100 g)	914kJ/215 kcal	9.2 g	41.6 g	2.5 g	5.8 g	550 mg
Baked potato (100 g)	581kJ/136 kcal	3.9 g	31.7 g	0.2 g	2.7 g	12 mg
Rice cooked weight (100 g)	599kJ/142 kcal	2.9 g	26.3 g	3.5 g	1.4 g	490 mg
Pasta (white) cooked weight (100 g)	442kJ/104 kcal	3.6 g	22.2 g	0.7 g	1.2 g	trace

Source – *The Composition of Foods*, 5th edition (plus supplements), Royal Society of Chemists

What is organic food?

Many supermarkets stock a range of 'organic' foods. These are normally more expensive than other foods, since it is more difficult to match the volume of perfect fruits and vegetables that are produced by intensive farming. Organic foods are grown using traditional methods of farming, without artificial fertilizers, pesticides or intensive growing systems. There are agreed standards for organic food production and organic food should be clearly labelled. People who eat organic food believe that it tastes better, and that it is better for the environment.

▬ Investigation ▬

What do you think are the advantages of organic foods? Carry out an investigation into the kinds of organic food on sale. What problems do you think the producers of organic food have in selling their products to the consumer?

WHOLEWHEAT FLOUR · NO ARTIFICIAL INGREDIENTS · SOYA FLOUR · SUNFLOWER SEEDS · LINSEEDS · CARROTS · ALL VEGAN INGREDIENTS · SESAME SEEDS · NORWEGIAN KELP

WHOLE EARTH BREAD - BALANCED NUTRITION
Eleven nutritious ingredients go into Whole Earth Organic Bread, including kelp and carrots. Linseeds, sesame, and sunflower seeds give extra flavour and fibre.

Whole Earth

ORGANIC BREAD

400g

INGREDIENTS: WHOLEWHEAT FLOUR*, WATER, SOYA FLOUR*, YEAST, SEASALT, SESAME SEEDS*, SUNFLOWER SEEDS*, LINSEEDS*, CARROTS*, OCEAN KELP

* ORGANICALLY GROWN TO SOIL ASSOCIATION SYMBOL STANDARDS

SA Symbol Holder Number P1117

Write to us for free recipes and organic foods information: Whole Earth Foods Ltd, 269 Portobello Road, London W11 1LR. Baked under license by Goswell's Bakeries Ltd, Caxton St. North, London E16 1JN

■ The ingredients for this bread are grown to agreed standards

▬ Questions ▬

1 Why is bread 'good for you'? Use the chart opposite, showing the nutritional value of starchy foods, to support your answer.

2 A government report recommended that everyone should eat at least four slices of bread per day, which for most people would mean a 50 per cent increase in consumption. How would you suggest that people can increase their bread consumption? Give some ideas for a week's menu to show how bread can be introduced into meals and snacks.

3 Look at the label for organic bread (above).

The list of ingredients includes sesame seeds, sunflower seeds and carrots. Copy the chart below and complete it to show what you think is the function of each of these ingredients. You can fill in the answer 'Yes' or 'No'. One example has already been put in.

	Adds bulk	Adds texture	Provides structure	Gives flavour	Nutritious	Fibre
Wholewheat flour	yes	yes	yes	yes	yes	yes

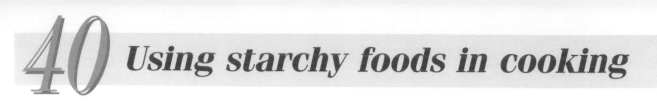

*S*tarchy foods change during cooking and this affects their cooking properties. With dry heat, starch changes to dextrin. This is what happens when bread is toasted and becomes golden brown.

Types of flour made from starchy foods

These include:
- wheat flour
- cornflour made from maize, potato flour, rice flour
- arrowroot made from a tropical root.

Most types of flour are mainly made up of the carbohydrate, starch.

What happens when starch is heated in a liquid?

Starch needs to be cooked since raw starch tastes floury and is not easily digested. When starch is heated in water, the water passes through the walls of the starch granules and the granules become swollen and may burst. This process is called **gelatinization** – a process in which starch, on heating, absorbs water and thickens liquids. This process is used to thicken sauces and soups.

   If gelatinization does not take place properly it could result in:
- lumpy sauce
- loss of flavour due to the taste of raw, uncooked starch
- the sauce having the wrong consistency.

Examples of how gelatinization is used to thicken liquids

- **Wheat flour** is used with butter or margarine and milk to make a thick, white sauce. Wheat flour gives a cloudy, creamy sauce and is used for white sauces and soups.
- **Arrowroot** is blended with water or fruit juice, heated until it thickens, then used to glaze fruit on flans. Arrowroot gives a clear, transparent sauce.
- **Cornflour** gives a less clear, more opaque **gel** and is used for sweet and savoury sauces. If the

■ Gelatinization is used in the production of soups and blancmanges

thickened liquid is left to cool, it will set and form a gel. For example, custard powder (made from coloured cornflour) thickens when heated with milk; when cooled it sets and can be used to top trifles. Blancmange is made from flavoured cornflour which is blended and heated with milk and sugar and sometimes set in a mould.

Ingredients that affect gelatinization

Acid foods such as tomatoes and lemon juice break down the starch granules slightly and this reduces the thickening power of the starch in a sauce.

Gluten in flour

When water is added to flour, the proteins present form another protein called **gluten**. The amount of gluten varies with the type of flour. Strong flours used for bread-making contain the most gluten. When flour mixtures are heated, the air, steam or carbon dioxide pushes up the mixture and the gluten strands set, providing the framework of the baked product.

— Investigation —

Investigate the ways different starches thicken liquids.

You will need small mixing bowls, teaspoons, a temperature probe, a microscope and microscope slides, cornflour, plain flour, arrowroot.

1 Blend two teaspoonsful of the cornflour with four tablespoonsful of water in a small bowl. Smear a little of the raw mixture onto a microscope slide. Cook the remaining mixture in a microwave oven until it thickens, stirring occasionally to avoid lumps. Record the temperature at which the mixture thickens, using a food probe.

2 Repeat step 1 for plain flour and arrowroot.

3 Compare the appearance of the three raw starches that you can see through the microscope.

4 Compare the cooked results for thickness and translucency (clearness). You could use a chart like the one below. You could give the thickness and translucency a rating score of 1 to 5, where 1 = not thick and 5 = very thick, 1 = not translucent and 5 = very translucent.

	Cornflour	Plain flour	Arrowroot
What does the raw starch look like?			
What temperature did it thicken at?			
Thickness			
Translucency			

Write a report on your findings to compare the results of the thickening ability of the different starches. Find out how each of these starches is used in cooking.

— To do —

Find out what each of the following flours is used for in cooking.

plain flour, self-raising flour, strong flour

Why is it important to use strong flour in bread-making?

— Investigation —

Compare the amount of gluten in different flours.

You will need mixing bowls, spoons, plain white flour, white self raising flour, white strong flour, J cloths, baking tray.

1 Mix 100 g of each flour with enough water to form a dough. Knead until smooth.

2 Wrap each dough in a J cloth. Hold it under the tap and run water over the dough.

3 The white starch runs out in the water. Wash until no more starch comes out. A piece of chewy gluten will be left inside the J cloth.

4 Bake the gluten balls in a hot oven at 220°C, Gas 7 until each ball is puffed up and golden. Make sure you can tell which ball is which.

5 Compare the sizes of the cooked gluten balls. Which is the largest? Comment on your results.

■ Which type of flour produces the biggest gluten ball when baked?

— Questions —

1 What happens to starch when it is heated in water?

2 Compare how wheat, arrowroot and cornflour thicken sauces.

3 How does gluten help form the framework of a baked product?

Pasta

'Pasta' means paste or dough. Pasta is made by simply mixing together flour and water to form a paste. It has been made for thousands of years in many parts of the world including China, Italy and Arab countries. Italian pasta is made from **durum wheat semolina** which is a variety of hard wheat that is higher in protein than other varieties and makes a pasta which is golden in colour and retains its shape and texture during cooking.

Nutrition

Pasta is a good source of carbohydrate and contains some protein, dietary fibre (NSP), B-group vitamins and potassium and iron. Wholewheat pasta made from the whole wheat grain will provide more fibre. The rich, brown-coloured pasta takes longer to cook than the refined produce because of its fibre content.

Coloured pasta

Pasta can be coloured with a variety of ingredients. Green lasagne and tagliatelle are coloured with spinach juice or powder. Tomato purée is used to produce orange pasta, beetroot juice produces red or pink pasta, saffron or turmeric makes yellow pasta. Black pasta – famous in Venice – is coloured with squid or octopus ink and there is even chocolate pasta!

■ Varieties of pasta

Dried versus fresh pasta

Dried pasta will keep for many months whereas fresh pasta needs to be eaten within a few days.

■ Question

This is the nutrition information from a spaghetti label.

	100 g dried weight	100 g cooked pasta
Energy	346 kcal/1468 kJ	318 kcal/1349 kJ
Protein	12 g	11 g
Carbohydrate	72.2 g	66.4 g
Fat	1 g	0.9 g
Fibre	2.1 g	21. g
Sodium	< 0.1 g	< 0.1 g

230 g of cooked product will typically be produced from 92 g of dry pasta.

Use the information from the spaghetti label to explain what happens to pasta when it is boiled in water.

■ Investigation

Visit a supermarket and buy a selection of different types of pasta.

Compare the cost per kilogram, and the cooking time. You could fill in a chart like the one shown below. Cook each type of pasta by boiling it for the time given on the packet. Taste the cooked pasta and compare the quality and flavour. For quality, taste and texture you could give each type of pasta a rating score of 1 to 5, where 1 = poor and 5 = excellent. Suggest how each type of pasta could be used in cooking.

Type of pasta	Cost per kg	Cooking time	Taste and texture	Comments	Uses
Fresh angel hair spaghetti	£2.89	1–2 minutes boiling	Taste 4 Texture 4 Fresh tastes better than dried version.	Cooks really quickly and can stick.	Main course with bolognaise sauce.

Rice

Nearly half the people of the world eat rice as their main staple food.

There are different kinds of rice which are used to make different dishes.

- **Long-grained rice** is usually used for savoury dishes, especially in Indian and Chinese cooking.
- **Short-grained rice** is used in the West for sweet rice puddings. In Japan short-grained rice is used to make sushi, small savoury snacks made from rice, fish, seaweed and pickles. In Spain short-grained rice is used for making paella which contains rice, shellfish, crayfish and fresh fish.

■ Varieties of rice.

The nutritional value of rice

Rice contains carbohydrate, a little protein and dietary fibre.

Questions

1 Use the chart below to compare the nutritional value of dry and cooked rice. Explain why the nutritional information has changed when the rice has cooked. How much dry rice would you need to get 100 g of cooked rice?

	100 g dry weight	100 g cooked weight
Energy	316 kcal/1344 kJ	127 kcal/537 kJ
Protein	5.8 g	2.3 g
Carbohydrate	70 g	28 g
Fat	1.4 g	0.6 g
Fibre	0.8 g	0.3 g
Sodium	0.2 g	0.1 g

100 g of cooked product will be produced by 40 g of dry product.

2 Explain why you think we are eating more pasta and rice dishes in Britain today.

3 Do you think pasta and rice are better foods than bread and potatoes? Give your reasons.

4 If you wanted to produce 100 g cooked pasta, how much dried pasta would you use?

Investigation

Visit a supermarket and buy a selection of different types of rice.

Compare the cost per kilogram, the size and quality of the grains of rice, and then the cooking time. You could fill in a chart like the one shown below. Cook each type of rice by boiling it for the time given on the packet. Taste the cooked rice and compare the quality and taste of the grains.

For quality, taste and texture you could give the rice a rating score of 1 to 5, where 1 = poor and 5 = excellent. Suggest how each type of rice could be used in cooking.

Type of rice	Cost per kg	Size of grain	Quality of grain	Cooking time	Taste and texture	Comments	Uses
American long grain	99p	*(Stick in sample)*	3	15 minutes boiling	Taste 3, Texture 3 Nutty, fluffy, separate grains.	Medium quality rice.	With curry, salad.

This chart shows nutritional information and advice about fatty foods.

Fatty foods	
Types of foods	Margarine, low-fat spread, butter, cooking oils, oily salad dressing, cream, chocolate, crisps, biscuits.
Main nutrients	Some vitamins and essential fatty acids but also a lot of fat.
How much to choose	Eat fatty foods sparingly – that is infrequently or in small amounts.
What types to choose	Some foods from this group will be eaten every day, but should be kept to small amounts, for example, margarine, low-fat spreads. Other foods in this group, such as fresh cream cakes and crisps, should be eaten only occasionally.

Source – 'The Balance of Good Health', Health Education Authority

The chart below shows the trend in fat consumption, per person per week.

Trends in fat consumption			
Consumption (ounces)	1991	1992	1993
Butter	1.54	1.44	1.41
Margarine	3.14	2.79	2.48
Low-fat and dairy spreads	1.66	1.80	1.83
Vegetable and salad oils	1.52	1.73	1.61
Other fats and oils	0.89	0.88	0.79

Source – National Food Survey

The types of fats used in cooking and food preparation also include oils such as sunflower and olive oil, butter, lard, suet, soft and hard margarine, dripping, low-fat spread.

Margarine

Margarine was developed in the 19th century as a cheap substitute for butter. It is made from a range of animal and vegetable fats which are hardened by the addition of hydrogen gas. This industrial process is called **hydrogenation**; it makes the fat more **saturated** which helps the product to keep longer. Unsaturated fats and oils are less stable and more likely to go rancid. Dietary guidelines suggest that we should eat less saturated fat so hard, saturated margarines should be avoided.

Reduced or low-fat spreads

These spreads contain 40–80 per cent fat compared with margarine and butter which are over 80 per cent fat. Reduced or low-fat spreads have been designed to meet the need to reduce fat intake. Because of their higher water content they are not suitable for frying, roasting or baking. They are called 'spreads' – not 'margarine' – since they do not meet the legal requirements for margarine.

Other fats used in cooking

- **Lard** is made from melted-down pigs' fat and is used for pastry and frying. Its use is declining, especially in ready-made food products – many religious groups do not eat pig or animal fats.
- **Dripping** is made from the fat left after roasting meat.
- **Suet** is the shredded fatty tissues from around the kidneys of animals and is used for suet and Christmas puddings. Vegetarian suet, made from vegetable fat, is now available.
- **Butter** is made by churning cream to remove the liquid buttermilk. Butter is high in saturates and should be used sparingly in a healthy diet – reduced-fat alternatives and concentrated cooking butters are available.
- **Ghee** is clarified, unsalted butter, used in Indian cookery.
- **Oil** is usually liquid at room temperature. The main oils used in cooking are sunflower, corn, soya, rapeseed and olive oil. Oil is used for salad dressings and frying, baking and roasting.
- **Low-fat spreads** contain added water which lowers the fat content but makes them unsuitable for cooking processes such as frying, baking and roasting.

Fats in pastry-making

Fats are used to **shorten** baked products by making them soft and crumbly.

Shortcrust pastry

Fat is mixed with flour and some fat forms a protective coating around the flour protein. Less water can mix with the protein so less gluten is formed and the mixture is softer.

Use of fats in food preparation and cooking

Type of fat	Baking	Frying	Roasting	Spreading
Butter (82% fat)	✓	✓	✓	✓
Soft margarine (81% fat)	✓	✓	✓	✓
Lard (100% fat)	✓	✓	✓	✗
Concentrated butter (96% fat)	✓	✓	✓	✗
Gold light (39% fat)	✗	✗	✗	✓
Margarine for baking (80% fat)	✓	✓	✓	✗
Solid vegetable oil (100% fat)	✓	✓	✓	✓
Dripping (100% fat)	✗	✓	✓	✓
Extra light half-fat spread (39% fat)	✗	✗	✗	✓

code ✓ = suitable, ✗ = not suitable
This information came from labels on fat products in a supermarket.

▬ Investigation ▬▬▬▬▬

Carry out a survey of the types of fat available in supermarkets. List the number of butters, reduced-fat spreads, margarines etc. on sale. Which are the most popular fats on sale?

Tip – Look at the amount of shelf space given to the various products. Those with the most space are usually the most popular products, or the products could be on special promotion to help them sell.

Name six of the fats and describe their use in cooking – you could use the headings: 'baking', 'frying', 'roasting' and 'spreading'. What does your survey tell you about the trends in using fats and spreads?

▬ Questions ▬▬▬▬▬

Refer to the chart from the National Food Survey (middle of page 96).

1 What is the trend in fat consumption in Great Britain?

Look at the table showing fat usage (above).

2 What types of fat can't be used for:
   a spreading   **b** cooking?

   What are the reasons for the limited use of these fats?

3 List the fats in order of their fat content. Which fat would you recommend for:
   a baking cakes   **b** spreading on toast
   c pastry-making   **d** lowering fat intake?

   In each case give your reasons.

# Sugars

The many forms of sugar that we eat include table sugar, sweets, preserves and sugary fizzy drinks. The main sugar used for cooking is **sucrose**.

How is sugar made?

Sugar can be made from sugar beet or sugar cane. The beet or cane is crushed and mixed with water and then the liquid is boiled to obtain sugar crystals.

Different types of sugar

- **Granulated sugar** is used to sweeten tea and coffee and for sprinkling on breakfast cereals.
- **Caster sugar** is finer than granulated sugar and is used for cakes and biscuit-making.
- **Icing sugar** is a fine sugary powder and is used for icings and sweets.
- **Brown sugars** have a stronger flavour than white sugars and are used for gingerbreads and biscuits.

Properties of sugar in cooking

Sugar has number of important properties which are used in cooking.

- Sucrose is a **preservative** and is used in jams and preserves such as jellies and chutneys. The high sugar content makes the water molecules in the food unavailable for the growth of micro-organisms and yeast.
- Sugar is often used, in small quantities, in yeast cookery to speed up the fermentation process which makes the dough rise.
- When cakes are made by the **creaming** method air is trapped by beating together the sugar and margarine or butter. The **whisking** method of cake-making involves beating together eggs and sugar. The sugar helps to trap air. This trapped air makes the cakes light and well risen. When egg whites are whisked to make **meringues**, sugar helps to keep the meringue foam stable.

The chart below shows the trend in sugar and preserve (jam) consumption per person per week.

Trends in sugar and preserve consumption			
Consumption (ounces)	1991	1992	1993
Sugar	5.88	5.51	5.33
Honey, preserves, syrup and treacle	1.79	1.59	1.50

Source – National Food Survey

Investigation

Carry out an investigation to find out the effect of sugar on a cake recipe. Use a basic recipe for the creaming method (100 g caster sugar, 100 g margarine, 2 eggs, 100 g SR flour) and change the amount of sugar in the recipe. Try several versions of this recipe, using less and less sugar. Cook the cakes in exactly the same size of tin or paper case, at the same temperature and on the same shelf of the oven. Try making the cake without any sugar.

Compare the results. Measure the height of each cake and comment on the texture. Taste the cakes. Which recipe produced the best result? Write a brief report to show the effect of reducing sugar in a cake recipe.

Questions

1 How is sugar useful in the preparation of some food products? Give examples in each case.
2 Refer to the chart from the National Food Survey (above). What is the trend in sugar and preserve consumption in Great Britain? What are the dietary recommendations for sugar (NME) consumption (see page 30)?

To do

Visit your local supermarket and find out about the range of sugars available for sale. What artificial sweeteners are available and how can these be used in cooking?

Eggs

Eggs have many different uses in cooking, and are used in many food products.

Where do eggs come from?

- **Battery farms** provide 90 per cent of the eggs sold in the UK.
- **Free range** eggs come from hens that are allowed to wander in open air runs or large hen houses. These eggs are labelled 'free range' on the packet and are different from 'farm fresh' eggs which come from battery farms.

Food poisoning and eggs

In 1989 the 'Salmonella in eggs' scare broke out. The Government warned people not to eat raw eggs and advised that eggs should be thoroughly cooked before being served to babies or pregnant, elderly or frail people. Research conducted in 1993 on eggs from high street outlets showed that **salmonellas** were isolated in the contents and shells of 0.2 per cent of the samples. It was a surprise to find salmonella on the outer egg shells. This means that as well as the health risk from undercooked or semi-cooked eggs there is also a direct risk from **cross-contamination** from the shells to other foods. To reduce the chance of salmonella multiplying at room temperature, eggs should be stored in the refrigerator after purchase and not kept for long periods.

Use of eggs in cooking

Eggs have many uses in cooking. On heating, the protein in the egg coagulates and sets. Some of the uses of eggs in cooking are listed in the chart below.

Nutritional value of eggs

The information below is from a packet of six eggs.

NUTRITION INFORMATION	
TYPICAL VALUES (BOILED)	PER 100g (3.5oz)
ENERGY	612 kJ.
	147 kcal
PROTEIN	12.5g
CARBOHYDRATE	less than 0.1g
of which SUGARS	less than 0.1g
FAT	10.8g
of which SATURATES	3.1g
MONO-UNSATURATES	4.7g
POLYUNSATURATES	1.2g
FIBRE	0.0g
SODIUM	0.1g
VITAMIN D	1.75µg (35% RDA)
VITAMIN B12	1.1µg (110% RDA)

RDA means Recommended Daily Allowance

PER 100g   147 CALORIES   10.8g FAT

Delivered to store within 48 hours of being laid

Store in a refrigerator or cool, dry place

6 FRESH eggs

SIZE
3
CLASS A

■ A typical label from an egg carton

Questions

Use the information from the egg packet to answer the questions.

1. What valuable nutrients are provided by eggs?
2. a What is the energy value of an egg?
   b What types of fat are found in an egg?
3. Why does the egg contain no dietary fibre?
4. Eggs are known to contain salmonella bacteria. Give some tips on safe handling and preparation of eggs during cooking.
5. Explain, with examples, the different uses of eggs in making food products.

Uses of eggs in cooking

Use	Example
Eggs can provide the main protein for a meal.	Omelette, poached egg, egg curry
Eggs can bind ingredients together.	Beefburgers, croquettes, cakes
Eggs can coat foods.	Fish cakes, batters used for tempura
Eggs trap air when they are beaten.	Swiss roll, meringues
Eggs thicken liquids.	Egg custard, egg sauces, egg soup
Egg yolk is used to emulsify ingredients by holding them together.	Mayonnaise, where the egg yolk binds with the oil
Beaten eggs are used to glaze foods.	Savoury pies, sausage rolls, Chinese buns

45 Fish

There are many types of fish available for us to eat. Fish may be **freshwater** species, such as trout, or **seafish**, such as cod, plaice, herring and tuna. Shellfish include crabs, lobsters, mussels and oysters. Shellfish are good sources of protein, low in fat and some are good sources of micro-nutrients.

Fish can be divided into three groups. The chart shows examples of the groups.

Name of group	Examples
White fish	cod, haddock, plaice, skate
Oily fish	herring, mackerel, salmon
Shellfish	crab, lobster, mussels

Nutritional value

Fish is a good source of protein and also contains B-group vitamins and minerals such as iodine and fluoride. Fish that is eaten with the bones, such as canned salmon and tuna, is a good source of calcium. White fish such as cod and plaice have very little fat in the flesh, as it is stored in their livers. Cod liver oil provides oil and vitamin A and is used as a food supplement.

Oily fish such as mackerel and salmon store fat in their flesh. Eating plenty of oily fish may reduce the risk of heart disease since the oil is rich in **omega-3 fatty acids** which seem to reduce the risk of blood clotting. We should try to eat fish several times a week.

Cooking fish

Fish is easy and quick to cook. You can even eat it raw as in Japanese sashimi and sushi.

- **Frying and deep frying** – this method can be used for battered and breaded fish fillets and whole fish.
- **Grilling and barbecuing** – small whole fish can be grilled, especially oily fish such as salmon.
- **Steaming and poaching** – fish can be cooked gently in a steamer or poached in water or milk.
- **Smoked fish** – many types of fish can be smoked including haddock, cod, salmon and herring (kippers). The fish is first dry salted or immersed in a salt solution, then smoked over a fire.
- **Dried and salted fish** – dried fish is usually dried in the sun and salted fish is covered in dry salt to preserve it. The fish must be soaked in plenty of water before cooking to remove the salt and rehydrate it.

▬ Questions ▬

1 We are told that we must increase the amount of fish we eat in Britain, but fish sales are not increasing. How would you encourage someone to eat more fish? Suggest some exciting fish recipes which might tempt them.

2 Refer to the chart showing nutritional values for selected foods. Give two reasons why fish is important in a healthy diet.

3 Give four examples of each of the following types of fish.

white fish, oily fish, shellfish

Explain how you could use each type of fish in a recipe.

The nutritional value of 100 g of selected foods	Energy (kcal/kJ)	Protein (g)	Fat (g)	Calcium (mg)	Iron (mg)	Vitamin A (μg)	Vitamin D (μg)
Haddock	73/308	16.8	0.6	18	0.6	tr	tr
Herring	234/970	16.8	18.5	33	0.8	45	22.5
Prawns	107/451	22.6	1.8	150	1.1	tr	tr
Beef (brisket)	252/1044	16.8	20.5	7	1.6	tr	tr
Chicken (meat and skin)	230/954	17.6	17.7	10	0.7	tr	tr
Lentils	304/1293	23.8	1.0	39	7.6	0	0
Cheddar cheese	406/1682	26.0	33.5	800	0.4	310	0.26

tr = trace

Source – The Composition of Foods, 5th edition (plus supplements), Royal Society of Chemists

46 Milk

Most of the milk that we drink comes from cows, but we also drink milk from goats and sheep. The milk of each animal provides for the needs of that animal's offspring. Human milk provides all the nutrients required by a human baby. Soya milk is not strictly a milk since it is made from soya beans and does not come from animals.

Nutritional value of milk

Milk is a good source of **protein** and **calcium** and also contains **fat**, **carbohydrate** and some B-group vitamins, including B12, and vitamin A (whole milk only).

The chart at the foot of the page compares the nutritional composition of Channel Islands, whole, semi-skimmed and skimmed milk per 100 ml.

Different types of milk

- **Channel Islands** (gold top) – comes from Guernsey or Jersey cows and is rich and creamy.
- **Whole milk** (silver top)   must have a minimum fat content of 3.5 per cent.
- **Homogenized milk** (red top) – has been homogenized so that the cream is mixed through the milk.
- **Semi-skimmed milk** (red and silver striped top) – has about half the fat of whole milk, and is suitable for anyone except children under the age of two.
- **Skimmed milk** (blue and silver checked top) – nearly all the fat has been removed to give this milk 0.1 per cent fat. The milk looks and tastes less creamy than other milks.

Many people prefer to drink semi-skimmed and skimmed milk, to lower the fat content of their diet. Semi-skimmed milk contains all the protein, minerals and most of the vitamins found in whole milk. Since skimmed milk has a low fat content, it contains less fat-soluble vitamins A and D than other milks.

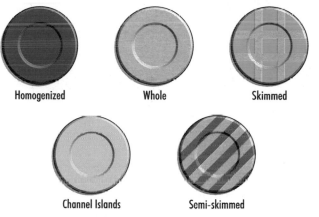

Homogenized   Whole   Skimmed

Channel Islands   Semi-skimmed

■ Different types of milk have different bottle-tops
Source – National Dairy Council

Questions

1 Describe the differences between the types of milk listed above.
2 Refer to the chart below, showing the nutritional value of different milks. Which milk has:
   a the highest   b the lowest
   energy value and fat content?
3 Which milk would you recommend for:
   a someone who likes creamy milk on their breakfast cereal
   b someone who wants to cut down on the amount of fat in their diet
   c a young child?

Comparison of the nutritional composition of milks (per 100 ml)				
	Channel Islands	Whole	Semi-skimmed	Skimmed
Energy (kcal/kJ)	81/337	68/284	49/204	34/146
Protein (g)	3.7	3.2	3.4	3.4
Carbohydrate (g)	4.7	4.7	5.0	5.0
Fat (g)	5.2	4.0	1.7	0.1
Vitamin A (μg)	60	58	24	1.0
Riboflavin (mg)	0.20	0.18	0.19	0.19
Calcium (mg)	134	119	122	124

Source – A–Z of Dairy Products, National Dairy Council

Consumption of milk and milk products

This chart shows the trend in milk consumption, per week, in Great Britain.

Trends in milk consumption			
Consumption (pints)	1991	1992	1993
Whole milk	1.90	1.69	1.51
Low fat milk	1.37	1.70	1.81
Total milk	3.27	3.39	3.32
Cream	0.03	0.03	0.03
Yogurt and fromage frais	0.19	0.21	0.21
Cheese	3.78	3.66	3.53

Source – National Food Survey

Milk and milk products

This chart shows nutritional information and advice about milk and milk products.

Milk and milk products	
Types of foods	Milk, cheese, yogurt and fromage frais.
Main nutrients	Calcium, protein, vitamin B12, vitamins A and D.
How much to choose	Eat moderate amounts and choose lower-fat versions whenever you can.
What types to choose	Lower-fat versions means semi-skimmed or skimmed milk, low-fat 0.1% yogurts or fromage frais and lower-fat cheeses. Check the fat content by looking at the labels – compare and choose the lowest.

Source – 'The Balance of Good Health', Health Education Authority

— Investigation —

Carry out a milk tasting of different types of milk. Include about six to ten people in your tasting panel. Choose whole milk, semi-skimmed milk, low-fat milk and soya milk for the tasting.

Compare the taste and 'mouth feel' of the milks and rank the milks in order of preference. Which is the most popular milk? Write a report on your findings.

Milk products

Milk can be made into many different products, including butter, cream, ice-cream, cheese and yogurt.

Butter

Butter is made by churning cream and contains not less than 80 per cent fat.

Cream

Cream is separated from whole milk and has a high fat content. There are different types of cream including single, whipping, double and clotted cream.

Ice-cream

Ice-cream is traditionally made from milk, cream, sugar and eggs. In the UK much of our ice-cream is made from air and water whipped into fat, sugar and milk powder. Types of luxury ice-cream can be made from cream. Ice-cream is rich in fat and sugar, and should be eaten in moderation.

Cheese

Cheese is made by coagulating the protein in milk to make a curd and leaving a watery whey. The curd is then pressed to make hard cheese such as Cheddar. Rennet is the natural extract from the stomach of a calf. Cheese that is suitable for vegetarians is made by using artificial rennet which is made by genetic modification (see page 118) but is identical in its reaction to calf rennet.

■ Milk can be made into a wide variety of cheeses

Nutritional value of cheese

Cheese is a good source of protein and calcium. Hard cheeses contain the least water and have the highest fat content and high energy values. A curd or cottage cheese contains more water and so has a lower energy value than hard cheeses.

Yogurt

Milk is heated, cooled and inoculated with a starter culture of bacteria to make yogurt. The yogurt thickens after being incubated at 40–45°C for 3–6 hours. This is due to the proteins coagulating. The yogurt is then cooled to 5°C for distribution and sale.

There are many different types of yogurt.

- **Low-fat yogurt** contains only 0.5–2 per cent fat.
- **Very low fat/diet/light yogurt** is virtually fat-free (less than 0.5 per cent).
- **Bio-yogurt** contains additional cultures which give it a mild taste and improve digestion.

- **Whole milk/thick and creamy yogurt** is usually made with whole milk products or added cream.
- **Long-life yogurt** is heat-treated after fermentation and has no active cultures.

The following yogurts will keep without refrigeration.

- **French yogurt or set yogurt** is yogurt in which fermentation takes place in the pot to give a more solid consistency.
- **Children's or infants' yogurt** is usually made with fruit purée rather than fruit pieces. Infants' yogurt normally has reduced sugar levels too.
- **Greek or Greek-style yogurt** is a higher-fat version of natural yogurt, with a rich flavour. Also available with fruit.
- **Split yogurt or corners** are plain or flavoured yogurts accompanied by a fruit or cereal in a separate compartment.
- **Fromage frais** is a cultured product with a creamy consistency which is, in fact, a form of soft cheese.

▬ Questions

1. What is the nutritional value of milk and milk products in our diet? Describe how people can make healthier choices with the milk and milk products they choose to eat.

2. Refer to the chart from the National Food Survey (page 102, top). What trend do you notice in the consumption of:
   a whole milk
   b low-fat milk
   c total milk sales?

   What is happening to sales of yogurt, cream and cheese? Explain why you think people are changing their choice of milks.

3. Why do you think people have been eating more yogurt products in recent years?

4. Refer to the list of different types of yogurt (above). Which yogurt would you recommend for:
   a a young child
   b someone watching their weight
   c mixing with fresh fruit?

▬ Investigation

Carry out an investigation into the types of milk products available in the supermarket.
You choice could include yogurt products, cheeses, creams or ice-cream.

Compare the cost, size, energy value and fat content per 100 g of each of the products. You could use a chart like the one shown below. Write a report on your findings.

Yogurt	Cost	Size	Energy per 100 g	Fat per 100 g

48 Meat

The range of meats to choose from includes beef, veal, lamb, pork and bacon. Offal is the name for the internal organs of the animal and includes liver and kidney. There are many popular meat products including beefburgers, sausages, meat pies and cook-chill meals.

Nutritional value of meat

Lean meat is a good source of high quality **protein**, **iron** and **B-group vitamins**, especially **B12**.

We should choose lower-fat versions of meat and poultry. This means cutting fat off chops and removing fatty parts such as the skin from chicken.

Why is meat cooked?

- Meat is cooked to kill bacteria and make the meat safe to eat.
- Cooking makes the meat tender and easier to eat.
- Different cooking methods improve the flavour of the meat.

Storage of meat

Raw and cooked meat should be stored separately and kept cool in the refrigerator. Raw meat needs to be stored at the bottom of the refrigerator so that the juices do not drip onto other foods. Minced meat must be eaten or cooked thoroughly on the day of purchase since it deteriorates quickly.

Poultry

Poultry includes chicken and turkey. Chicken is increasing in popularity as people choose to eat less red meat. There is also an increase in the amount of chicken cuts and products available, from portioned chicken, such as drumsticks and breasts, to products such as Chicken Kiev.

Chicken is good value for money and is versatile in the way it can be used. Poultry contains as much protein as meat, but is lower in fat. It also provides B-group vitamins.

■ A selection of cuts of meat

■ Beefburgers are a popular meat product

Chicken and salmonella

Much of the chicken sold in the UK contains the food poisoning bacteria, **salmonella**. Care is needed when handling and cooking chicken to avoid **cross-contamination** from one food to another. Chicken must be thoroughly cooked to a high enough temperature, for sufficient time, to kill off any bacteria which might be present.

The chart below shows nutritional information and advice on meat, fish and alternatives

Meat, fish and alternatives

Types of foods	Meat, poultry, fish, eggs, nuts, beans and pulses. Meat includes bacon and salami, meat products such as sausages, beefburgers. Beans such as canned baked beans are in this group. Fish includes frozen and canned fish, fish fingers and fish cakes.
Main nutrients	Iron, protein, B-vitamins, especially B12, zinc and magnesium.
How much to choose	Eat moderate amounts and choose lower-fat versions whenever you can.
What types to choose	Lower-fat versions include meat with the fat cut off, poultry without the skin and fish without batter. Cook these foods without added fat. Beans and pulses are good alternatives to meat as they are naturally very low in fat.

Source – 'The Balance of Good Health', Health Education Authority

The chart below shows the trend in consumption of meat, fish and eggs in the UK per person per week.

Trends in consumption of meat, fish and eggs

Consumption (ounces)	1991	1992	1993
Beef and veal	5.35	4.98	4.68
Mutton and lamb	3.02	2.49	2.33
Pork	2.88	2.53	2.83
Bacon and ham	3.00	2.73	2.71
Poultry	7.14	7.64	7.84
Other meat and meat products	12.54	13.15	13.32
Fresh fish	1.15	1.02	1.05
Processed fish and shellfish	0.56	0.55	0.54
Prepared fish including fish products	1.64	1.92	1.96
Frozen fish and fish products	1.53	1.50	1.55
Eggs (number)	2.25	2.08	1.92

Source – National Food Survey

Questions

1 What is the nutritional value of meat and poultry?
2 Refer to the chart from the National Food Survey, above. Explain whether the consumption of each of the foods has gone up or down over the three years since 1991. Why do you think we are eating less of some types of food and more of others?

Investigation

Carry out an investigation into ready-prepared food products. Find out:

a how meat and poultry has been prepared to make cooking easy

b the range of meat and chicken products which are sold as meals or snacks in supermarkets.

Write a report on your findings.

Beans, pulses, nuts and seeds

Beans, pulses, nuts and seeds are good sources of **protein** and **dietary fibre** (NSP), as well as **carbohydrate**, **B-group vitamins** and some **iron**. Many seeds such as peanuts and sunflower seeds are rich sources of **fat** and are used to make vegetable oils for cooking.

Cooking beans

Beans and pulses are often dried and need soaking before they can be cooked. Some beans, including red and black kidney beans, contain **toxins** in their outer skins. They must be boiled vigorously for fifteen minutes to destroy these toxins. Beans and pulses are used for many famous dishes thoughout the world including **dhal** made from lentils, **chilli-con-carne** from red kidney beans, **baked beans** from navy beans and **hummus** from chickpeas.

■ Beans and pulses

— To do

Use recipe books to find out how beans, pulses, nuts and seeds are used in cooking. Why do you think these ingredients are important in traditional recipes in dishes from around the world? Give examples to show how these ingredients are used in different countries.

Sprouting beans, peas and seeds

Sprouting beans and seeds add crispness to salads and can be added to stir-fry dishes to improve texture and flavour. Many seeds can be sprouted, including aduki beans, chickpeas, lentils, mung beans, soya beans and alfalfa. Sprouted seeds are good source of protein, fibre and vitamins and minerals.

Plant-based meat replacements

Quorn, **tofu** and **textured vegetable proteins** (**TVP**) are all products which are used to replace meat as a 'meal centre'. These products are low in fat and there is no waste.

Tofu is soya milk curd and it is made by curdling soya milk with calcium sulphate. The soya curds are pressed and drained and the firm curd that is left is called tofu. Tofu needs to be eaten very fresh and can be used for tofu burgers, in ready meals such as tofu stir-fry, and in desserts such as ice-cream.

How beans, pulses and seeds are used in meals and snacks

Type of bean, pulse, nut or seed	Use in cooking
Red kidney beans	Chilli-con-carne, bean soup, Mexican refried beans
Pine nuts	Pesto sauce
Chickpeas	Hummus and falafel
Sesame seeds	Burger buns, tahini
Lentils – brown, green, yellow, red, puy	Dhal, lentil soup, lentil curry
Borlotti beans	Italian dishes, tuna and bean salad
Butter beans	Cooked with bacon in casseroles
Navy beans	Baked beans
Peas	Pease pudding, mushy peas, split pea soup
Soya beans	Bean sprouts, tofu, soups, salads
Coconut	Curries and sweet foods
Peanuts	Roasted, salted and served as a snack

Textured vegetable protein or TVP is made from soya bean flour which has had its oil removed. The soya flour is mixed to a dough with water and then extruded in a process that cooks the dough and gives TVP its fibrous meat-like texture. TVP is used for vegetable burgers, burger mixes, sausages and dry meal mixes such as vegetable curry.

■ A vegetarian curry

Quorn (see also pages 74–5) is made from a tiny fungus which is processed and cut into slices, dice or chunks. *Quorn* can be used to make ready meals such as sweet and sour dishes, curries and savoury casseroles.

The chart below shows the nutritional composition of meat and some alternatives. The figures are for typical portion sizes.

— Investigation

1 People say that beans and lentils are difficult and time-consuming to cook. Find some recipes which use beans or lentils which can be prepared and cooked within 20 minutes. List the nutritional values of these dishes.

2 Sales of vegetarian sausages and burgers made from beans and lentils are increasing in the UK. Carry out an investigation with a group of people to find out if they are eating more products made from beans and lentils. Identify the range of products they like and report on your findings.

Nutritional content of meat and some alternatives

	Energy (kcal)	Protein (g)	Total fat (g)	Saturated fat(g)	Fibre (g)	Sodium (mg)	Calcium (mg)	Iron (mg)
Plain tofu (71 g)	64	8.2	3.2	0.6	0	Tr	157	0.9
TVP rehydrated (114 g)	81	16.7	0.3	0.05	8	96	107	6.1
Quorn (63 g)	53	7.7	2.0	0.4	3	150	13	0.4
Chicken breast (115 g)	163	30.5	4.6	1.5	0	82	10	0.6
Rump steak lean grilled (115 g)	193	32.9	6.9	2.9	0	64	8	4
Pork sausages (2) grilled (70 g)	222	9.3	17.2	6.8	0.4	700	38	1.0

Source — *Which?*, October 1991

— Questions

Use the information on the chart above, which shows the nutritional composition of meat and some alternatives.

1 Which foods have:
   a the highest and lowest energy value
   b the highest and lowest fat content
   c the highest and lowest saturated fat content
   d the highest and lowest fibre content

   for the portions shown on this chart?

2 Why do you think the chart shows the information in portion sizes, rather than 100 gram weights of each food as are shown on food labels?

3 Are the meat alternative foods – tofu, TVP and *Quorn* – as nutritious as meat or poultry? Give your reasons.

Nutritional value of fruit and vegetables

Fruits and vegetables – except for avocado pears – are **low in fat**. Many fruits and vegetables are **low in energy value** (kJ/kcal), and are good sources of **dietary fibre** (NSP). Citrus fruits and blackcurrants are rich sources of **vitamin C**, and yellow, red and orange fruits and vegetables supply the anti-oxidant pigment **beta-carotene** (a form of **vitamin A**). Medical research suggests that the **anti-oxidant vitamins A, C and E** protect against certain diseases.

The chart below shows nutritional information and advice about fruits and vegetables.

Nutritional information for fruits and vegetables	
Types of foods	Fresh, frozen and canned fruit and vegetables and dried fruit. A glass of fruit juice. Beans and pulses can be eaten as part of this group.
Main nutrients	Vitamin C, carotenes. Folates, fibre and some carbohydrate.
How much to choose	Try to eat up to five portions of fruit and vegetables a day.
What types to choose	Eat a wide variety of fruit and vegetables. Try to avoid: • adding fat and rich sauces to vegetables • adding sugar and syrupy dressings to fruit e.g. adding chocolate sauce to banana.

Source – 'The Balance of Good Health', Health Education Authority

■ Fruit and vegetables form part of a healthy diet

Why five fruits and vegetables a day?

For a healthy diet, we are advised to eat five portions of fruit and vegetables a day. These portions can include fresh, frozen, dried fruit and fruit juice or canned vegetables but do not include potatoes. Our consumption of vegetables in the UK is the lowest in Europe.

Fruits and vegetables provide us with a range of nutrients which form part of a healthy diet, so by eating five portions a day we can improve our nutritional intake. We often think of snack foods as crisps, biscuits and sweets which are high in sugar and fat. Fruits such as bananas, pears and apples can be eaten as snacks and provide us with dietary fibre (NSP) and vitamins and minerals.

The chart below shows trends in consumption of vegetables and fruit in Great Britain per person per week.

Trends in consumption of fruit and vegetables			
Consumption (ounces)	1991	1992	1993
Potatoes	33.81	31.78	30.88
Fresh greens	9.13	8.81	8.46
Frozen, and vegetable products	7.04	7.00	7.17
Other processed vegetable products	12.19	13.03	12.64
Fresh fruit	21.53	21.80	21.75
Fruit juices	8.80	7.81	8.31
Other fruit products	3.23	3.18	3.06

Source – National Food Survey

Healthier cooking with fruit and vegetables

Water-soluble vitamins are destroyed by cooking and are also lost over time. Minerals and vitamins leach out into cooking water.

- Buy good quality fruit and vegetables and store in a cool, dark place.
- Vitamins, minerals and fibre are often located just under the skin of fruit and vegetables. Peel very thinly and use cleaned and unpeeled if possible. (You need to check with current Government advice on peeling vegetables such as carrots.)
- Cook vegetables as quickly as possible in very little water. Steam or microwave if possible.

- Don't chop fruit and vegetables into small pieces – it exposes more of the surface and means more nutrients are lost.
- Prepare fruit and vegetables just before you need them – don't leave them to keep warm as vitamin C is destroyed by warmth and time.
- Use vegetable water for soups and sauces – so the minerals and vitamins that may have leached out are recycled!
- Try to eat fruit and vegetables raw – vitamins and minerals are then not lost by cooking.
- Don't leave vegetables to stand in water – vitamin C and B-group vitamins dissolve out and are lost.

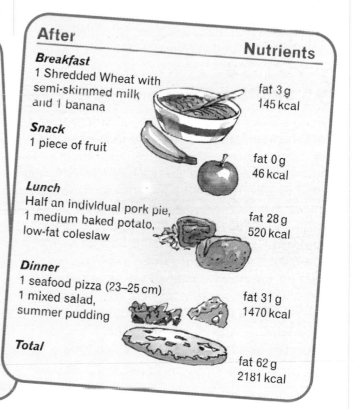

Before — **Nutrients**

Breakfast
1 bowl cornflakes with semi-skimmed milk — fat 2 g / 160 kcal

Snack
2 digestive biscuits — fat 5.5 g / 122 kcal

Lunch
1 individual pork pie, coleslaw, chips — fat 71 g / 1070 kcal

Dinner
Small piece garlic bread, 1 pepperoni pizza (23–25 cm) chocolate cheesecake — fat 81 g / 1840 kcal

Total — fat 160 g / 3192 kcal

After — **Nutrients**

Breakfast
1 Shredded Wheat with semi-skimmed milk and 1 banana — fat 3 g / 145 kcal

Snack
1 piece of fruit — fat 0 g / 46 kcal

Lunch
Half an individual pork pie, 1 medium baked potato, low-fat coleslaw — fat 28 g / 520 kcal

Dinner
1 seafood pizza (23–25 cm) 1 mixed salad, summer pudding — fat 31 g / 1470 kcal

Total — fat 62 g / 2181 kcal

■ How to add more vegetables and fruit to your diet – 'before' and 'after'

Source – *Healthy Eating on a Plate*, Janette Marshall, published by Vermilion

— Questions

1 What is the nutritional value of fruits and vegetables in our diet?

2 Study the chart on page 108, column 2, which shows the trends in fruit and vegetable consumption. Explain the data – what is happening to our eating habits?

3 Refer to the 'before' and 'after' recipes above. Describe how the day's meals have been changed to increase amounts of fruits and vegetables eaten. Why has the amount of total fat in the day's meals decreased?

4 How can you reduce loss of nutrients when preparing and cooking vegetables?

51 Additives

Many packaged foods contain additives. In the UK there are over 300 listed additives and more than 3000 flavourings. Additives are used to help food keep safe longer, to stop oils and fats from going rancid and to add colour. Our choice of foods would be reduced if additives were not used in food products, since they would not last as long, and many new lower-fat products would not be available. Some additives have been used for many years. Potassium nitrate (E251) has been used for curing bacon and ham, and pectin (E440a) in jam-making. Some people are sensitive to certain additives and need to avoid them. Tartrazine (E102), used to colour soft drinks, has been linked to food allergies.

Are additives safe?

Additives used in the UK have been strictly tested. An 'E-number' shows that the additive has been accepted as safe by the countries of the European Union. Some additives must wait for the European Union to give them an E-number, before they can be used.

The 300 listed additives fall into three groups:

- **natural** – made from natural products, such as **paprika** and **beetroot juice**
- **nature identical** – made to the same chemical formula as those extracted from natural products, for example **caramel** used for colouring
- **artificial** – made entirely from chemicals, for example **saccharin** used to sweeten foods.

New additives can cost a food company over £1 million to develop and the additive has to be approved by the Government's Food Advisory Committee.

The food label gives people the information they need to make choices. Some people are allergic to certain additives – the food label tells them if the additive is in the food.

Questions

1 What is an E-number? What is the difference between additives with and without E-numbers?
2 Why are additives used in food products? Use the chart at the bottom of this page to help with your answer.
3 What are your views on food additives? Give the case for and against using additives in food products.

   Use the information about the cake (opposite) for these answers.
4 Why are emulsifiers and stabilizers used in this cake recipe?
5 Explain how additives can help to increase the shelf-life of this cake.

Investigation

Investigate how additives are used in food products. Keep a record of your findings. You could fill in a chart like the one shown below. Comment on your results.

Additive	Use in food product	E-number

Examples of additives used in food products

Additive	What it does	Number
L ascorbic acid	Anti-oxidant used in fruit drinks to prevent harmful effects of oxidation.	E300
Butylated hydroxytoluene (BHT)	Anti-oxidant used in chewing gum.	E321
Curcumin	Used to colour margarine and flour confectionery.	E100
Beetroot red	Used to colour ice-cream.	E162
Lecithins	Used to emulsify oils and fats with water in foods.	
	Used in low-fat spreads and chocolate.	E322
Sorbic acid	Used as a preservative in soft drinks, fruit yogurt and processed cheese slices.	E200
Calcium sorbate	Used as a preservative in frozen pizza and flour confectionery.	E203
Aspartame	Intense sweetener used in soft drinks, yogurts, dessert and drink mixes.	—

Additives in food

Additives and labels

The ingredients list must show all additives which perform a function in the final product.

The category or function name must show either the serial number identifying the additive or its chemical name, or both. Flavourings do not need this information.

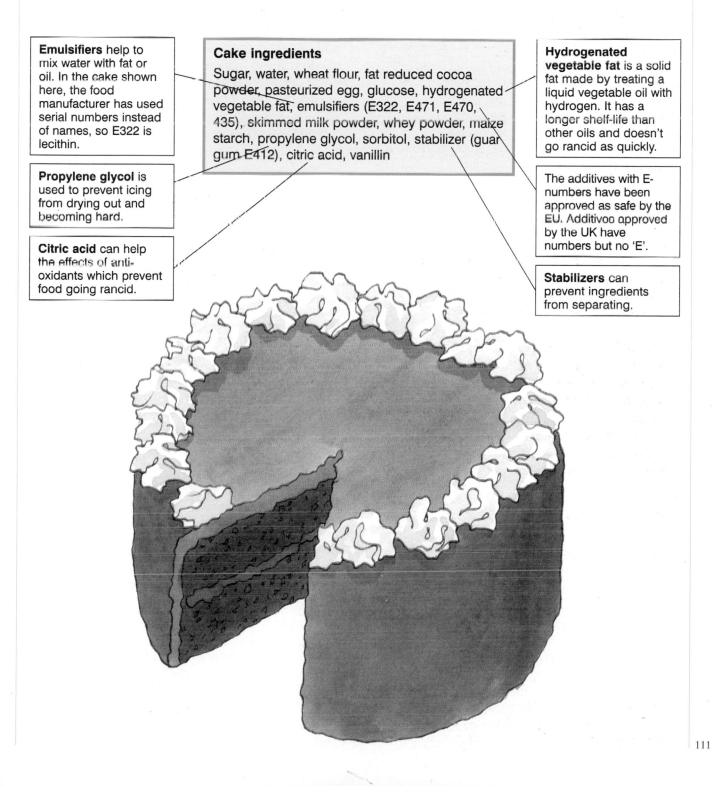

Emulsifiers help to mix water with fat or oil. In the cake shown here, the food manufacturer has used serial numbers instead of names, so E322 is lecithin.

Propylene glycol is used to prevent icing from drying out and becoming hard.

Citric acid can help the effects of anti-oxidants which prevent food going rancid.

Cake ingredients

Sugar, water, wheat flour, fat reduced cocoa powder, pasteurized egg, glucose, hydrogenated vegetable fat, emulsifiers (E322, E471, E470, 435), skimmed milk powder, whey powder, maize starch, propylene glycol, sorbitol, stabilizer (guar gum E412), citric acid, vanillin

Hydrogenated vegetable fat is a solid fat made by treating a liquid vegetable oil with hydrogen. It has a longer shelf-life than other oils and doesn't go rancid as quickly.

The additives with E-numbers have been approved as safe by the EU. Additives approved by the UK have numbers but no 'E'.

Stabilizers can prevent ingredients from separating.

Preservatives

Preservatives help food to keep longer by protecting it against deterioration caused by micro-organisms such as bacteria, fungi and moulds. This means that food can be transported and the storage time is increased. Preservatives are found in meat that has been cured, such as bacon and ham. Preservatives are used in baked goods, soft drinks and fruit juices.

Anti-oxidants

Anti-oxidants prolong shelf-life, stop fatty food from going rancid and protect fat-soluble vitamins from combining with oxygen. Anti-oxidants are used in dried soups, cheese spreads and sausages. Ascorbic acid (vitamin C) is a natural anti-oxidant which is found in fruit and prevents other fruits going brown – this is why lemon juice is added to peeled apples.

Colours

Colours are added to food to make it look more attractive and to replace the colour which might be lost during processing. During canning, peas and strawberries both turn brown so colouring can make them look more attractive. Some people think that we should cut down on the quantity of food colouring added to food products since colour is not necessary for food to be nutritious and tasty. Caramel (E150) is the most popular colouring used for gravy powder, soft drinks and sauces. Many food colours used today come from or are copied from plant sources, such as beetroot red (E162). Baby foods are only allowed to contain the three colours which are also sources of vitamins.

Emulsifiers and stabilizers

Emulsifiers and stabilizers allow fats and oils to mix with water to make low-fat spreads and salad dressings. They give food a smooth and creamy texture, and help to improve the shelf-life of baked goods. Lecithin, found in eggs, is a natural emulsifier used for mayonnaise and for low-fat spreads. Carob gum made from locust beans is used to thicken foods such as salad cream.

Sweeteners

There are two types of sweetener:
- intense sweeteners
- bulk sweeteners.

Intense sweeteners (artificial sweeteners) such as saccharin, aspartame and acesulfame-K are many times sweeter than sugar and only a little is needed. These intense sweeteners are useful to help people eat less sugar since they are very low in calories. They are used for low-calorie drinks and reduced sugar products.

Bulk sweeteners such as hydrogenated glucose syrup are used in the same sort of quantities as sugar.

Flavourings and flavour enhancers

Flavourings are used to restore flavours lost in processing and to add flavours to foods, such as in vanilla ice-cream. Flavourings must meet the requirements of the Food Safety Act 1990 and Regulations on Flavourings. Over the next few years, flavourings will be coded. A flavour may be classified as natural, nature identical or artificial. Monosodium glutamate (MSG) is a flavour enhancer used in many Chinese meals and savoury foods. It has no flavour of its own but intensifies the flavours of other foods. Some people try to avoid foods containing monosodium glutamate as they don't like the increase in flavour and aftertaste. A small number of people may be allergic to monosodium glutamate. Food producers now try to avoid using monosodium glutamate and replace it with herbs, spices and other seasonings.

Other additives

- **Raising agents**, such as sodium bicarbonate, are used to give a lighter texture to baked products.
- **Anti-caking agents**, such as calcium silicate, stop crystals and powders like salt and cocoa from sticking together.
- **Flour improvers**, such as ascorbic acid (E300), help to make bread dough stronger and more elastic.

- **Thickening agents** are used to form a gel to thicken sauces.
- **Nutrients**, such as vitamins and minerals, are used to enrich certain foods such as breakfast cereals, and to replace nutrients lost during processing.

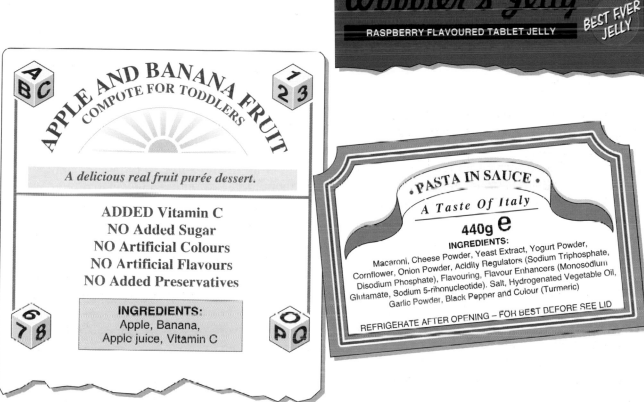

INGREDIENTS: Sugar, Glucose Syrup, Invert Sugar Syrup, Water, Gelatine, Citric Acid, Colours (Carmine, Anthocyanin), Flavouring, Acidity Regulator (Sodium Citrate), Acetic Acid, Raspberry Juice, Lemon Juice.

135g ℮

Wobbler's Jelly ®

RASPBERRY FLAVOURED TABLET JELLY

BEST EVER JELLY

APPLE AND BANANA FRUIT COMPOTE FOR TODDLERS

A delicious real fruit purée dessert.

ADDED Vitamin C
NO Added Sugar
NO Artificial Colours
NO Artificial Flavours
NO Added Preservatives

INGREDIENTS:
Apple, Banana, Apple juice, Vitamin C

• PASTA IN SAUCE •

A Taste Of Italy

440g ℮

INGREDIENTS:
Macaroni, Cheese Powder, Yeast Extract, Yogurt Powder, Cornflower, Onion Powder, Acidity Regulators (Sodium Triphosphate, Disodium Phosphate), Flavouring, Flavour Enhancers (Monosodium Glutamate, Sodium 5-rihonucleotide). Salt, Hydrogenated Vegetable Oil, Garlic Powder, Black Pepper and Colour (Turmeric)

REFRIGERATE AFTER OPENING – FOR BEST BEFORE SEE LID

■ Food labels often show the use of additives

Questions

1 Explain why each of the following types of additive are used in food products.
   a preservatives   b anti-oxidants
   c colours   d emulsifiers
   e sweeteners   f flavour enhancers
   Give an example in each case.

Examine the three food labels (above).

2 In the apple and banana fruit compote for toddlers the label states there are no artificial colours, flavours or added preservatives. What is the advantage of this statement:
   a to the parent of the toddler
   b to the food manufacturer?

3 a What colours are used in the raspberry flavoured jelly?
   b What ingredients are used to give it acidity and flavour?

4 Why do food manufacturers use flavour enhancers in products such as 'Pasta in Sauce'?

52 Raising agents

Raising agents are added to sweet and savoury mixtures to make them rise. There are three types of raising agent:

- **air**
- **steam**
- **carbon dioxide gas.**

How does a raising agent work?

The raising agent produces bubbles of gas. In a hot oven or in a steamer, the gas expands, pushing up the surrounding mixture. Some gas escapes and some is trapped in the mixture as it cooks and sets.

How is air introduced into mixtures as a raising agent?

Air can be introduced into mixtures by:

- **sieving** the flour for cakes and scones
- **beating** mixtures such as batters
- **whisking** egg whites to make meringues
- **creaming** fat and sugar to make cakes
- **rubbing** fat into flour for pastries and scones
- **rolling and folding** pastry such as flaky pastry.

How is steam used as a raising agent?

Water changes to steam when it reaches boiling point, 100°C. If mixtures such as batters contain a lot of water, this evaporates as steam in a hot oven. The steam escapes from the mixture, pushing it up, and the mixture sets on cooking.

Steam is used as a raising agent in Yorkshire pudding, eclairs, some cakes and breads.

How is carbon dioxide used as a raising agent?

Carbon dioxide, for use as a raising agent, is produced in two ways in doughs.

- Chemicals such as baking powder or bicarbonate of soda release carbon dioxide gas.
- Yeast grows and ferments.

The carbon dioxide gas is released into the dough. When heated the gas expands and pushes up the surrounding mixture. The dough cooks and sets.

How do chemical raising agents work?

Baking powder is added to rich fruit cakes and scones. Baking powder is made from acid sodium pyrophosphate, rice flour and sodium bicarbonate which react with the cake mixture to produce carbon dioxide gas.

Bicarbonate of soda (sodium bicarbonate) is used in gingerbread and chocolate cake and reacts with the cake mixture, releasing carbon dioxide gas.

Yeast

Yeast is a single-celled plant fungus which needs food, warmth and liquid to ferment. During fermentation carbon dioxide gas is produced.

How does yeast work in bread-making?

Most types of bread are made with yeast. The yeast uses the flour for food, and ferments with the liquid to produce carbon dioxide and alcohol. The dough increases in size during a process called **proving**, when the dough is left in a warm place which encourages the yeast to grow. During the baking of the bread, the carbon dioxide gas expands, pushing up the dough. The yeast is killed by the heat, the alcohol evaporates and the bread dough cooks and sets.

Questions

1. Why are raising agents needed to make some food products?
2. Explain how the different types of raising agent work. Give examples to show how each raising agent is used in a food product.
3. Find recipes which use raising agents. Give an example of recipes which use the different types of raising agent – air, steam and carbon dioxide.

— Investigation —

Find out how raising agents work.

You will need four test tubes, four balloons, a test tube rack, baking powder, bicarbonate of soda, teaspoons and a timer.

1 Label the test tubes A, B, C and D.
2 Put a level teaspoonful of baking powder into test tubes A and B.
3 Put a level teaspoonful of bicarbonate of soda into test tubes C and D.
4 Pour 3 cm of cold water into test tubes A and C and cover each with a balloon, shake and store in the test tube rack.
5 Pour 3 cm of hot water into test tubes B and D and cover each with a balloon, shake and store in the test tube rack.
6 Watch carefully what happens to each of the test tubes over a period of 10 minutes and record your results on a chart like the one below.

Test tubes	What happened
A – baking powder and cold water	
B – baking powder and hot water	
C – bicarbonate of soda and cold water	
D – bicarbonate of soda and hot water	

Write a report on your findings from this experiment. Taste each of the mixtures and comment on the result of adding cold and hot water.

What happens?

As each mixture bubbles, carbon dioxide gas is given off. Bicarbonate of soda changes during this effervescence to washing soda, so the mixture should taste soapy. This is one reason why bicarbonate of soda should only be added to strong-tasting mixtures that will disguise the soapy taste.

— Investigation —

Find out what conditions yeast needs for fermentation.

You will need six test tubes, six balloons, a test tube rack, fresh or dried yeast, sugar, teaspoons and a timer.

1 Label the test tubes A, B, C, D, E and F.
2 Put a small piece of fresh or dried yeast into each test tube.
3 Fill each test tube as follows:
   Test tube A – the control which just contains the yeast
   Test tube B – yeast + a pinch of sugar
   Test tube C – yeast + a pinch of sugar + 3 cm cold water
   Test tube D – yeast + a pinch of sugar + 3 cm warm water
   Test tube E – yeast + a pinch of sugar + 3 cm boiling water
   Test tube F – yeast + 3 cm warm water.
4 Shake each test tube, place a balloon over the top and put it in the test tube rack. Stand the rack in a bowl of warm water.
5 Watch carefully what happens to each of the test tubes for a period of 10 minutes and record your results on a chart like the one below.

Test tubes	What happened
A – yeast	
B – yeast + sugar	
C – yeast + sugar + cold water	
D – yeast + sugar + warm water	
E – yeast + sugar + boiling water	
F – yeast + warm water	

Write a report on your findings from this experiment.

What happens?

Yeast needs sugar, liquid and warmth to grow. The boiling water should kill the yeast cells and stop growth. The balloon which blows up the most should be the one over the tube containing the yeast, sugar and warm water since these are the ideal conditions for yeast to grow.

53 Convenience foods

Trends in eating convenience food

We are eating more and more ready-prepared, convenience foods at all times of the day. In 1993, convenience foods accounted for 35 per cent of the average food bill.

The graph below shows the trend in convenience foods since 1971.

'Single adult' households – adult people living alone – spend the most money on convenience foods. In 1993 single people spent, on average, £5.32 per person per week on all types of convenience food. Convenience foods are also very popular with families with children.

What is convenience food?

In 1959, the Ministry of Agriculture, Fisheries and Foof (MAFF) defined convenience foods as:

Products of the food industries in which the degree of culinary preparation has been carried out to an advanced stage and which are purchased as labour-saving versions of less highly processed products.

For research purposes, this definition was still used in 1993 for products such as cake mixes, but:
- 'convenience foods' do not include products such as yogurt
- 'frozen convenience food' does not include ice-cream or frozen meat.

What are convenience foods?

Convenience foods are ready prepared foods, including cans of food, bottles, cartons, frozen food, dried food, chilled food.

─Questions─

1 Why do you think there has been such an increase in the amount of convenience foods eaten? Give three reasons and explain your answer.
2 List six examples of convenience foods.
3 Explain the trends in the graph below.

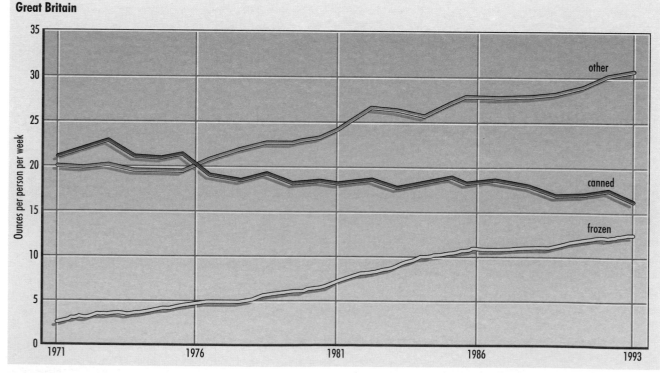

■ Trends in eating convenience foods, 1971–1993

Source – 'Social Trends', CSO

Process	Types of convenience food
Canned food	Soup, baked beans, dhal, curry, sweet and sour
Cartons of food	Soup, sauces, drinks
Dried food	Dried soup, mixed vegetables, ready meals, rice dishes
Dried food mixes	Cake mix, pancake mix, custard, biscuit mix
Frozen food	Battered fish, beefburgers, cheesecake
Chilled food	Ready meals, garlic bread, desserts

— Investigation —

1 The table below lists some examples of convenience foods.
   For each one, explain what ingredients you would need to buy to make the food product
   and roughly how long it would take to make. Add some more examples of your own. Carry
   out some research to compare the cost of convenience food with the freshly prepared
   version. Is convenience food good value for money? Write a report on your findings.

Convenience food	Ingredients to make the fresh version	Time to make from fresh ingredients	Cooking time of convenience food	Cost of convenience food	Cost of fresh version
Canned tomato soup Chilled lasagne Squeezed orange juice Canned treacle sponge Frozen cod in cheese sauce Chilled pizza Frozen beefburgers					

2 Carry out some research to find examples of different types of convenience food using the
   headings on the chart below. Fill in as many examples as possible.

Process	Types of convenience food
Canned food Cartons of food Dried food Dried food mixes Frozen food Chilled food	

*B*iotechnology is using biological processes to make useful products such as foods. Bread, beer and wine are made by using yeast which ferments and helps to produce foods and drinks by a biological process. Food products that are made using traditional biotechnology include beer, cheese, bread, vinegar, wine, cider, soy sauce, yogurt, pickles, salami and the mould in blue cheese.

Biotechnology and the future

Genetic modification is sometimes described as modern biotechnology. Scientists can identify the gene that makes up certain characteristics of food and modify it. This process has been used to slow down the softening of fruits. Flavr Savr R tomatoes are the first genetically modified whole food on sale in the USA. The tomatoes are picked when they are red and their full flavour has developed. They stay firm for some time without going soft and this makes transport and handling easier.

How is genetic modification carried out?

A copy is made of the gene responsible for the softening enzyme and this gene is 'switched off'. This results in tomatoes that soften more slowly, and therefore there is less waste.

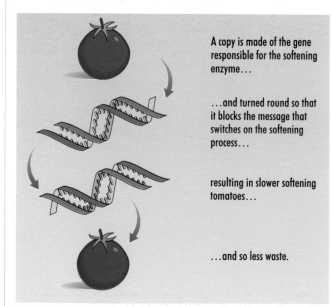

A copy is made of the gene responsible for the softening enzyme…

…and turned round so that it blocks the message that switches on the softening process…

resulting in slower softening tomatoes…

…and so less waste.

■ A vegetarian cheese produced using gene technology

Vegetarian cheese

This cheese can be made without using animal rennet, which comes from calves' stomachs. The genetic information for the chymosin enzyme in calf rennet has been identified and copied into yeast cells. These yeast cells produce pure chymosin, which is the same as the animal enzyme but is made by a yeast cell which is not of animal origin. Co-op vegetarian cheese is made using this product and the label shows that it is 'produced using gene technology and so free from animal rennet'.

What are the benefits of biotechnology and genetic modification for the future?

Biotechnology could be used for:
- reducing losses in food supplies – for example, crop diseases could be controlled
- improving the nutritional value of food products – for example, increasing the protein in rice or altering the saturated fat content of crops used for oil, such as corn, soya beans and oil seed rape

■ How Flavr Savr R tomatoes were developed

- making longer lasting fruit and vegetables – for example, the Flavr Savr R tomato described opposite
- modifying micro-organisms and adapting their use – for example, as in vegetarian cheese.

Genetic modification and the law

In the UK all food must be fit for human consumption as required by the Food Safety Act. The safeguard controls for genetic modification of foods are assessed by several committees including the Advisory Committee on Novel Foods and Processes (ACNFP).

Food labelling and genetic modification

The European Commission has set up a group of advisers on the **Ethical Implications of Biotechnology** which stated that consumers should be provided with 'appropriate and understandable information' on genetic modification of ingredients used in food products. The food industry is trying to find ways to meet these needs.

A recent Government committee sought the views of religious groups on genetic modification.

- Most Christian and Jewish groups find genetic modification acceptable.
- Muslims, Sikhs and Hindus have ethical objections to consuming organisms which contain copy genes from animals which are included in dietary restrictions for their religions.

- Strict vegetarians would object to using copy genes of animal origin in a plant.

Clear labelling would be needed to help these groups make an informed choice.

There is concern among many people about the use of genetically modified foods. Some people feel that we should not tamper with nature. Others think that the science can be used greatly to improve the world sources of food.

— Investigation

What are your views on the used of genetically modified foods? Carry out some up-to-date research on the issues and present the cases for and against this process. Support your work with newspaper or magazine articles on this issue. You can use the library and CD Roms for this research.

— Questions

1 What foods and drinks are made by traditional biotechnology? Explain how one of these same foods can be made using biotechnology.
2 What is meant by 'genetic modification'? Give an example of its use in a food product.

The information in this unit is sourced from *Food for our Future – Food and Biotechnology*, published by the Food and Drink Federation.

55 *Novel and functional foods*

Novel foods

The Government's Advisory Committee on Novel Foods and Processes (ACNFP) defined novel foods as:

Foods or food ingredients which have not hitherto been used for human consumption to a significant extent in the UK and/or which have been produced by extensively modified or entirely new food production.

Margarine, invented in the 19th century, might have been called a novel food, as it was intended as a substitute for butter. *Quorn*, a low-fat protein food made from mycoprotein (a type of fungus), was the first novel food to be accepted by ACNFP.

Artificial sweeteners such as aspartame and saccharin are also novel foods in everyday use. Novel foods developed in recent years include genetically modified enzymes used in cheese-making and fat replacers which imitate fat but have fewer calories.

▬ *Questions* ▬

1 What is meant by the following terms?
 a novel foods **b** functional foods
2 Do you think novel and functional foods have a role to play in our diets now or in the future? Explain your answer.

Functional foods

One definition for functional foods is:

Functional foods are food and drink products derived from naturally occurring substances, which are consumed as part of the daily diet and have a particular physiological benefit when eaten.

This food trend started in Japan where the Ministry of Health and Welfare supported the development of functional foods to help increase the health of the population. Functional foods have alleged benefits to health and extra vitamins, minerals or dietary fibre are added to increase their healthy image.

The range of functional foods includes soft drinks, breakfast cereals, ready meals and baby foods. Bio-yogurts are one type of functional food. Active bacillus cultures are added to the yogurt and these are thought to promote the growth of beneficial bacteria in the gut and act as an aid to digestion.

For some Japanese, the consumption of a range of functional foods with different health properties is a daily routine. Dietary habits play an important part in keeping healthy. In Europe attitudes to healthy eating are different. People tend to take cures and medicine only when ill. So Europeans may not be so attracted to regular use of functional foods in their daily diets.

■ Which of these products are novel foods and which are functional foods?

There are several reasons for cooking food, including:

- to **make it tastier**, **more attractive** and **easier to eat** – for example, potatoes cannot be eaten raw so they are boiled, roasted, fried or cooked in other ways
- to **make it safer to eat**, as harmful bacteria are killed if heated to a high enough temperature for a long enough time – for example, raw meat needs cooking to make it safer to eat
- cooked food **keeps longer** because any yeasts, moulds or bacteria present are destroyed by heating over a sufficient time – for example, stewed soft fruit such as raspberries will keep longer than fresh
- cooking can **change and improve the flavour** of foods by combining them – for example, lentils, spices and garlic are cooked together to make dhal (lentil curry).

How is food cooked?

The three ways that heat energy can be passed to food are by conduction, convection and radiation.

Conduction

Heat is conducted from molecule to molecule in solids or liquids. Heat is conducted round a metal pan and through a joint of meat as it roasts. Metals conduct heat easily; wood and plastic are poor conductors of heat which is why they are used for stirring spoons and saucepan handles. Copper is a good conductor of heat and is sometimes used on the base of pans to speed up heat transfer. Water is a good conductor of heat, so boiling food such as potatoes is quicker than baking

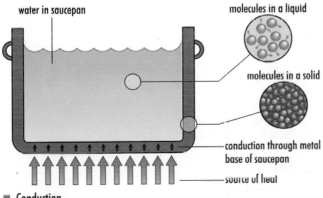

■ Conduction

Convection

Heat travels round liquids and air by convection currents. Ovens are heated by convection currents. The hot air rises and cool air falls which is why a conventional oven is hotter at the top. Cooking methods which use convection currents include boiling food in a saucepan and baking in the oven.

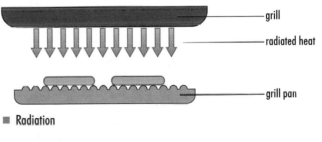

■ Convection currents in a saucepan

Radiation

Heat travels in waves or rays that heat up objects such as food. Food that is grilled or toasted is cooked by radiation – the direct rays heat the food.

Most food is cooked by a combination of methods of heat transfer. For example, a baked potato is cooked in the oven by convection currents carrying the heat around the oven to the potato, and the heat is conducted through the potato to cook it.

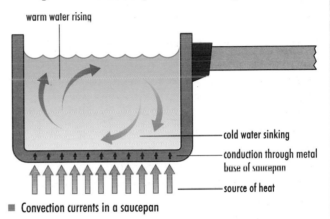

■ Radiation

Questions

1 Give examples of how food can be cooked by conduction, convection and radiation of heat.
2 Explain the following.
   a Why should you stir hot foods with a wooden or plastic spoon?
   b Why are solid metal handles unsuitable for cooking pans?

57 Cookers

Types of cookers

A cooker usually has a grill, hob and oven. It may be powered by gas, electricity, solid fuel or calor gas.

What do people want from a cooker?

The most popular features include:
- good, reliable performance
- split-level cookers with separate oven, hob and grill
- choice of using both electricity and gas
- hotplates which give a range of cooking speeds – normal, rapid and simmer
- automatic hobs that can bring food to the boil and reduce the temperature to pre-set simmer
- halogen hobs which have very quick-to-use halogen cooking areas that also cool down quickly
- a grill which cooks evenly and quickly
- a grill at eye level or in the oven

- choice of colours
- the controls being easy to operate
- glass doors to the oven so you can see inside
- catalytic oven coating so the oven cleans itself
- storage for pans and trays
- oven and hob lights so you can see what is cooking
- drop-down door or hinged door
- fan-assisted cooking so hot air circulates throughout the oven for even cooking on every level
- child safety switches that protect against the hob being switched on in error.

Fan-assisted ovens

In fan-assisted ovens the convection currents are disturbed as the fan moves the hot air around. The temperature should therefore be the same in all parts of the oven so the cooking temperature will be the same for food cooked on all of the shelves.

In the gas oven, the air closest to the burner is heated first. It rises and is replaced by cold air which in turn is heated and rises creating convection currents. Because of the convection currents, the hottest air moves towards the top and the coldest towards the bottom. This creates zones of heat.

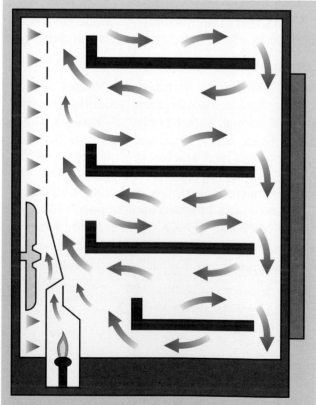

Air is heated by the gas burner and then drawn up into the fan and distributed evenly throughout the oven.

■ Convection currents in a gas oven

■ A fan-assisted oven distributes heat evenly

■ Popular features for cookers include easy-to-use controls, a choice of colours and drop-down glass doors

Cooking methods on the pasta packet

Below are the instructions for cooking pasta in boiling water on the hob or in the microwave oven.

COOKING INSTRUCTIONS

1 Empty contents into a large saucepan of boiling water, adding salt if required.

2 Bring back to the boil and simmer for 3–4 minutes until tender.

3 Drain and serve immediately.

MICROWAVE INSTRUCTIONS

1 Place 250 g pasta into a large non-metallic bowl and pour over enough boiling water to cover.

2 Cover and microwave on full power for:

Heating category		Wattage (IEC 705)	
B	D	650	750
5	4	5	4
minutes		minutes	

Select appropriate time for your oven.

3 Stir halfway through cooking. Drain and serve.

Questions

1 Use the list of features, at the top of page 122, to help you describe the sort of cooker you would choose for the following people.
   a a person living on their own
   b a family with two or more children
   c an elderly couple
   d a house rented out to students.

Refer to the cooking methods on the pasta packet to answer these questions.

2 Which method of cooking do you think is:
   a the quicker
   b the one which uses less fuel?

3 When might you choose to cook pasta:
   a on top of the stove
   b in the microwave cooker?

What are the advantages and disadvantages of each method of cooking?

Investigation

Carry out a survey to find out what sort of cooker people want to use. Ask them why they chose the cooker they use and what sort of cooking facilities they would like if they had the choice. Find out what foods they cook, and how they cook them. Explain how they could use other methods for cooking these foods, which may be more economical in the use of fuel.

58 Cooking methods

*F*ood is cooked in many ways to make it tasty and also safer and easier to eat.

Cooking with water

There are several cooking methods which need water or other liquids.

- **Boiling** – foods such as vegetables are boiled in water in a saucepan.
- **Simmering** – foods which need more gentle cooking, including eggs, are cooked in liquids.
- **Stewing** – this method is used to cook meats, vegetables or fruit in a liquid.
- **Poaching** – eggs and fish are cooked very gently in a liquid.
- **Steaming** – food is cooked in steamers over boiling water. This is a popular method for Chinese cooking.
- **Pressure cooking** – food is cooked in liquid at a temperature above the boiling point of water, and this reduces the cooking time.

Cooking with fat

Fats such as vegetable oils and butter are used to fry food and add flavour during the cooking process.

- **Frying** – fat cooks the food at a higher temperature than water. Food cooks more quickly, and often becomes crisp. Frying increases the energy value of the food.
- **Dry frying** – this method uses no fat at all. The food itself contains a little fat. It is best to use a non-stick pan. Foods which can be dry-fried include bacon and sausages.
- **Shallow frying** – food is cooked in a very little fat. This method is used for fried eggs and sausages.
- **Deep fat frying** – foods are cooked in plenty of very hot fat. This method is used in fish and chip shops. Delicate foods such as fish need to be protected with batter.

■ A barbecue in Hong Kong. Barbecuing gives food a special flavour

Cooking in the oven

- **Roasting** – this method involves basting the food with fat during cooking to improve the flavour. Meat, chicken and potatoes are traditionally roasted in the oven.
- **Baking** – foods are cooked on their own in an oven. Baked foods include baked potatoes, cakes, breads and fish.

Other methods of cooking

- **Grilling** – food is cooked under the grill of an oven. This is a quick method of cooking by radiant heat. The heat is then conducted through the food. Food which can be grilled includes burgers, fish and toast.
- **Barbecuing** – food is cooked in the open air over wood or charcoal. This gives a special flavour to the food. Foods which can be barbecued include sweetcorn, chicken and many kinds of meat.

How is heat energy transferred into the food?

Method of cooking	How the heat energy transfers to the food
Boiling	Heat is conducted through the pan to the liquid and convection currents pass the heat around to the food.
Steaming	Steam rises around the food by convection currents and then is conducted through the food.
Frying	Heat is conducted through the pan to the fat and convection currents pass the heat around to the food.
Roasting and baking Grilling	Heat passes around the oven by convection currents and is conducted into the food. The grill radiates heat to the food.

Questions

1 Give examples of three foods which are cooked by each of the methods.

Method of cooking	Examples of food cooked by this method
Boiling	
Stewing	
Poaching	
Steaming	
Shallow frying	
Deep frying	
Roasting	
Baking	
Grilling or barbecuing	

2 Explain what methods of cooking you could use for the following foods. In each case there may be several choices of methods of cooking.
  a a cake   b a pizza
  c vegetable burgers   d noodles
  e chapatis   f spring rolls
  g chicken drumsticks

3 Which alternative method would you choose to cook the following foods if you wanted to reduce the fat content?
  a roast potatoes   b fried noodles
  c fried rice   d deep fried fish or falafel
  e chips   f pineapple fritters

59 *Microwave cooking*

*O*ver 70 per cent of households in the UK have a microwave oven. Most people use the microwave oven for reheating, defrosting food and cooking vegetables, fish and hot puddings quickly.

What are microwaves?

Microwaves are electronic waves, similar to radio and television waves. A microwave oven is basically a metal box with a door; inside, the microwaves are produced by a magnetron which converts electrical energy into microwave energy. A stirrer or paddle helps to distribute the microwaves evenly into the microwave cabinet.

When the microwaves pass into the cooker they:
● reflect off metal walls and bounce around inside the cavity
● are transmitted by the cooking container
● are absorbed by food.

How do microwaves heat food?

Microwaves penetrate food to a depth of 3–5 cm. The microwave energy is absorbed by the food molecules, especially the water and fat molecules. The molecules become agitated and start to vibrate. This creates heat which cooks food.

Safety and microwave ovens

Microwave ovens provide a safe and effective method of heating food if the instructions are followed properly. Doors and hinges of microwave ovens are fitted with several locks and automatic cut-outs to prevent microwaves escaping. The holes in the metal mesh in the door are not large enough to allow microwaves through.

Food safety

When food is cooked or reheated, the destruction of food-poisoning bacteria depends on a high temperature being maintained for sufficient time. Microwaves will not themselves kill bacteria. The heat produced by the vibration of the food molecules will kill bacteria if food is heated to 72°C and this temperature is maintained for two minutes.

■ A typical microwave oven

You can check the temperature by using a food probe. Insert the probe into the centre and outside edge of the food. Keep the probe clean by wiping it with antibacterial wipes to avoid cross-contamination by bacteria. Make sure that the temperature is 72°C or above in several places.

What are 'cold spots'?

Microwaves do not cook food evenly. The food can have areas which are cold – areas where the food does not reach 72°C for two minutes. These areas are called 'cold spots' and the food may not reach a temperature that is high enough to destroy food–poisoning bacteria such as salmonella and listeria.

To solve this problem, food is usually cooked in the microwave oven on a rotating turntable and there may be a stirrer fan inside which distributes the microwaves evenly. Food should be stirred or turned during cooking to help even out the temperature. Observe the 'standing time' which is shown in recipes or on packets. This allows the food to reach an even temperature by allowing heat to be conducted to cold spots from hot spots.

Basic principles for cooking food in a microwave oven

● Always reheat until 'piping hot', that is 72°C for two minutes.
● The more food there is in the oven, the longer it will take to cook.
● It is better to overheat than underheat, as bacteria will be killed by overheating.
● Dense foods such as meat take longer to cook than less dense foods such as cake mixture.

What containers can and cannot be used in the microwave oven?

- Solid materials such as glass, plastic and china absorb only a few microwaves and so don't get hot. These materials can be used in the microwave oven. However, as the microwaves do not pass through the dishes, this can add up to 25 per cent to the cooking time.
- Some plastic materials, such as roasting bags and boil-in-the-bags, are designed for use in microwave ovens.
- Metal containers such as foil cannot be used in a microwave oven as they reflect the microwaves and cause sparking and, over time, the metal on the oven walls becomes damaged and pitted.
- If ovenware decorated with metal rims is used in the microwave oven, the rims may turn black. Very small pieces of foil can be used to protect food such as fish tails and these will not cause damage.
- Some clingfilms are not suitable for use in microwave ovens so check the label. Clingfilm is used to cover bowls of food but should not come into direct contact with the food itself.

Microwave cookware

Special cookware has been developed for use in microwave ovens. This is made from a type of plastic which resists microwaves and does not distort or melt during cooking. Examples of such cookware include a roasting dish for cooking bacon, meats and chicken, a jug for heating milk and coffee, and small dishes for reheating food.

■ These containers have been designed for use in a microwave oven

Advantages of microwave ovens

- They are versatile and can be used for thawing, cooking and reheating.
- Cooking is fast, cooking times can be cut by as much as 60–75 per cent.
- They are economical and can use as little as 25 per cent of the power used by a conventional cooker. Cooking times are shorter and the lower the power level used the less electricity is used.
- They are convenient; you can prepare snacks and meals quickly when needed.
- They are easy to use, can be plugged in anywhere with a 13 amp socket and the controls are simple to use.
- They save washing up as food can be served in the cooking dish.
- It is a safe and cool way of cooking, suitable for the elderly, disabled and children.
- Food usually keeps its quality and taste when reheated.
- There is less waste since you can cook what you need when you want it.
- Foods can be cooked from frozen without defrosting first.
- Vitamin C content of vegetables cooked in a microwave oven is higher than in boiled vegetables, due to shorter cooking time and less water added.

The chart below compares the time taken to cook a potato and a fish fillet in a microwave oven and in a conventional oven.

Comparison of microwave and conventional cooking		
Food	Cooking time in a microwave oven	Cooking time in a conventional oven
Baked potato	4 minutes	60 minutes
Small fillet of fish	1 minute	15 minutes

▬ Questions ▬

1. Explain how microwaves are used to cook food.
2. How would you make sure that food is cooked safely in a microwave oven?
3. What are the advantages and disadvantages of cooking food in a microwave oven?

Limitations of microwave ovens

- Browning and crisping are not possible except in ovens with grills or in a combination cooker.
- Frying (deep or shallow) is not possible.
- Microwave ovens cannot be used for toast or pancakes and they don't cook pastry well.
- Eggs cannot be cooked in their shells as they explode.
- Heating more than 300 ml of water is more economical in an electric kettle.
- Foods which develop flavour by long, slow cooking, such as stews or baked potatoes, do not have the same taste when cooked in the microwave oven.
- Microwaves do not cook food evenly so care must be taken to avoid 'cold spots'.

Types of microwave ovens available

- **Microwave** – cooks with microwaves only.
- **Microwave with grill** – cooks with microwaves and browns the top of foods. Not all ovens allow microwaves and grill to be used at the same time.
- **Combination** – can be used in several ways: microwave only, grill only, convection only (like a conventional oven), microwave and grill, microwave and convection, grill and convection. You can cook fish in tomato sauce using microwaves and then grill the cheese on top.

Some microwave ovens provide extra features. At least one has **sensors** which recognize the temperature and quantity of food in the cooker by sensing the level of humidity given off as the food heats. The cooker can then calculate the time and power level needed to cook the food.

Microwave oven labels

Since 1992 most new microwave ovens have displayed special labels. This voluntary labelling scheme for microwave ovens and food packs has been developed by MAFF, food manufacturers and shops. Microwave ovens vary in their ability to reheat food. A system was needed to make sure that people using different ovens could get the same result when they cooked food.

The labels on ovens and food packs include the following details.

- **Heating category** – how quickly the oven can heat small quantities of food. Ovens are given categories A to E. The category helps you to calculate the time it takes to cook small portions of food or microwave meals. If you had two ovens with a power output 650 watts and one was heating category B and the other D, they would both cook a large casserole in the same time, but the category B oven would take longer to heat small portions of food.

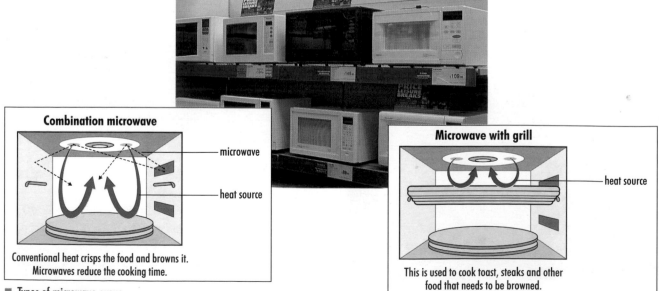

Combination microwave

microwave

heat source

Conventional heat crisps the food and browns it.
Microwaves reduce the cooking time.

Microwave with grill

heat source

This is used to cook toast, steaks and other food that needs to be browned.

- **Power output** – the wattage which gives a guide to how quickly an oven can heat large quantities of food. The oven wattage affects the amount of time the food takes to cook. The higher the wattage the faster the food cooks. If you were cooking the same food these would be the times.

To find out about your microwave oven:
- check the model against the list of power outputs in the booklet 'The new microwave labels'
- contact the manufacturers.

Wattage (W)	550	600	650	700	750
Cooking time (minutes)	9	8	7	6	5

the microwave symbol — 800W — the power output (watts)

D — the heating category for small packs

■ Microwave labels can be found on ovens and food packs

— To do

1 Choose a main course dish or a dessert which can be reheated in a microwave oven. Test the reheating time to make sure the food is piping hot (72°C) for two minutes. Write out detailed instructions for reheating for category B or D ovens.

2 Use a food probe to measure the changes in temperature when heating food in the microwave oven. Demonstrate in this experiment the importance of standing time (the time the food should be left to rest after cooking).

— Questions

1 Why has the labelling scheme for microwave ovens been introduced? Where will you find these labels? Why are they useful for the consumer?

2 Give two examples of suitable containers which can be used in a microwave oven. Give reasons for your answers.

   Give one example of a container which could not be used in a microwave oven. Give one reason for your answer.

3 A young person who lives alone wants to buy a cooker. Write down the advantages and disadvantages to them of a conventional electric cooker or a microwave oven. What sort do you think they should buy? Give your reasons.

4 Use the chart below to work out cooking times for a roast meal and explain which method of cooking you would use to cook this meal. You can use all three types of cooker but remember that the combination microwave and microwave usually cook one dish at a time.

Cooking times for a roast meal

	Conventional method	Combination microwave and convection oven	Microwave only
Chicken 1.5 kg (3 lb)	oven 190°C 1 hour 20 mins	190°C + simmer power 12 mins for every 450 g = 36 mins	medium power 10 mins for every 450 g = 30 mins
Carrots fresh	hob and pre-boil water 6 mins		no boiled water required 7 mins
Peas frozen	hob and pre-boil water 8 mins		no boiled water required 7 mins
Roast potatoes	oven 190°C 50 mins	230°C + warm power 25 mins	
Apple pie	oven 200°C 40 mins	210°C + simmer power 20 mins	
Custard	hob 11 mins		4–6 mins

Source – Panasonic UK Ltd

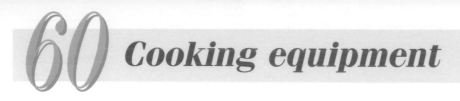

There are many types of cooking equipment which can help speed up the cooking process, or save time and money.

Pressure cooker

What does it do?

A pressure cooker is a heavy saucepan with a tight-fitting lid. A pressure regulator is fitted to the top of the lid to increase the pressure inside the saucepan. The trapped steam increases the pressure inside the cooker so the water boils at 110–120°C instead of 100°C.

Why is it useful?

The increase in temperature inside the cooker allows food to cook much faster than normal. A pressure cooker is very useful for cooking meat stews, curries and dishes using dried beans.

Food processors, food mixers and liquidizers

What do they do?

Food processors usually have a range of blades which fit into a large bowl or jug. A variety of foods can be processed, including bread doughs, pastry, soups and cakes.

Food mixers are bowls with electric beaters used for whisking food such as cake mixes and making bread.

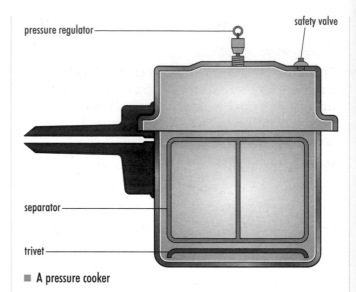

A pressure cooker

(labels: pressure regulator, safety valve, separator, trivet)

A **liquidizer** can churn chunky food such as fruit and vegetables into liquid, and can also make breadcrumbs.

Why are they useful?

Food processors, food mixers and liquidizers all speed up food preparation tasks which are time-consuming and difficult if they are done by hand.

Examples of food preparation tasks that can be speeded up by a food processor are shown in the following chart.

■ Food processors have a variety of attachments for different functions

Tasks that can be speeded up by a food processor	
Task	*Attachments needed*
Bread-making	dough hook
Mincing raw and cooked meats	special mincing attachment
Making pastry	blending blade to rub in the fat
Making meringues	beater to beat air into egg whites
Chopping vegetables such as chips and sliced cucumber	chopping blade
Grating and shredding vegetables such as carrots and cabbage	shredding and grating blade
Making breadcrumbs	blade to break up sliced bread
Puréeing food such as baby food	blending blade
Making soup	blending blade to chop up vegetables
Making burgers	blending blade to mix meat and onions

Electric frying pan

What does it do?

This is a large frying pan that can be plugged into the electricity, so that the base of the pan heats up. The pan can be used for frying foods such as eggs, bacon and sausages, as well as making meat stews and curries, and steaming vegetables.

Why is it useful?

The electric frying pan is useful for people who live on their own who do not wish to buy a cooker. It can cook a wide variety of foods and is safe to use.

▬ Investigation ▬

What labour-saving equipment can be used in the kitchen? Visit a kitchen shop or department store, or refer to a catalogue or magazine. Collect pictures and make lists of the labour-saving equipment which can be used to speed up food preparation tasks or save fuel. Draw up a chart like the one shown below and fill in your own comments.

Cooking equipment	Why it is useful

▬ *Questions* ▬

1 Make a list of different types of cooking and kitchen equipment that could be used in food preparation. For each example, give the main advantages and disadvantages.

2 Choose four types of cooking equipment. Explain how food would be prepared if you could not use each of these pieces of equipment.

The range of cooking equipment and its uses

Cooking equipment using electricity	Use in the kitchen
Toaster	Toasts bread quickly and evenly.
Food processor	Speedy preparation of soups, breadcrumbs and pastry mix.
Coffee maker	Makes filter coffee without attention.
Slow cooker	Cooks food slowly with low fuel costs.
Juice extractor	Efficient at getting juice out of fruits and vegetables.
Electric kettle	Boils water and switches off when ready.
Microwave oven	Cooks food quickly using little fuel.
Food mixer	Useful for making cakes and whisking egg whites.
Deep frier	Fries food safely at an even temperature.
Pressure cooker	Cooks food in less time than normal cooking.
Electric sandwich maker	Toasts filled sandwiches.
Electric frying pan	Cooks food without using the hob and can be used for frying, stewing, and steaming.

Equipment for food preparation

There is a huge variety of equipment which could be used for food preparation.

The following chart lists some basic items which can be used for a variety of tasks.

Basic equipment for preparing food

Equipment	What it looks like	What it is used for
Kitchen knives:		
1 cook's knife		1 a large sharp knife, used for chopping and cutting food
2 paring knife		2 small knife used for preparing fruit and vegetables
3 palette knife		3 used to lift and mix food
4 serrated knife		4 used for cutting fruit and vegetables
Spoons:		
1 tablespoon		1 measuring, stirring and serving food
2 dessertspoon		2 measuring and eating
3 teaspoon		3 small measurements and stirring tea
4 plastic stirring spoon		4 stirring and mixing food such as sauces
Whisks:		
1 balloon whisk		1 beating and whisking, especially sauces
2 rotary whisk		2 beating and whisking batters and meringues
Mixing bowls		mixing food
Wok		used for Chinese cooking such as stir-frying
Bamboo steamer		used to steam food above boiling water as in Chinese cooking.
Sieve		sieving flour
Colander		draining vegetables
Graters		useful for grating cheese and vegetables such as carrots
Autochop		easily chops parsley and onions
Chopping board		best made of polypropylene for food hygiene, used for chopping food
Measuring jug		measuring liquids and dry ingredients

— Investigation

Compare kitchen equipment to find out which is best for the task.

1 Peeling and chopping vegetables

You will need carrots.

Compare the tools you could use to peel and chop some carrots. You could use a food processor in your comparative testing. Write a report on your findings.

2 Whisking egg whites

You will need several egg whites and a selection of whisks and electric mixers.

Whisk the egg white until it is stiff, using a different piece of equipment for each egg white. Time how long it took for the egg white to become stiff.

Rate the effort involved: 1 = easy, 2 = OK, 3 = difficult. Write a report on your findings.

Non-stick cookware

Non-stick cookware can be made from different materials such as aluminium, stainless steel, enamelled steel and cast iron. Even glass and ceramic ware can be made non-stick. The non-stick coating is made from PTFE (polytetrafluoroethylene) which can resist almost any substance sticking to it at high temperatures. After use, it just needs rinsing in hot, soapy water.

There is a wide range of non-stick cookware including saucepans, milk pans, frying pans, baking trays, cake tins, and jam tart tins.

The advantages of using non-stick cookware

- Food does not stick so this saves cleaning time.
- Less food is wasted as it does not stick to the pan.
- Food can be cooked more healthily since the amount of fat used for frying can be reduced.

Equipment from around the world

Chinese wok

A traditional Chinese wok is a large iron pan used for stir-frying Chinese food. Modern, non-stick woks are available with non-stick linings. The wok is best used over sources of high heat such as gas burners, and food is cooked quickly by tossing and stirring the ingredients with oil – hence the term 'stir-frying'.

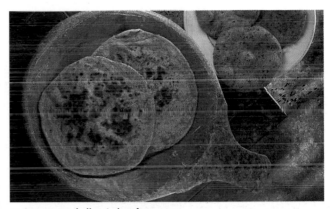

■ A tawa is a shallow Indian frying pan

Tawa

A tawa is a shallow Indian frying pan, made from cast iron and used for cooking chapatis.

Tajine

A tajine is a Moroccan stewing pot used for stews of meat or vegetables. It is often used over a charcoal burner and has a decorated lid which keeps the food warm.

— Investigation

Compare a non-stick frying pan with an ordinary frying pan.

You will need some eggs.

Fry an egg in a tablespoonful of oil for the same amount of time in each pan. Wipe out the non-stick frying pan and fry the egg without any oil.

Compare your results. How do the texture and colour of the cooked eggs compare? Taste them and make comments on the flavour. How much oil is left in the pan after the egg is cooked? Estimate the amount, since it is difficult to measure. Look up nutritional information on fried and boiled eggs (the equivalent data for an egg cooked without fat). Compare and comment on this information. What are the advantages of using a non-stick pan?

— Investigation

Research and describe ten different types of cooking equipment and tools which are used in food preparation and cooking around the world. What materials are used to make the different types of equipment? In each case, explain why these materials have been chosen and how this affects the cost of the product. Show how they are used for a variety of cooking purposes. Find out the cost of the equipment by visiting shops, using magazines or catalogues. Write a report on your research.

— Question

What basic cookware would you choose for someone to carry out simple cooking?

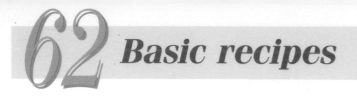

*T*here are several basic recipes which can be adapted and made into many other food products. There are many ways these recipes can be cooked, such as baking, steaming or cooking in the microwave oven or on the hob.

Adapting basic recipes to make different food products

The chart below shows how each of the basic recipes can be made into many other dishes. Different flavours can be added and the shape and size of the recipe can be changed.

To do

For each of the basic recipes shown on these pages, suggest four ideas to show how the recipe has been adapted and used to make a variety of food products. Use recipe books to help with the research. You can use a chart like the one shown below. Try out some of the recipes you have chosen.

Basic recipe	Recipe ideas

Using basic recipes

Basic recipe	What it can be made into
Shortcrust pastry	pies, tarts, pasties, flans
Scone mixture	sweet and savoury scones. pizza base, cobbler
Bread	sweet and savoury breads, rolls, plaits, loaves, pizza base
Creamed cake mixture	small cakes in different flavours, Victoria sandwich, topping for pies
Whisked cake mixture	Swiss roll, large iced cakes, gateaux, small cakes
Biscuits	variety of flavourings can be added such as nuts, chocolate chips and dried fruit, shapes can be changed
White sauce	sweet and savoury flavours can be added such as fruit purée and vanilla, cheese, onion, parsley

WHOLEMEAL BREAD

Ingredients

200 g strong wholemeal flour
25 g fat (margarine, butter, lard)
1 level tsp salt
1 sachet quick dried yeast
about 150 ml warm water to mix

Method

1 Sieve the flour into a bowl and add the fat cut into pieces.
2 Rub the fat into the flour until the mixture looks like breadcrumbs.
3 Add the salt and dried yeast and mix with enough warm water to make a dough.
4 Knead the dough. Put into a tin to prove inside a greased bag until the dough has doubled in size.
5 Bake in a very hot oven.

PLAIN SCONE MIXTURE

Ingredients

100 g self raising flour
25 g fat (margarine, butter, lard)
cold water or milk to mix

Method

1 Sieve the flour into a bowl and add the fat cut into pieces.
2 Rub the fat into the flour until the mixture looks like breadcrumbs.
3 Mix with enough cold water to make a dough.
4 Roll out to the required thickness.

WHISKING METHOD FOR CAKE MAKING

Ingredients

2 eggs
50 g caster sugar
50 g self-raising flour

Method

1 Whisk the eggs and sugar until they are thick and creamy.
2 Gently fold in the flour.
3 Pour the mixture into a tin for baking.

SHORTCRUST PASTRY

Ingredients

100 g plain flour
50 g fat (margarine, butter, lard)
cold water to mix

Method

1 Sieve the flour into a bowl and add the fat cut into pieces.
2 Rub the fat into the flour until the mixture looks like breadcrumbs.
3 Mix with enough cold water to make a dough.
4 Roll out to the required thickness.

CREAMED CAKE MIXTURE – VICTORIA SANDWICH

Ingredients

100 g soft margarine or butter
100 g caster sugar
2 beaten eggs
100 g self-raising flour

Method

1 Cream the margarine or butter with the sugar in a mixing bowl.
2 Gently add the beaten egg and then stir in the flour to make a soft dough.
3 Spoon into greased tins and cook in an oven.

Note – as an alternative, put all the ingredients together in a food processor with 1 tsp of baking powder, and mix.

BASIC BISCUIT MIXTURE

Ingredients

100 g self-raising flour
50 g soft margarine or butter
50 g caster sugar
1 beaten egg

Method

1 Sieve the flour and sugar into a bowl and add the fat cut into pieces.
2 Rub the fat into the flour until the mixture looks like breadcrumbs.
3 Add enough beaten egg to form a stiff dough.
4 Roll to the thickness required.

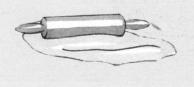

WHITE SAUCE

Ingredients

25 g soft margarine or butter
25 g plain flour
300 ml milk or water

Method

1 Melt the margarine or butter in a saucepan.
2 Stir in the flour and cook slowly for 1–2 minutes.
3 Gradually add the milk or water, stirring all the time. Bring to the boil.

Note – this can also be made by the 'all-in-one' method, where all the ingredients are placed in a pan then heated and whisked to make a thick sauce.

To make sure that our food is safe and clean to eat, we need to store, prepare and cook it hygienically.

Good food hygiene practice includes:
- good personal hygiene
- careful buying and storing of food
- safe preparation of food and thorough cooking
- good kitchen hygiene.

What is good personal hygiene?

This is the way we make ourselves ready to prepare food, and the way we handle food. Our hands, ears, nose and mouth can carry dangerous food-poisoning bacteria which can be passed onto food by poor hygiene.

Tips on good personal hygiene
- Always wear a clean apron or overall when preparing food.
- Wash hands thoroughly before handling food – use hot water and liquid soap and dry hands thoroughly.
- Always wash hands after visiting the toilet, after handling raw food and waste food products.
- Dry hands using a hot air drier or clean paper towel.
- Never cough or smoke during food preparation.
- Cover all cuts with waterproof dressings – cuts can carry bacteria.
- Tie back hair before working with food – food-handlers should wear head coverings.
- Do not work with food when suffering from diarrhoea or sickness.

■ Now wash your hands

Careful buying and storing of food

Make sure that food is as fresh as possible when it is bought, and that it is stored safely to reduce risks of cross-contamination and deterioration.

Tips on buying food
- Buy from shops that are clean and well run.
- Check the date mark on the food before buying it – make sure it is not out of date.
- Pack raw and cooked foods separately to avoid cross-contamination.
- Pack chilled and frozen foods in a cool bag which is insulated to prevent heat loss.
- Avoid leaving perishable food in warm cars or at room temperature.
- Store food as soon as you arrive home or at school.

■ People who handle food should wear special clothing when working with food

■ A cool box can be used to take frozen or chilled food home from the shops

Tips on storing food

- Check the date mark on stored foods and throw away food that is out of date.
- Store food according to instructions on the packaging.
- Store food in a cool, dry, clean place away from pests and pets.
- Keep food covered.
- Store perishable food in a refrigerator that is operating at 5°C or below – check by using a refrigerator thermometer.
- Store frozen food in a freezer that is operating at –18°C or below and do not refreeze frozen food that has defrosted.
- Cool food quickly before storage.
- Avoid cross-contamination of food during storage by keeping raw food such as meat away from cooked food such as ham.

Good hygiene practice during food preparation

Food can be contaminated during preparation and cooking, so it needs careful handling and storage. Food must be cooked or reheated properly to make sure it reaches a high enough temperature for a long enough time to kill any harmful bacteria which may be present.

Tips on good hygiene practice during food preparation

- Don't lick your fingers or smoke during food preparation – bacteria from your mouth can pass onto food.
- Avoid cross-contamination of raw and cooked foods – use separate chopping boards and equipment when preparing raw meat and other foods, wash the boards and equipment thoroughly in hot, soapy water after use, then dry them.
- Wash your hands after handling raw foods to avoid cross-contamination.
- Control the amount of time perishable food is kept in the **danger zone** (5–63°C) – prepare foods quickly then refrigerate or cook them. Do not leave them at room temperature for more than two hours as bacteria multiply in these conditions.
- Keep raw and cooked food separate during preparation.

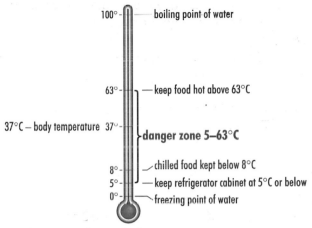

■ A thermometer showing the danger zone

Cooking food

- Cook food thoroughly: make sure food is cooked to at least 72°C at the centre – you can test with a food probe.
- Follow the instructions on packets carefully and always use the suggested oven temperature and cooking time.
- Always cook poultry thoroughly – most chickens are contaminated with bacteria.

Reheating food

- Cool food quickly if you want to reheat it later. Divide food such as cooked rice into smaller portions and leave in a cold place to cool for up to 90 minutes, then refrigerate or freeze.
- Reheat food thoroughly by cooking to a temperature of at least 72°C for at least two minutes.
- Food reheated in a microwave oven should be stirred half way through the heating time and left to stand after cooking to help avoid cold spots developing in the food.
- Reheat food only once.

═ Questions ═

1 Why is it important to prepare food hygienically?
2 Write ten important 'kitchen rules' for people to follow to make sure that food is safely prepared, cooked and stored.

Kitchen hygiene

The kitchen needs to be kept clean for safe food preparation.

Tips on kitchen hygiene

- Wash worktops and equipment in hot, soapy water before and after use and use an anti-bacterial spray or liquid before and after working with ingredients.
- Leave washing-up to air-dry if possible.
- Make sure kitchen equipment is clean before it is stored and used.
- Bleach, disinfect or change kitchen cloths regularly.
- Empty and wash rubbish bins regularly.
- Don't have pets in the kitchen.
- Keep the stock cupboard, refrigerator and freezer clean and check that food is not out of date.

Using the refrigerator and freezer

Refrigerators keep food cool, and freezers keep food frozen so it is important that this equipment operates at the correct temperature and is kept clean.

Safe use of the refrigerator

- The refrigerator should operate at between 2°C and 5°C – check using a refrigerator thermometer. Don't overload the refrigerator with food – this prevents cold air from circulating.
- Don't open the door more than is necessary – this lets in warm air.
- Prevent cross-contamination – store raw foods below cooked foods to prevent drips.
- Keep food covered.
- Defrost the refrigerator regularly to prevent a build-up of ice on the ice box.
- Don't put hot food in the refrigerator – hot food heats up the refrigerator cabinet. Allow hot food to cool rapidly for $1\frac{1}{2}$ hours, then place in the refrigerator.
- Do not keep food beyond its date code.

■ A fridge should be used carefully, with foods stored in the proper places

Safe use of the freezer

- The freezer should operate at −18°C or below – check with a freezer thermometer.
- Defrost and clean the freezer once every six months.
- Keep the freezer as full as possible – empty freezers take more energy to keep cool.
- Wrap food well before freezing to avoid damage to the frozen food and show the 'use-by' date.
- Never refreeze thawed food – bacteria could multiply to a dangerous level in the thawed food.
- Store food according to the star markings on the packet.
- Always thoroughly defrost joints of meat or poultry, otherwise it may not reach a safe temperature (63°C or above) during cooking.

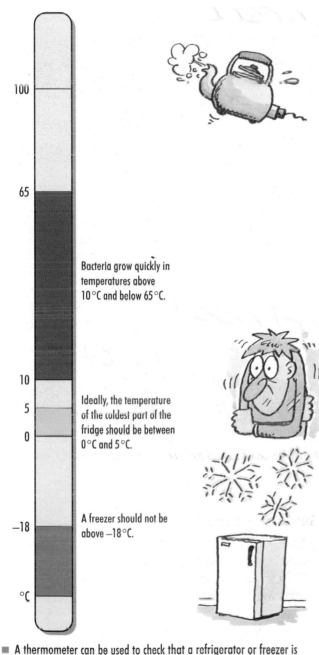

Bacteria grow quickly in temperatures above 10°C and below 65°C.

Ideally, the temperature of the coldest part of the fridge should be between 0°C and 5°C.

A freezer should not be above −18°C.

°C

■ A thermometer can be used to check that a refrigerator or freezer is operating at the correct temperature

Star markings

A special symbol is used for freezers to show how to store frozen food. This is shown on frozen food packets.

Star marking symbols	
Produce stored in	*Consume within*
Main compartment of refrigerator	24 hours of purchase
* Frozen food storage compartment	1 week of purchase
** Frozen food storage compartment	1 month of purchase
*** Frozen food storage compartment	3 months of purchase

To do

1 Make a collection of food hygiene rules used by caterers and food businesses. You could visit some of your local food businesses, food stores and your school meals supervisor to obtain this information. Ask them what kind of training they receive in food hygiene and safety when they start work. Record the answers to these questions.

Write a paragraph to explain why food hygiene rules and training are important in the food business. Write a report on your findings.

2 Find out the operating temperature of your refrigerator and freezer. You can use a thermometer or food probe to measure the temperature of the refrigerator and freezer cabinet. Take the measurement in different parts of the refrigerator cabinet and record your findings on a chart like the one shown below. Comment on your results.

Refrigerator cabinet temperature (°C)
top of cabinet
middle of cabinet
bottom of cabinet

Questions

1 List five rules for keeping food safely in:
  a a refrigerator
  b a freezer.

2 List five important rules for good kitchen hygiene.

64 Food spoilage

*F*ood spoilage is caused by micro-organisms which are too small to see without the use of a microscope. The three types of micro-organisms are **yeasts**, **bacteria** and **moulds**.

Yeasts

Yeasts are microscopic, single-celled fungi which reproduce by budding. Yeasts use sugar to grow and produce carbon dioxide gas in the process called **fermentation**. Yeasts can attack foods such as jams and cause spoilage, but they are also very useful in making many food products. Through fermentation, they help bread to rise and change grapes into wine. Yeasts are killed by heat.

Bacteria

Bacteria are single-celled organisms which are widely found in soil, air and on our bodies. Some bacteria are useful to us, and others cause food spoilage and serious illness. Useful bacteria are used to make foods such as yogurt and cheese. Most bacteria are killed by heat.

■ Yeasts

Moulds

Moulds are a form of fungi. Mould spores are carried in the air and settle and grow on the surfaces of food such as bread, meat and cheese. Mould is used in the production of some foods such as blue cheese. Certain moulds produce harmful toxins. The mould which grows on peanuts produces aflotoxin which causes serious illness, even death, if eaten. Moulds are killed by heat.

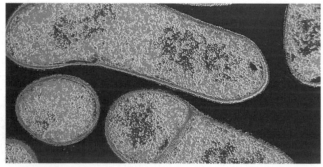

■ Bacteria

■ Moulds

The effects of micro-organisms on food		
Micro-organism	*Useful effects in making food products*	*Harmful effects*
Bacteria	Certain types of bacteria are used to make cheese and yogurt.	Certain types of pathogenic bacteria cause food poisoning.
Yeasts	Fermentation is used in beer and wine making as well as bread.	Ferment food and cause 'off' flavours in jams.
Moulds	Certain cheeses have mould introduced into them to turn them blue — e.g. Stilton.	Mould grows on the outside of food and affects taste and appearance; certain types of mould can be dangerous.
Enzymes (not micro-organisms)	Used to cause changes in food products such as junket.	Enzymes cause browning in apples and loss of vitamins.

Enzymes

Food can be changed by enzymes which are chemicals found in food. Enzymes cause fruits such as apples to go brown, and enzymes can destroy the vitamin content of food. Enzymes are destroyed by heat.

The chart at the bottom of page 140 shows the effects of micro-organisms on foods.

Food-poisoning bacteria

Food-poisoning bacteria can enter food at any stage during production, shopping, storage, preparation and cooking. To avoid illness, it is important to reduce the risk of letting dangerous pathogenic bacteria enter food. Most food poisoning in this country is caused by *Campylobacter* and *Salmonella* bacteria which are mainly found in raw meat and poultry.

To enable them to grow, bacteria need:
- the correct **temperature**
- **time**
- **food** and **moisture**.

If one or more of these conditions are controlled, there is less chance of food-poisoning bacteria multiplying.

Temperature control

This is the most effective way to control or destroy bacteria.

The danger zone

Bacteria grow rapidly at 20–50°C. To prevent their growth, food should be kept below 5°C and cooked to above 63°C. This temperature range 5–63°C is known as the **danger zone**.

> **For food safety, keep perishable, high risk-food out of the danger zone.**

Some bacteria can produce spores which survive above 63°C.

Keep food cool

If food is kept cool in a refrigerator, the bacteria are not killed, but their growth is slowed down. Refrigerators should operate at 5°C or below. This can be checked using a refrigerator thermometer.

Keeping food in freezers can stop bacteria growing but does not kill them, so once the food is defrosted, the bacteria can multiply in warm conditions.

Food Hygiene Regulations require that most short-life food is stored at 8°C or colder when it is being processed, during distribution and on display in shops. Buy food from reputable shops which have refrigerated units for this type of food storage.

Cook food to a high enough temperature

Bacteria are destroyed at high temperatures, so if food is thoroughly heated to at least 72°C at its centre, for a sufficient time, harmful micro-organisms, including bacteria, will be destroyed. Food can be tested using a temperature probe to see if a high enough temperature has been reached. Bacteria such as *Staphylococcus* produce toxins which can survive normal cooking temperatures.

■ A chicken can be checked with a roasting thermometer to see if it is cooked thoroughly

Questions

1 Name the three types of micro-organisms which can cause food spoilage. Give an example of how each type of micro-organism causes deterioration in the food.

2 Give four examples of how micro-organisms are useful in food production.

3 Why is temperature control important in food safety?

Time

Some bacteria can divide in two every ten minutes by a process called **binary fission**. So, after two or three hours, food which contains a few food-poisoning bacteria will contain enough to cause an outbreak of food poisoning if the food is kept in the danger zone.

Controlling time

- The length of time that food is kept in the danger zone (5–63°C) should be as short as possible so that bacteria do not begin to multiply quickly.
- The time between buying the food and storing it in the refrigerator or freezer should be as short as possible.
- The shelf-life of food should be controlled so that food is not kept past its '**use-by**' or '**best-before**' date, when it might be unsafe to eat.
- The preparation of food should be carried out as quickly as possible.

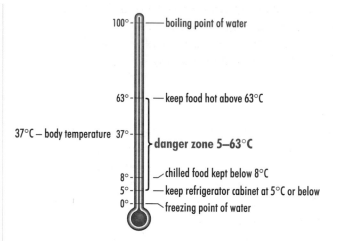

■ A thermometer showing the danger zone

- Food should be cooked for sufficient time so that it is piping hot right through. Salmonella bacteria are killed if they are heated to 72°C and maintained at that heat for two minutes. This is temperature and time control.
- When food is kept warm, such as in a self-service canteen, it should be for as short a time as possible and the food should not be reheated.
- Food cooked in a microwave oven should be cooked according to the instructions, and standing time allowed for the temperature to even out.
- Left-over food should be cooled quickly and kept cool.

Controlling the food available for bacterial to grow on

Bacteria like moist, high-protein foods, especially meat, chicken and dairy products. Foods that have been preserved may have their moisture made unavailable so that the bacteria cannot multiply.

Examples of preserved food where the water is unavailable

- **Frozen food** – moisture is frozen so it is unavailable.
- **Dried food** – most of the moisture has been driven off in the drying process.
- **Pickles, jams and salted foods** – the water is unavailable since it has been replaced by vinegar, sugar and salt.

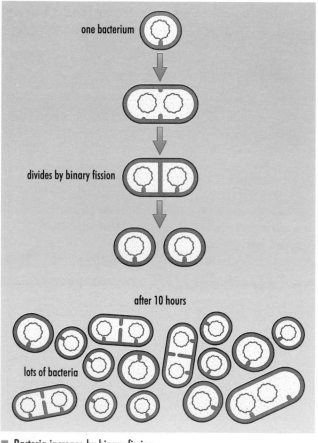

■ Bacteria increase by binary fission

Once frozen food is defrosted and dried food has been rehydrated, it must be treated as fresh food since the moisture is once again available for bacteria to grow and multiply.

Food poisoning

The number of food poisoning cases is increasing. Most of the reported cases of food poisoning outbreaks occur when food is served to large numbers of people such as at parties and weddings. Food poisoning can happen in the home too.

Can you tell if food contains food-poisoning bacteria?

The answer is 'No'. An egg may contain enough salmonella bacteria to cause food poisoning, but you cannot smell or taste that it is contaminated. Other foods such as milk, fish or meat can smell 'off' and you should throw them away rather than risk illness.

These are the ten main reasons for food poisoning.

1 Food prepared too far in advance and stored at room temperature i.e. not under refrigeration.
2 Cooling food too slowly prior to refrigeration.
3 Not reheating food to high enough temperatures to destroy food-poisoning bacteria.
4 The use of cooked food contaminated with food-poisoning bacteria.
5 Undercooking.
6 Not thawing frozen poultry for sufficient time.
7 Cross-contamination from raw food to cooked food.
8 Storing hot food below 63°C.
9 Infected food handlers.
10 Use of left-overs.

Source – *The Food Hygiene Handbook*, The Institution of Environmental Health Officers, by courtesy of Dr D Roberts, Food Hygiene Laboratory, Central Public Health Laboratory, Colindale

Where are food-poisoning bacteria found?

These are the main sources of food-poisoning bacteria:

1 **People** – bacteria are found in the nose, mouth, intestine and skin and can reach food by poor hygiene, coughing, spitting, cuts on the hands and not washing the hands after going to the toilet.
2 **Raw food and soil** – foods which might contain bacteria include raw meat, chicken, eggs and shellfish. Raw food must be stored separately from other foods to avoid cross-contamination. Soil from vegetables can contaminate other foods.
3 **Pests and pets** – flies, cockroaches, rats, mice and household pets can all carry food-poisoning bacteria and transmit them to food. Care must be taken to keep pests and pets out of the food preparation area.
4 **Waste food and rubbish** – bacteria can multiply in rotting food and parts of the food preparation area which are not cleaned. Clear up food waste daily, and wash hands after handling rubbish.

▬ *Questions* ▬

1 Give examples of how time is used as a control to prevent the growth of bacteria in food.
2 Explain why bacteria cannot multiply easily in
   a frozen food
   b dried food
   c preserves such as jams and pickles.
3 What are the main sources of food poisoning?

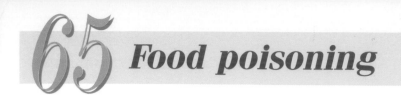

Food poisoning

How does food become contaminated with food-poisoning bacteria?

This is the food poisoning chain.

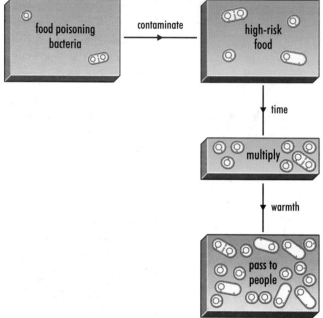

■The food poisoning chain

Food-poisoning bacteria can pass from one area to another by cross-contamination to high-risk food.

- Prevent raw foods from touching cooked foods.
- Prevent blood or juices dripping onto cooked food.
- Prevent bacteria from being transferred from raw to cooked food via hands, knives and utensils.

Examples of cross-contamination

- Bacteria from raw meat can pass onto cooked rice.
- A chopping board used for raw meat could be used to slice cooked ham.
- A bowl used for mixing raw eggs could be used unwashed to mix a sandwich filling.

— Did you know? —

The name *Salmonella* comes from the American vet, Dr Salmon, who in 1855 was the first to identify this type of bacteria.

High-risk foods

These are foods in which harmful bacteria can grow. High-risk foods are usually eaten without further cooking, and are good sources of protein.
  High-risk foods include:
- cooked meat such as ham
- cooked chicken
- milk, cream, custard and milky desserts
- cooked eggs
- shellfish
- cooked rice.

Equipment for food preparation

Food preparation equipment can harbour bacteria.
- Equipment that is used for food should not be chipped, cracked or badly worn – cracks in mixing bowls can provide hiding places for bacterial growth.
- Wooden chopping boards and spoons should not be used as they are absorbent to moisture and cannot be easily cleaned or disinfected.
- Chopping boards and spatulas should be made from polypropylene which can be easily cleaned.
- Chopping boards in catering kitchens should be colour-coded so that they can be used just for preparing certain foods such as meat or vegetables.

Food-poisoning bacteria

There are many types of bacteria which cause food poisoning and each one produces its own symptoms, has its own food sources and responds to certain methods of control. Some bacteria, such as **listeria**, grow at low temperatures, so may even grow in the refrigerator.

  Most bacteria are killed by thorough heating, but some, such as *Clostridium botulinum*, produce spores which can survive high cooking temperatures. The chart on page 145 shows the most common types of food-poisoning bacteria.

The most common types of food-poisoning bacteria

Food-poisoning bacteria	Symptoms	Period before onset of illness	Likely sources	Control
Salmonella	Abdominal pain, diarrhoea, nausea, vomiting and fever.	12–36 hours	Many types of raw meat, poultry, eggs	Keep food cool, cooked to 75°C at centre, avoid cross-contamination.
Campylobacter	Most common cause of fever, diarrhoea.	3–5 days	Raw poultry and other meats	Avoid cross-contamination from raw meat to other food, cook meat and poultry thoroughly.
Listeria monocytogenes	Mild and flu-like, but can invade bloodstream and cause brain disease. Dangerous for pregnant women because of risk of abortion.	variable	Soft cheeses and patés	Buy cooked meats and soft cheeses from good suppliers, store food below 8°C.
Escherichia coli (E coli)	Bloody diarrhoea, vomiting, kidney disease.	3–4 days	Raw meat	Avoid cross-contamination from raw meat to cooked food, cook meat thoroughly.
Clostridium perfringens	One of the most common causes of food poisoning; causes cramps and pain.	variable	Raw meat, vegetables, herbs and spices.	Grows very fast at 45°C, so reheat quickly, cool food quickly and store below 8°C.
Clostridium botulinum (caused by toxin)	Attacks the nervous system and causes impaired vision and paralysis. Rare but often fatal.	12–36 hours	Spores form toxin and are found in a variety of foods.	Does not grow well in acid foods below pH 4.5 or below 8°C. Do not use blown cans.
Staphylococcus aureus	Nausea, vomiting, diarrhoea.	1–6 hours	Main source is food handlers, since found in nose and throat and infected cuts.	Good personal hygiene, cover cuts, store food below 8°C.
Bacillus cereus	Nausea, vomiting, diarrhoea.	1–5 or 8–16 hours	Pre-cooked rice dishes and other grains.	Avoid cooking rice and pasta dishes in advance, cool quickly, store below 8°C, reheat thoroughly.

Questions

1 What is meant by the following terms?
   a cross-contamination
   b high-risk foods

2 What are the most common symptoms of food poisoning?

3 Which foods are the most likely sources of food-poisoning bacteria?

4 Give three examples to show how the risk of food poisoning can be reduced.

What about raw eggs?

Eggs are known to be a source of salmonella bacteria which causes food poisoning. The Government warns that we should not eat raw eggs or dishes made with raw eggs such as mayonnaise or home-made mousses. People who are sick, pregnant or frail, as well as small children, should make sure that their scrambled, boiled or fried eggs are thoroughly cooked. For healthy people there is little risk from eating cooked eggs.

What about listeria?

Healthy people are unlikely to suffer if they eat food which contains listeria bacteria. However, pregnant women or people who are sick should avoid eating foods which could be contaminated with listeria. These foods include paté and soft cheeses.

What if you get food poisoning?

The most common symptoms of food poisoning are stomach aches, vomiting or diarrhoea. You may feel ill within an hour of eating the contaminated food or it could be five days later. Most symptoms of food poisoning go away in time. You need to rest, drink plenty of water and avoid solid food for a while. If you are very ill, consult your doctor. Don't prepare food for other people if you are ill from food poisoning – you could pass the infection on to them.

If you or your doctor thinks that the infection was linked to a particular food, shop or eating place, then the local **Environmental Health Officer** needs to be contacted. An investigation will be carried out, since other people may have been infected and the cause of the food-poisoning outbreak needs to be removed.

Barbecues

The number of cases of food poisoning increases during summer time. This is partly due to the warm weather, but also to the increase in the amount of food cooked outdoors on barbecues.

Tips for food safety when using a barbecue

- Make sure that raw foods such as chicken and sausages are cooked right through.
- Keep a separate pair of tongs for handling cooked and raw food to avoid cross-contamination.
- Prepare food hygienically – wash your hands before handling food.

■ Barbecue equipment. Seperate tongs must be used for raw and cooked food

Defrosting food

When food is frozen solid, bacteria cannot multiply, as they are dormant. Once the food is defrosted, it must be treated like fresh food, as any bacteria present can become active again and start to multiply in warm conditions.

Tips on defrosting food

- Thaw meat and poultry well away from other foods – to avoid contamination, they must not drip on or make contact with other uncooked foods.
- Once food is defrosted do not refreeze it.
- Once food has been thawed, treat it as fresh.

Food poisoning

The charts on this page show the notified cases of food poisoning in England and Wales.

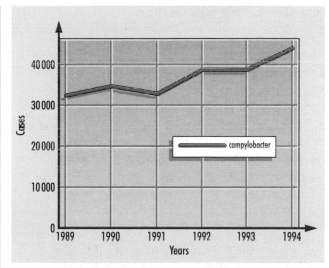

■ Chart B Notified isolates of campylobacter in England and Wales

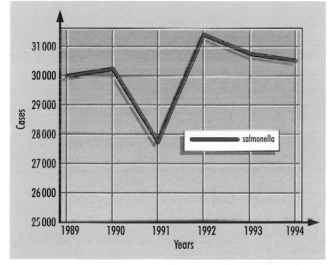

■ Chart A Confirmed isolates of salmonella in England and Wales

Source – *The Food Hygiene Handbook*

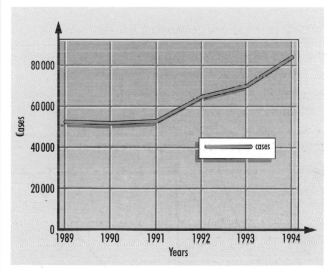

■ Chart C Notified cases of food poisoning in England and Wales

▬ *Questions* ▬

1 What is the trend in food-poisoning outbreaks in England and Wales? Refer to charts A, B and C for the information.

2 What is the current Government advice about eating raw eggs?

3 What should you do if you get food poisoning?

4 Why are barbecues likely food hazards? What can be done to reduce the risk of food poisoning when using a barbecue?

66 Food handling

*H*ere are some tips on the safe handling of food.

Good food handling guide

1 When you have bought chilled or frozen foods, store them quickly.
2 Keep hot food hot and cold food cold.
3 Store raw meat in the refrigerator below food that is not going to be cooked or reheated.
4 Keep raw and cooked foods apart.
5 Wash chopping boards, knives and other equipment *and* your hands after they have been used for preparing raw food.
6 Cool left-over food quickly and keep it cool.
7 Don't keep food beyond its 'use-by' or 'best-before' date.
8 Keep all food covered.
9 Keep pets out of food preparation areas.
10 Wash your hands before handling food.

FOOD POISONING QUIZ

1 At what temperature should fresh food be kept to minimize the risk of food poisoning?
a −18°C   *b* 8°C or colder
c 10°C   *d* room temperature

2 If there is a power cut for three hours, what should you do about the food in the freezer?
a Throw everything away.
b Distribute the food among your neighbours and tell them to eat it straight away.
c Leave the whole thing alone until several hours after the power has been restored.
d Keep opening the door/lid to see what is happening.

3 Which of these should you not cook from frozen?
a rib of beef
b a whole salmon
c chicken nuggets
d a rolled shoulder of lamb

4 Some foods such as meats, fish and bacon are now packed in gas-flushed packs to extend their storage lives. Where and for how long should you keep them?
a in the fridge for up to three days
b in the larder for up to three days
c in the fridge for up to five days
d in the fridge for the time stated on the pack

5 You have a chilled recipe dish containing chicken. It is two days past the 'use-by' date. You think it has been kept in the fridge so what do you do?
a Throw it away.
b Cook it in the usual way and eat it.
c Cook it for a few minutes longer than stated and eat it.

6 Which of these is the most important time to wash your hands?
a before handling raw meat/poultry
b after handling raw meat/poultry
c before handling cooked meat/poultry
d *a*, *b* and *c* are equally important.

THE ANSWERS

1 *b*   Fresh food should be kept at 8°C or colder.

2 *c*   A three-hour power cut won't have any significant effect on a well-stocked freezer, provided you don't keep opening the lid/door.

3 *a, b, d*   Thorough cooking of these foods is very difficult unless they are thawed before cooking begins.

4 *d*

5 *a*   It is recommended that all food is eaten by the 'use-by' date.

6 *d*

67 Preservation

Why does preservation stop food from going bad?

The bacteria micro-organisms **yeast** and **mould** cause changes in food which can be harmful. Micro-organisms need **food**, **warmth**, **moisture** and **time** to multiply. If these conditions are removed, the food is **preserved** and will keep for longer. **Enzymes** in food also cause deterioration and these enzymes must be destroyed to improve the keeping quality of food.

Many methods of food preservation have been used for thousands of years. The chart below shows the methods and how they work.

Questions

1 What conditions do micro-organisms need to be able to multiply and grow?
2 Explain why food needs to be preserved.

■ Foods can be preserved by canning, drying, smoking, freezing, vacuum or MAP packing

Methods of preserving food

Method of preservation	How does it work?	Examples of foods
Drying	Water is removed, and micro-organisms and enzymes are inactive.	Vegetables, herbs, beans, soups
Freezing	Water is frozen and therefore not available, so micro-organisms and enzymes are inactive.	Fish, chicken, meat, vegetables
Use of chemicals – pickling, salting, smoking and jams	Chemicals in preserving agents such as vinegar, salt, smoke and sugar destroy micro-organisms.	Pickled vegetables, chutneys, jams, salt fish, olives, smoked salmon
Heating – bottling and canning	Heat kills micro-organisms and destroys enzymes. Food must be sealed in jars or cans.	Bottled fruit and vegetables, most food can be canned
Chilling	Cools food to a low temperature so that micro-organisms cannot multiply.	Chilled ready meals, salads, desserts
Vacuum packing or MAP (modified atmosphere packaging)	Vacuum packing removes air, so micro-organisms cannot multiply. MAP changes gas so micro-organisms do not multiply so quickly.	Bacon, chopped salads
Irradiation	Kills all micro-organisms.	Spices and herbs

Drying

Micro-organisms need water to grow and multiply. Drying (dehydration) is a very old method of preservation, in which much of the water is removed from food. Many fruits such as apricots and figs are dried, grapes are dried to make sultanas and raisins.

Drying as a method of food preservation is used to preserve fruits, vegetables especially beans and pulses, meat and fish. Water is removed so that micro-organisms will not grow.

Methods of drying food commercially

- **Spray drying** – a fine liquid is blown into a chamber of hot air and the liquid turns into powder. This method is used to dry liquids such as milk and soups.
- **Hot air beds** – the food is placed on a tray with holes in it, and hot air is blown through to dry the food. This method is used to dry solid food such as meat, fruit, vegetables and pulses.
- **Accelerated freeze drying** (AFD) – this is a modern system of drying frozen food under vacuum at reduced pressure. This method of drying causes little damage to the food, since ice is driven off as water vapour, and is useful for heat-sensitive foods. This process preserves the flavour and colour of the food and is used for soups and instant coffee granules. These foods can be easily rehydrated by adding water.

■ Many products are preserved using modern mechanical drying methods

Nutritional value of dried food

Dried foods contain concentrated sources of nutrients since much of the water has been removed during processing. Fruits and vegetables have lost most of their vitamin C but they are good sources of vitamins A and D and iron. Dried pulses are valuable sources of protein and high in dietary fibre.

Dried foods can be stored for long periods of time but they must not be allowed to get damp.

Advantages of using dried foods

- Foods can be eaten out of season.
- They occupy less space than fresh foods and keep for a long time.
- Dried foods such as prunes and sultanas taste different from the fresh fruits.

Using chemicals

Chemicals have been used to preserve foods for thousands of years. Many chemicals are found naturally in foods and other products.

Examples of chemicals used in food

- **Salt** (sodium chloride) is used to salt meat and fish.
- **Sodium nitrate** and **sodium nitrite** are used to make bacon.
- **Sugar** is used for jams and jellies which are methods of preserving fruits.
- **Vinegar** is used for pickles and chutneys to preserve vegetables.

■ The traditional method of drying chillies

- **Alcohol** is used for fruits such as peaches which can be preserved in brandy.
- **Smoking** over burning wood is a way of preserving fish and meat.
- **Spices** are used to preserve meats, e.g. salami.

How do chemicals work?

Chemicals remove the available water from food so that micro-organisms cannot multiply. There is a range of chemicals used as **preservatives** for food products. They protect food against micro-organisms and food-poisoning bacteria and **increase the shelf-life** of food products. For example, E200 (sorbic acid) is used as a preservative for soft drinks and fruit yogurt; E203 (calcium sorbate) is used for frozen pizza. The E-number shows that the additive is accepted as safe all over the European Union.

■ Fish can be smoked over smouldering wood

■ Sugar is used as a preservative in jam-making

Questions

1 Give ten examples of foods which have been preserved by drying. Explain why drying helps the food to keep longer.

2 Describe the different methods of drying food commercially. What is the nutritional value of dried food? What are the advantages of using dried foods in cooking? Give three reasons.

3 Explain how chemicals are used to preserve foods. Give examples in each case.

Investigation

Look at food in a store cupboard or visit a supermarket to find examples of different foods that have been preserved by:

a drying

b using a range of chemicals.

You could fill in a chart like the one shown below. Find out which food additives are used to preserve food, and give examples of their use in food products. Write a report on your findings.

Examples of foods preserved by drying	*Examples of foods preserved by using chemicals, and the chemicals used*

Freezing

Why does freezing preserve food?

Freezing turns water into ice. Micro-organisms need food, warmth, liquid (moisture) and time to multiply. In freezing, both the warmth and the liquid are removed.

Quick freezing

The rate at which food is frozen is important. Quick freezing produces smaller ice crystals, so there is less chance that the food will be damaged on defrosting. Quick freezing means that the food must pass through the freezing zone 0°C to −4°C within 30 minutes.

Quick freezing is ideal for producing good-quality frozen foods. The food freezes immediately and keeps its shape and appearance. Slow freezing breaks down the walls of cells in the food and changes it appearance. Strawberries become mushy if they are frozen too slowly.

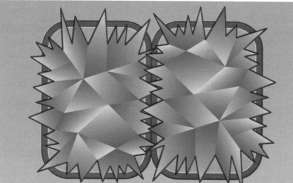

Slow freezing produces large ice crystals which break the cell walls in the food.

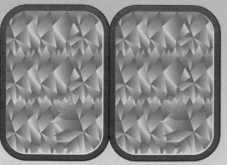

Quick freezing produces smaller ice crystals so there is less damage to cell walls.

How is food frozen?

Factories where food is frozen use three different methods.

- **Plate freezing** – flat products such as beefburgers and fish are frozen on plates.
- **Blast freezing** – cold air is blasted over food such as vegetables.
- **Cryogenic freezing or immersion freezing** – the food is immersed or sprayed with liquid nitrogen. The food is frozen immediately but this is an expensive process and is usually used for delicate foods such as raspberries and strawberries.

Blanching

Before freezing vegetables, it is important to blanch them by dipping them in boiling water, to stop enzymes from working and to prevent browning and loss of vitamins.

Nutritional losses in frozen foods

The nutritional loss in frozen foods is very small. Blanching causes some loss of the water-soluble vitamins C and thiamin but the final cooking time is reduced, so frozen vegetables can be just as nutritious as fresh. Many frozen vegetables are more nutritious than the fresh version since they are frozen very soon after harvesting. When food is defrosted, valuable nutrients can be lost in the liquid which comes out of the food as it thaws.

Keeping frozen food

Food can be stored for a long time by freezing it. Micro-organisms become inactive at around −10°C and enzymes are inactive at −18°C. Domestic freezers, used in the home, should operate at −18°C or below and commercial freezers used by canteens or supermarkets should operate at −29°C.

Defrosting

Follow instructions for defrosting food products. Do not refreeze defrosted food.

Cook-freeze foods

These foods have been fully cooked and then quickly frozen and stored at temperatures below −18°C. This process is used for hospital meals and some airline food.

Chilling food

If food is kept at low temperatures, micro-organisms do not multiply so quickly as at room temperature. Chilled food is kept at below 8°C. Chilling as a method of food preservation has grown rapidly in the past few years and has been helped by the development of efficient chilled storage and distribution systems. Chilled food must be handled under strict hygiene conditions to prevent contamination by bacteria and other micro-organisms. The food is stored in cold conditions where temperatures are low enough to prevent the growth of most bacteria which may cause food poisoning.

Cook-chill foods

The UK food industry has led the world in developing cook-chill ready meals. Food such as a ready-to-heat chilli-con-carne is cooked and chilled to just above 0°C then stored for sale at a temperature low enough to prevent food micro-organisms from multiplying.

Cook-chill meals are sold in supermarkets but are also used in hospitals and restaurants. Cook-chill foods are expensive, compared with making a similar meal from the basic ingredients. Food manufacturers call these 'added value' foods since the preparation and presentation has added value and the product can be sold at a high price compared with the cost of the raw ingredients.

The cook-chill process

Types of cook-chill foods include ready meals and desserts which are already cooked to destroy pathogenic bacteria. The food must be chilled as soon as possible after cooking (within a period of one and a half hours) to a temperature of just above 0°C to prevent bacteria from multiplying.

Cook-chill foods need to be stored and distributed in controlled temperatures between 0° and 8°C and can only be kept for a few days, as shown on the 'use-by' date code.

The food should be reheated until the centre reaches a temperature of at least 72°C, and should be consumed within two hours of reheating. Cook-chill food should only be reheated once.

This type of food needs very careful temperature control and should not be kept at temperatures above 8°C.

■ Cook-chill foods have a limited shelf-life and should be eaten by the 'use-by' date on the packaging

— *To do* —

Visit your local supermarket and make a list of ten different types of:

a frozen food

b chilled food.

Which are the most successful types of frozen food – the ones with the largest display area? Give reasons for the popularity of this type of frozen food.

▬ *Questions* ▬

1 Why is it best to freeze food as quickly as possible?
2 Why does freezing preserve food?
3 How are cook-chill meals produced?
4 What is meant by the term 'added value'?

Heating food to preserve it

Heat kills micro-organisms and destroys enzymes.

Bottling

Fruit and vegetables can be bottled in the home by heating them in liquid in glass jars and then covering them with an airtight seal. The food is sterilized in the jars and the seal prevents micro-organisms from entering the food.

Canning

Canning is an industrial version of bottling. Food is placed in a can made of tinned steel, liquid is added and the can is sealed and heated until harmful micro-organisms and spores are killed. Most food can be preserved by canning. Canned vegetables and meat are usually heated to 115°C and fruits to a lower temperature.

High temperature short time canning (HTST)

Using very high temperatures reduces processing time and prevents food from becoming over-processed and losing texture.

Nutrition

Some loss of nutrients occurs during heating – thiamin is lost from meat and vitamin C from fruit and vegetables. Canned foods are nearly as good as corresponding fresh foods in terms of nutritional value. Fruit and vegetables are canned within hours of picking so few nutrients are lot.

Canned foods will keep for several years. Canned foods such as fish, tomatoes and beans are good value for money. Cans have a 'best-before' date to show how long they can be kept. The chart below shows how long food in undamaged cans will keep.

How long canned foods can be kept	
Food product	*How long it can be kept in a sealed can*
Soft fruits such as blackberries, plums, strawberries	2 years
Carrots, butter beans, baked beans, cured meats, fish products	3 years

Once cans have been opened, the contents should be emptied out and treated like fresh food. Otherwise, with exposure to oxygen, the contents can react with the metal in the can.

Pasteurization

Heat treatment can lengthen shelf-life and make a product safer to eat. For milk, pasteurization involves heating to 72°C, holding this temperature for at least fifteen seconds and then cooling rapidly to 10°C. Pasteurization destroys many but not all of the micro-organisms present. Other products that can be pasteurized include orange juice, cream, beer and wine.

Sterilization

This involves heating food to a high temperature. Milk is heated to 104°C for 40 minutes.

Ultra heat treatment (UHT)

Ultra heat treatment destroys all bacteria. This process is used to heat milk and fruit juices to a very high temperature. Milk is heated to 132.2°C for not less than one second to kill all bacteria, then cooled quickly. This makes the milk sterile but alters the taste. The product is sealed to prevent contamination. UHT milk will keep for several months without refrigeration.

■ UHT milk will keep for several months. Canned food can be kept for two or three years

— To do

Visit a supermarket and make a list of 20 different preserved food products. Show how they are preserved to prolong their shelf life. Make a note of the 'use-by' or 'best-before' date on each food and compare results. From your survey, find out which is the most popular method of preservation used today. You could use a chart like the one shown below to fill in your results.

Food product	Method of preservation	'Best-before' date

Shelf-stable foods

These foods have been heat-treated to sterilize them and then sealed in plastic trays in an oxygen-free atmosphere.

Vacuum packaging and MAP

If the gas in the food package is changed, the growth of micro-organisms can be delayed. **Vacuum packing** removes all gas from the package and keeps food in anaerobic conditions with no oxygen.

Modified atmosphere packaging (MAP) changes the type of gas in the pack. It replaces most of the oxygen in food packaging with carbon dioxide and nitrogen gas so that the food does not deteriorate so rapidly. This process is used to pack ready prepared salads, minced beef and other meats including bacon. The food looks, tastes and smells just like fresh food, but the change of gas slows down the growth of micro-organisms. The European Union is proposing that MAP foods should be labelled. Both these processes increase the shelf-life of foods.

Food irradiation

Food is irradiated by bombarding it with ionizing radiation to make it keep longer. This method of preservation has been permitted in the UK since 1991 but so far only herbs and spices have been irradiated. By law, any food which has been irradiated must be labelled as such. None of the major supermarket chains have yet decided to sell irradiated food.

Some advantages of irradiation

- It reduces or eliminates harmful micro-organisms such as salmonella and listeria.
- It kills insect pests and parasites.
- It delays the ripening of fruit.
- It prevents sprouting of vegetables.

Some disadvantages of irradiation

- Vitamins are lost during processing and storage.
- Not all harmful bacteria may be removed and toxins may remain in the food.
- Old food could be 'cleaned up' and sold as fresh.
- No test is available to find out if foods have been irradiated.

— Questions

Explain what is meant by the following terms.

AFD	cryogenic freezing	HTST canning
UHT	shelf-stable foods	vacuum packing
MAP	irradiation	

Give examples of foods which may be preserved by each of the processes.

*T*here are several regulations which affect the way food is prepared, stored and sold.

The Food Safety Act 1990

The Food Safety Act came into force in January 1991 to replace the Food Act 1984. The Food Safety Act 1990 was introduced to take account of the changes in food technology and eating habits. It was designed to help reduce the number of cases of food-borne illness such as food poisoning and contamination. It strengthens and updates the law on food safety and consumer protection in the food business throughout Great Britain.

The Food Safety Act 1990 covers the whole of the food chain, from the farm to the food shop, and refers to the sale of all food, including takeaways. Food premises must be registered and anyone preparing food for sale must come under the control of the Act. The Act applies to food businesses in England, Scotland and Wales. In Northern Ireland the Food Safety (Northern Ireland) Order 1991 applies.

■ Environmental Health Officers at work

What does the Food Safety Act do?

- It makes sure that all food produced and sold is safe to eat.
- It increases penalties and legal powers.
- It meets changing technology.

What is meant by 'food' under the Act?

Food includes:
- anything used as a food ingredient
- animals that are eaten, such as oysters
- drinks
- slimming aids and dietary supplements.

Who does the Food Safety Act affect?

The Act covers:
- the whole of the food chain, from farm to food shops and restaurants
- the sale of all food
- anyone working in the food business, from small to large businesses, sandwich bars to supermarkets and including non-profit making organizations such as lunch clubs for the elderly.

Food safety requirements

Food must not be:
- injurious to health
- unfit – putrid or toxic
- contaminated.

Enforcement

The day-to-day **enforcement** of the Food Safety Act is carried out by officers in local government including:
- **Environmental Health Officers** who cover hygiene of food premises and food safety
- **Trading Standards Officers** who cover weights and measures and deal with food labelling and the composition of food.

Officers can enter food premises to investigate complaints, inspect food to see if it is safe and detain, seize or condemn food. When the officers go into premises they can take away food samples, and make videos to record what they see.

Control of Substances Hazardous to Health Regulations 1994 (COSHH)

These regulations provide a framework for the control of hazardous substances in all types of businesses including food businesses. The 1994 Regulations replace the 1988 Regulations.

Sale of Goods Act

The Sale of Goods Act 1979 is the law which protects consumers when they buy goods. In 1994 a new law (The Sale and Supply of Goods Act) replaced the term 'merchantable quality' with 'satisfactory quality'.

BASIC

Food Hygiene

CERTIFICATE

A N Other

has completed a course of Basic Food Hygiene training and has achieved a satisfactory degree of competence in the assessment which concluded the course.

Course Director

Date *16th March 1992*

Centre *B00039*

Chief Executive
The Chartered Institute
of Environmental Health

Certificate No. 0000003

■ The Basic Food Hygiene Certificate from the Chartered Institute of Environmental Health

Food Safety (General Food Hygiene) Regulations 1995

These regulations lay down the 'rules of hygiene', and require food businesses to assess the risks in making their food products and take any required action to ensure the safety of the food. **Hazard Analysis and Critical Control Points** (HACCP) is an example of a system that ensures controls are appropriate. The 'Industry Guide to Good Hygiene Practice: Catering Guide' provides practical advice to the catering industry on how to comply with the general food hygiene regulations.

Training in food hygiene

Food handlers must be supervised and instructed and/or trained in food hygiene matters to a level appropriate to their job. For staff handling high-risk foods, it would be advisable for them to be trained to a standard equivalent to the basic or certificate food hygiene course run by a number of accredited bodies.

Food Safety (Temperature Control) Regulations 1995

A maximum chill temperature of 8°C is a specific requirement, subject to certain exemptions, for foods that pose a potential microbiological hazard. Cooked or reheated food that needs to be kept hot must be kept at a temperature at, or above, 63°C.

Food Labelling Regulations 1984

The labelling, description and presentation of food are regulated to stop them from being misleading.

▬ *Questions* ▬

1 What is the purpose of the Food Safety Act? How does it protect consumers?
2 How is the Food Safety Act enforced?
3 Give five reasons to explain why do you think regulations are needed for the sale and consumption of food.

Food labels

A food label provides information from the food manufacturer to the consumer. Detailed labelling requirements are laid down under the Food Safety Act. Food labels help to tell us what we are buying.

Advantages of food labels

Food labels help people:

- to know what they are buying by giving information about the food product
- to use foods and food products correctly with preparation and storage information
- to make food choices for dietary or other reasons with nutritional information
- to compare food products for value for money.

People can choose foods that are low in fat or high in fibre by reading and comparing the nutritional label. If someone wants to lose weight they can work out the energy value of the food product from the label.

Manufacturers can promote their products with attractive labels.

Requirements for labelling

For most food products, the label must include the following information, unless exempt from one or more of these particulars:

- the product name
- an ingredients list – in descending order of weight so the first ingredient is the largest
- the shelf-life – 'use-by' or 'best-before' date
- storage instructions
- the name and address – may be that of the manufacturer, packer or EC seller
- the origin
- instructions for use
- the weight of product.

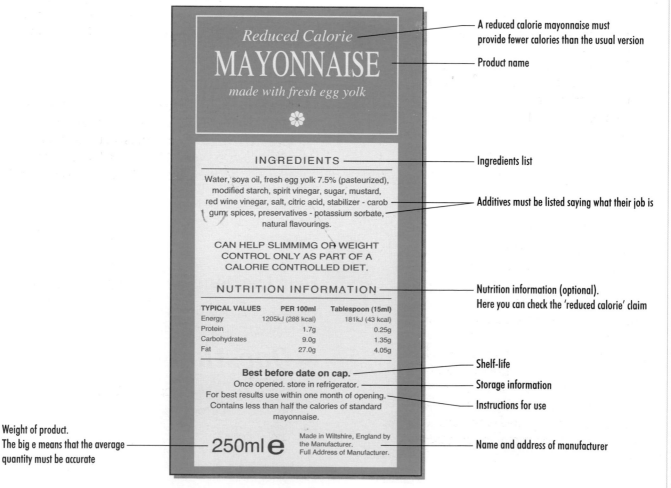

A reduced calorie mayonnaise must provide fewer calories than the usual version

Product name

Reduced Calorie

MAYONNAISE

made with fresh egg yolk

INGREDIENTS — Ingredients list

Water, soya oil, fresh egg yolk 7.5% (pasteurized), modified starch, spirit vinegar, sugar, mustard, red wine vinegar, salt, citric acid, stabilizer - carob gum, spices, preservatives - potassium sorbate, natural flavourings.

Additives must be listed saying what their job is

CAN HELP SLIMMIMG OR WEIGHT CONTROL ONLY AS PART OF A CALORIE CONTROLLED DIET.

NUTRITION INFORMATION

Nutrition information (optional). Here you can check the 'reduced calorie' claim

TYPICAL VALUES	PER 100ml	Tablespoon (15ml)
Energy	1205kJ (288 kcal)	181kJ (43 kcal)
Protein	1.7g	0.25g
Carbohydrates	9.0g	1.35g
Fat	27.0g	4.05g

Best before date on cap. — Shelf-life
Once opened. store in refrigerator. — Storage information
For best results use within one month of opening. — Instructions for use
Contains less than half the calories of standard mayonnaise.

Weight of product. The big e means that the average quantity must be accurate

250ml e

Made in Wiltshire, England by the Manufacturer. Full Address of Manufacturer. — Name and address of manufacturer

The name of the food

A name may be:
- established by law
- customary in the area where the product is sold, or
- a product description.

If this name does not explain the food, a subtitle must be added. As an example, in the name 'Jump – moist, chewy cereal bars with chocolate chips', the words, 'moist, chewy cereal bars with chocolate chips' explain what the 'Jump' bar is; the name 'Jump' may be included on the label, but may not be used instead of the descriptive product name.

The name must show if the food has gone through any sort of process, for example, **smoked** mackerel, **dried** apple slices.

A few well known or traditional foods are allowed to keep their names, for example, Swiss rolls do not have to come from Switzerland.

The picture on the packet must not mislead the consumer – a yogurt with artificial strawberry flavours cannot be sold with a picture of strawberries on the pot.

List of ingredients

This list tells consumers the ingredients that have been used in manufacturing the food. The list of ingredients is in descending order by weight, so the first ingredient on the list is the largest. Permitted additives are included in this list.

The food company must declare the specific name of an additive number and/or its E number, which indicates that it has been approved by the European Community. Before each name the label says what sort of additive it is, for example 'preservative'.

QUID – The EC wants to introduce a system showing the percentage of the main ingredients used in a food product. QUID stands for 'quantitative ingredient declaration'.

Below is the label for an apple pie which shows the percentage of apple used in the pie.

Ingredients:
wheatflour, sugar, hydrogenated vegetable fat, apple (10%), dextrose, modified starch, flavouring

How long will it keep?

The shelf-life of a product is the length of time the food is expected to last and remain good to eat if it is stored according to instructions. This is shown with a date mark which can be a 'use-by' or 'best-before' date (see page 160 for more information).

Nutrition information

Nutrition labelling provides valuable information about the nutritional aspects of a product's composition. This information is voluntary unless a nutrition claim such as 'high in fibre' or 'low in sugar' is made (see page 161 for more information).

Questions

1. Name three advantages of labelling food.
2. Make a collection of food labels. Compare the information they provide under the following headings.
   Product name
   Ingredients list
   Shelf-life
   Storage instructions
   Name and address of manufacturer
   Origin
   Instructions for use
   Net quantity

Date coding

After purchase, food must be stored, prepared and cooked properly if it is to be safe to eat. Otherwise, harmful bacteria could multiply and cause food poisoning. Food labels carry date codes and, to maintain the safety and quality of food, it is important to check that food is not out of date.

Date codes only refer to the product before the pack is opened. After opening, the food should be handled and stored according to instructions and eaten within two days.

Different types of date code

'Use-by'

This date code is often used for chilled foods such as sandwiches and cook-chill meals which should be stored in the refrigerator. The 'use-by' date must be used for foods that are microbiologically highly perishable and as a result likely after a short time to be a danger to human health. After the use-by date shown, the product will start to deteriorate and may no longer be safe to eat.

'Best-before'

Where the 'use-by' date is not applicable, a 'best-before' date must be given, with the date in the form: day, month and year in that order, although the regulations permit alternatives to this format. For a product with a shelf-life of three months or less, such as bread, biscuits, crisps and sweets the 'best-before' date may be expressed as a day and month only. Sometimes there is a number after the date for example 11 Sept (2), which shows the number of days, before the date marked, when the product should be removed from sale, in this example two days, although this is not a legal requirement.

'Best before end'

This is an alternative form of the 'best-before' date for a product with a shelf-life of more than three months, such as canned and bottled foods, drinks and frozen goods. It may be expressed in terms of a month and year only, or if the product has a shelf-life of more than 18 months, in terms of a month and year, or a year only.

'Display-until'

The 'display-until' date code is not required by the regulations, but may be used by the store to tell them when to remove the product from the shelves. The 'display-until' date is normally a few days before the 'use-by' date so that there are a number of days life left when the customer purchases the product. Foods such as fruits and vegetables are not legally required to be marked with a 'best-before' or 'use-by' date but may have a 'display-until' date.

■ Examples of date codes on food labels

Food not date coded

Some products are not required to be date marked, e.g. wines and spirits, which have a long shelf-life, and fresh fruits and vegetables. In addition, food that is not pre-packed, such as delicatessen products, does not require a date mark.

Food labelling

Many food labels show nutritional information which helps us make healthier choices of food products. Food companies do not have to provide nutritional information, but if they make a claim such as 'low-sugar' or 'high-fibre' they need to support it with nutritional labelling.

Information is given per 100 grams or 100 ml. This allows you to compare different foods. Some companies give details for a serving portion as well.

Nutrition labelling

There are two systems of nutrition labelling which have been agreed by the European Community:
● **Group 1** – energy, protein, carbohydrate, fat
● **Group 2** – energy, protein, carbohydrate, sugars, fat, saturates, fibre and sodium.

Nutrition claims

If a nutritional claim is made on a label, the food must be capable of fulfilling the claim. The Government has issued recommendations on commonly-used nutrition claims such as 'low-fat'. Other nutrition claims are controlled by food law.

Garlic rolls

Nutrition information

	Per 100 g	per roll
energy	1551 kJ, 370 kcal	558 kJ, 133 kcal
protein	7.6 g	2.7 g
carbohydrate	44.9 g	16.2 g
fat	17.8 g	6.4 g

■ Group 1 Nutrition information for garlic rolls

CHEESE AND TOMATO PIZZA

NUTRITION INFORMATION

	Per 100 g	Per $\frac{1}{2}$ pizza
energy	1245 kJ, 295 kcal	1422 kJ, 337 kcal
protein	13.1 g	15 g
carbohydrate	41.4 g	47.3 g
of which sugars	7.8 g	8.9 g
starch	33.6 g	38.4 g
fat	8.6 g	9.8 g
of which saturates	4.7 g	5.4 g
fibre	2.4 g	2.7 g
sodium	0.7 g	0.8 g

■ Group 2 Nutrition information for a cheese and tomato pizza

— To do

1 Collect a range of packaging with date codes. Make a list of the different types of date code and give an example of a food product which uses that code. Choose one of your food products and explain why you think that type of date coding has been used.

2 Collect examples of food labels which have nutrition claims. Show how the nutritional information supports these claims.

Questions

1 Why is it important for food labels to show date codes?

2 What is the difference between the date codes 'use-by', 'best-before' and 'best before end'? Give an example of a food product which uses each type of date code.

3 Why is it useful to have nutritional information on a food label?

Other information on a food label

Suitable for vegetarians

Many food labels have easy-to-identify vegetarian symbols to show that the ingredients have been checked and do not involve the slaughter of animals. The products may not necessarily be suitable or vegans.

■ Vegetarian symbol

Microwave symbol

This is used on packs to show that the food is 'microwavable', with details of how long and at what power the food should be heated in the microwave oven. Some food is already packed in microwavable containers so that it is ready to reheat.

■ Microwave symbol

Cooking instructions

Cooking instructions are given for food products that need to be cooked in an oven. Manufacturers use different symbols to show this.

■ Symbol that food may be cooked in an oven

Freezing instructions

If the product can be frozen, this is shown on the label with instructions.

■ Freezing symbol

Bar code

Most packets and labels contain a bar code. When the pack is passed over the scanner in the checkout, the scanner reads the code, registers the price and records the sale of the product for stocktaking.

■ Bar code

Litterman symbol

This symbol is used to encourage people to dispose of their litter properly in a suitable litter basket. It is most frequently used on snack foods such as crisps and cans of drink.

■ Litterman symbol

Environmentally friendly symbols

When recycled material has been used for packaging, these symbols are included.

■ Recycled symbol

▰ *Question* ▰

Explain why it is useful to have the following information on food packaging.
a nutrition information
b ingredients
c barcode
d litterman
e environmentally friendly symbol
f microwave instructions
g freezing instructions

Refer to the pizza label (opposite) in your explanation. Show how these instructions could be used for other foods. You could fill in a chart like the one shown below.

	Why is this information useful on the pizza label?	Why is this information useful on other foods?
Nutrition information		
Ingredients		
Bar code		
Litterman		
Environmentally friendly symbol		
Microwave instructions		
Freezing instructions		

REAL ITALIAN PIZZAS
• The taste of Italy •
MARGHERITA

400g ℮

`8 297421 001697`

COOKING INSTRUCTIONS

If serving to young children, allow to cool slightly.

For best results. COOK FROM FROZEN

1. Pre-heat oven to 200°C (400°F) or gas mark 6.
2. Remove all packaging.
3. Place pizza directly onto oven shelf and bake for 14-16 minutes until golden brown and the pizza is piping hot throughout.
4. Serve immediately.

NOT SUITABLE FOR MICROWAVE COOKING

As oven temperatures vary, cooking times may need to be adjusted to suit your own oven. For fan assisted ovens adjust temperature/time according to the manufacturer's handbook.

NUTRITIONAL INFORMATION

Typical Values	Amount per 100 g	Amount per Half Pizza
Energy	802 kJ/190 kcal	1798 kJ/405 kcal
Protein	9.3g	19.9g
Carbohydrate (of which sugars)	26.6g (0.2g)	56.6g (0.5g)
Fat (of which saturates)	5.2g (2.0g)	11.0g (4.2g)
Fibre	2.1g	4.4g
Sodium	0.5g	1.1g
Calcium	124mg (15% RDA*)	264mg (33% RDA*)
Iron	1.3mg (9% RDA*)	2.8mg (20% RDA*)

* Recommended Daily Allowance

STORAGE INSTRUCTIONS

Food Freezer	✱✱✱✱	†Until best before date
Star marked	✱✱✱	†Until best before date
frozen food	✱✱	1 month
compartment	✱	1 week
Ice making compartment		3 days
Refrigerator		24 hours

† Should be - 18°C or colder. Do not refreeze once thawed.

INGREDIENTS

WHEATFLOUR, WATER, MOZZARELLA MEDIUM FAT SOFT CHEESE, TOMATOES, OLIVE OIL, SALT, YEAST, OREGANO

Best Before End – NOV 96

Paganuzzi Pizza Company
Peckenham
ZZ14 2YZ

■ Note the symbols used on this pizza box

— To do —

Make a collection of food labels and make a display to show a range of the many symbols and information provided by the labels. Draw or cut out each symbol and explain why it is useful. You could fill in a chart like the one on the right. Suggest other symbols which could be included on food packaging labels. Write a report on your findings.

Symbol	Why is it useful?
Vegetarian symbol	Useful for vegetarians to make food choices when buying food

What is the function of packaging?

Packaging helps to:
- reduce food waste by protecting food from damage – e.g. eggs in cartons
- increase the life of a food – e.g. putting food in a can, gas-flushed packs
- give information on contents and shelf-life
- make food easier to handle, transport and store
- improve hygiene since food cannot be touched by hand.

Information on packaging

Packaging should carry the following information:
- product name and description
- instructions for use
- storage, shelf-life, weight, and name and address of the supplier.

Changing the gas inside packaging

With the introduction of new plastics, food manufacturers can adapt the types of gas used in the pack in order to increase the shelf-life of the product.

Modified atmosphere packaging (MAP) replaces most of the oxygen in food packaging with carbon dioxide and nitrogen gas. This process is used to pack ready-prepared salads, minced beef and other meats including bacon. The food looks, tastes and smells just like fresh food, but the change of gas slows down the growth of micro-organisms.

Vacuum packing removes all the air from a pack and keeps food in anaerobic conditions with no oxygen. Both these processes increase the shelf-life of foods. The EC is proposing that MAP foods should be labelled. Once the packs are opened, they have a normal shelf-life.

■ **A typical range of packaging**

Different types of packaging		
Packaging	*Advantages*	*Disadvantages*
Paper and board	Renewable resource, can be recycled, easily printed, strong and lightweight.	Doesn't protect food from damp, crushes easily. Food should not touch recycled paper because it could be contaminated with chemicals and other products which might be harmful to food it comes into contact with.
Plastic (PET, PVC, polyethylene, polypropylene, polystyrene)	Strong, but not as strong as glass or metal, lightweight, good barrier to moisture, flexible, can be printed, does not react with foods.	A limited resource, can be recycled but not easily. A litter problem.
Metal – aluminium and steel	Can be recycled – steel can be separated from aluminium using magnets. Strong and rigid, good barrier to water and gas, can be printed on easily.	Uses a lot of energy in extraction, cannot be microwaved, must be coated on inside, otherwise reacts with product.
Glass	Re-usable, easily recycled, good barrier to water, transparent, can be printed, can be microwaved.	Brittle and heavy and easily broken.

Tamper-proof packaging

After an number of scares in 1989 when baby food was contaminated with slivers of glass, many manufacturers have developed tamper-proof packaging. Examples include shrink-wrapped jars, paper strips over jam pot lids and plastic collars on lids.

■ Packaging showing tamper-proof devices

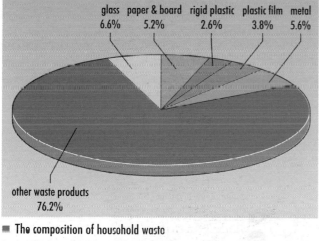

glass	paper & board	rigid plastic	plastic film	metal
6.6%	5.2%	2.6%	3.8%	5.6%

other waste products
76.2%

■ The composition of household waste

Source – 'Packaging', Sainsbury's *Living Today* leaflet

Waste from packaging

Nearly 25 per cent of the waste products we throw away in household rubbish is made up of packaging. The waste from packaging is made up of paper and board (5.2 per cent), rigid plastic (2.6 per cent), plastic film (3.8 per cent), glass (6.6 per cent), metal (5.6 per cent), which together give 23.8 per cent of the total waste produced.

Reducing the amount of packaging

We have already seen that nearly 25 per cent of our rubbish is made up of packaging. Here are some ways that packaging can be reduced.

- Manufacturers are trying to reduce the packaging for food products and use only what is essential.
- Shoppers are being encouraged to re-use containers and recycle them at centres such as bottle banks.
- In some parts of the country, tests on recycling plastic containers are being carried out.

— Questions —

1 Why is food packaging needed? Give five reasons.

2 Choose one type of material used for packaging and list its advantages and disadvantages.

3 What is meant by the following terms?
   a MAP   b vacuum packing
   c tamper-proof packaging

4 Suggest ten ways that the amount of packaging that we use for food products can be reduced.

— To do —

Carry out some research to find out how food is packaged. How necessary is all the packaging? Write a short report on your findings. You could use a chart like the one below. State your views on food packaging. What recommendations would you give food manufacturers on how to package their food products in the future, to reduce the amount of packaging used for their products?

Food product	Type of packaging	Is all the packaging needed?

When you buy goods, there are many ways in which you are protected. The law (Sale and Supply of Goods Act 1994) says that goods must be:

- **of a satisfactory quality** – which covers the appearance, finish, safety and durability of the goods. Goods must be free from defects, except where the seller has told you about them.
- **fit for their purpose** – so a non-stick pan should be non-stick
- **as described** – so the goods should be as described on the label.

All goods are covered by these statutory regulations.

What if things go wrong?

When you buy something, you and the seller have made a contract. The law gives you statutory rights. If there is something wrong with the goods, you must tell the person who sold them to you as soon as you can. The seller must sort out the complaint for you. It is not the responsibility of the manufacturer. If the goods are faulty, for example a jumper may have a hole in it, you are entitled to your money back. Most shops will ask for proof of purchase to deal with your complaint.

How to make a complaint

- Go back to the shop as soon as possible and take the goods with you.
- Take some proof of purchase.
- Explain the problem and say what you want to be done.
- If you are not satisfied with the reply, write to the customer services manager or think about taking the matter to court.

Writing to make a complaint

- If you write a letter, make your complaint very clear.
- Describe the goods, and when and where you bought them.
- Explain the problem, what action you have taken, who you dealt with and what happened.
- Say what you want done.
- Keep copies of anything you send.

Who can help?

Trading Standards Departments

The address and telephone number of your local Trading Standards Department can be found in the telephone book, under your county, metropolitan district or London borough council. They

■ Citizens' Advice Bureaux are found all around the country

investigate false or misleading descriptions or prices, inaccurate weights and measures and the safety of goods.

Citizens' Advice Bureaux (CAB)

The addresses and telephone numbers of these organizations can be found in the telephone book. They give advice on shopping problems and going to court.

Environmental Health Departments

These are part of your county, metropolitan district or London borough council and their addresses and telephone numbers can also be found in the telephone book. Environmental Health Departments deal with health matters such as unfit food and drink, dirty shops and restaurants.

The Office of Fair Trading

The Office of Fair Trading is a Government department with a wide range of duties for protecting consumers. This includes watching out for trading practices which might be bad for consumers, and identifying traders who might mislead or deceive consumers.

Questions

1 How does the Sale and Supply of Goods Act 1994 protect you when you buy goods?
2 If the goods you buy are not up to standard, how would you complain and sort things out?
3 What officials can help you to get information to support your complaint?

What about food?

The law gives protection when you buy food. The Food Safety Act 1990 makes it an offence to sell unfit food, or to describe food falsely, or to mislead people about its nature, substance or quality, including nutritional value.

Regulations cover food hygiene where food is sold, made, packed, processed or stored for sale.

Food Labelling Regulations 1984, which are replaced by **Food Labelling Regulations 1995**, state that food should be clearly labelled so that you know what you are buying.

Labels must include the name of the contents, a list of ingredients in descending order of weight, any food additives used and the address of the manufacturer. The label must also show the date by which the food must be eaten. Local authorities are responsible for enforcing these regulations.

The Weights and Measures Act 1985 states that the quantity of the contents must be marked on the packaging to show the contents by weight, volume or number. There are exceptions to this. The Act makes it an offence to give short weight or inadequate quantity, or to mark goods with the wrong amount. Most pre-packed goods must be sold in prescribed metric quantities. For example flour should be sold in quantities of 125 g, 250 g, 500 g, 1000 g and larger amounts.

The **average system** of quantity control has been in operation since 1979. The packer must make up the packages so that the quantity is within limits laid down by law. Trading Standards Officers are responsible for enforcing the law and making sure that weights, measures and scales are accurate. Packers, importers and traders who do not conform to the weights and measures regulations can be prosecuted and fined.

Questions

1 How are consumers protected by law if they buy faulty goods?
2 What Acts and Regulations protect us when buying food?

To do

Imagine that you have bought faulty goods from a shop. Write a letter of complaint to the shop suggesting what action you want to be taken. What information would you include with your letter?

We care about the quality of everything we buy. Look around a food market and count the signs for, for example, 'best quality tomatoes', 'finest English celery' or 'freshly picked strawberries'.

'Quality' means different things to different people. In recent years the European Union and the food industry have agreed terms for the quality of many foods.

Food and the European Union

The UK is a member state of the European Union. Common EU legislation is being developed in many areas including food. The aim is to establish a common market with similar standards for each member state. This means food labels will be similar throughout the European Union and there will be standards for food quality.

The Food Safety Act 1990 includes a statement on quality: 'it is an offence to sell any food which is not of the nature, substance or quality demanded by the purchaser.'

How do consumers judge food quality?

When people buy food, they want to know:
● How fresh is it?
● Does it look good?
● Does it smell right?
● How reliable is the person selling the food?

All these statements refer to the quality of the food.

Taste is also an important food quality which is sometimes forgotten. Strawberries, for example, may arrive in the shop looking red and delicious but with little taste.

Here are some terms used by the food industry in relation to quality.

Quality standards

As food technology has increased in complexity, quality standards and controls during production have increased too.

Quality control is a system for testing and inspecting food during its production and distribution.

■ Tesco Quality symbol

Quality assurance is a system which can apply to all levels of food production to make sure that the end product is safe and meets quality standards.

British Standards 5750 (ISO9000 in US and EN2900 in Europe)

This certificate (BS5750) was developed for the engineering sector and is used by many UK businesses. To get a certificate a company has to show that it has quality controls for all levels of management.

Hazard Analysis and Critical Control Points (HACCP)

This system assesses the **hazards** for every stage of manufacture and identifies critical control points at which risks need to be monitored. A HACCP system helps to make sure that the food product is safe to eat. An egg is a high-risk food. When it is used to glaze food products such as sausage rolls to make them shiny and golden, the glazing process is a risk which needs to be controlled. This involves trying to avoid cross-contamination with other foods (see page 144 for explanation of cross-contamination). The point at which the egg is used for glazing is a **critical control point** in the making of the sausage roll. Every effort must be made to avoid cross-contamination of other foods by clearing away the egg glaze once it is used and thoroughly washing any brushes used for glazing, in very hot water. The sausage rolls must also be baked to a high enough temperature to make sure the egg glaze is cooked. By this process the risk of salmonella poisoning from the egg (see page 146) will be reduced or eliminated.

═ *Questions* ═

1   What do you think is meant by the 'quality' of a food product?
2   What is meant by the following terms?
    a quality control   b quality assurance
    c BS 5750   d HACCP

Where do most people shop for food?

There is a wide choice of places to buy food. You can use corner shops, supermarkets, superstores, street markets, and even buy food by post and have home deliveries of food like pizza.

Supermarkets and the local stores

Supermarkets and superstores are able to buy large quantities of food in bulk and can cut the cost of food products to their customers. Many people travel to these stores by car or public transport since the stores are often situated on out-of-town sites. This can increase traffic. Out-of-town shopping also means that local, smaller shops are likely to suffer from loss in trade, since they have to charge higher prices for their goods. However, local shops can sell local produce such as vegetables and fruit.

The chart below shows the decline of small shops and rise in supermarket shopping since 1950.

Shopping in the future

By the year 2000 it is possible that one in six families will be shopping for food from home. In 1994 in Britain we spent £6.52 billion on goods bought from home. Seventy per cent of women in Britain go out to work, and supermarkets are developing ways that people can place orders using their home computers.

Virtual reality shopping could be a trend in the future. Shoppers will put on a virtual reality headset and 'move' around the supermarket from their armchair at home. Researchers are investigating how shoppers can choose what they want to buy by pressing buttons as they whiz down the aisles. The supermarkets may then arrange home deliveries.

■ Despite the growth in supermarket shopping many people still buy food at local shops and markets

▬ *Questions* ▬

1 List the advantages and the disadvantages of buying food from:
   a supermarkets **b** small corner shops.
   Give three ideas in each case.

2 Look at the chart on this page which shows the changes in shopping habits. Use the information to explain what is happening to shopping trends in Britain.

3 How do you think people will be buying food in the year 2100?

▬ *Investigation* ▬

1 Investigate the differences in prices of similar foods sold in a small shop compared with a large supermarket. You need to choose products with the same label for this comparison, for example Heinz Baked Beans. Comment on your findings. What do you think will happen to small food shops in the future? What is the function of the small shop for the local community? Give examples to explain your answer.

2 Do you think small food shops are losing business if people are buying their food from large supermarkets? Carry out some research to find out what is happening to small food shops in your area. Are they losing business? Has the amount of food they sell declined over recent years? You could ask them to explain the shopping trends for food in your area. Write a report on your findings.

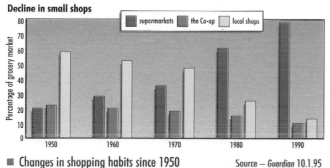

Decline in small shops

Legend: supermarkets | the Co-op | local shops

(Percentage of grocery market, years 1950, 1960, 1970, 1980, 1990)

■ Changes in shopping habits since 1950   Source — *Guardian* 10.1.95

Shopping trends

*H*ow do we know how people in the UK shop for food and other products?

The **National Food Survey** investigates the changing patterns of household food consumption in the UK. Each year about 8000 households take part in the survey. The person who does the shopping is asked questions about the household and its food purchasing. They keep a diary for seven days, recording the food that comes into the household – the amount and how much it costs – and details of household meals. The survey has been run for over 50 years so the report can show long-term trends in eating and shopping habits. For example, since the 1940s people are gradually eating fewer fresh potatoes and since the 1980s people have been buying more low-fat spreads.

Nutrition information

Food scientists use the survey results to estimate the average amount of foods people eat and work out the average nutrition intake. Nutritional information covers calories and about 40 vitamins, minerals, sugars and fats. Nutrient intakes can be compared with the recommendations by the Department of Health to show how diets meet current dietary guidelines.

Trends for 1991–3
- People spent less on eggs, fats, fruit and drinks.
- People spent more on meat and meat products.
- More soft and alcoholic drinks and sweets were consumed.

Source – National Food Survey

The pie chart below shows the percentage of household spending on the main food groups in 1993.

Family spending on food

Research shows that the amount spent on food per head decreases as the number of adults and children in the household increases. This may be because there is less wastage of food and ingredients, and that meals for six can cost only a little more than meals for four, but there are many other factors which could contribute to the results of this research.

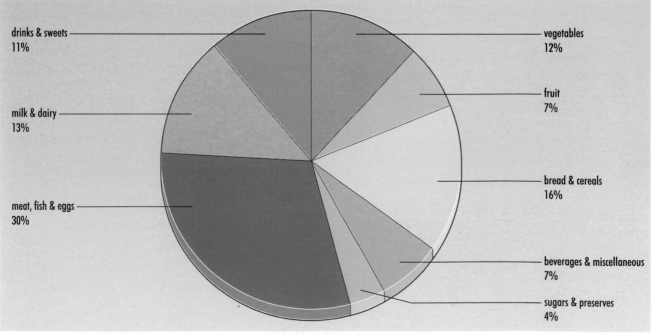

drinks & sweets 11%

milk & dairy 13%

meat, fish & eggs 30%

vegetables 12%

fruit 7%

bread & cereals 16%

beverages & miscellaneous 7%

sugars & preserves 4%

■ Household spending on food and drink for 1993

Source – National Food Survey

Consumption figures for the main food groups (per person per week)			
	1991 (ounces)	1992 (ounces)	1993 (ounces)
Milk and cream	3.74	3.91	3.84
Cheese	4.11	4.01	3.85
Meat and meat products	33.93	33.52	33.71
Fish	4.90	4.99	5.10
Eggs (number)	2.25	2.08	1.92
Fats and oils	8.76	8.66	8.11
Sugar and preserves	7.67	7.10	6.82
Vegetables	78.42	77.36	75.98
Fruit	33.56	32.79	33.12
Cereals including bread	51.30	51.57	51.53
Soft drinks (fl oz)	22.92	25.39	27.25
Confectionery (g)	not available	50.92	52.27

Source — National Food Survey

This chart shows the consumption for main food groups. The weights are in ounces, except where indicated (1 ounce ≈ 25 g).

Questions

1 How does the National Food Survey gather information about people's eating habits?
2 Why is the information useful?
3 What were the changes in food trends from 1991 to 1993?

To do

Write a brief report which could be used as a newspaper article explaining the trends in our eating habits. Support your article with data from the table from the National Food Survey.

For example:

Since 1991 egg consumption has dropped from 2.25 to 1.92 eggs per person each week. This may be due to the 'salmonella in eggs' scare in 1989.

■ The National Food Survey shows that we are eating more fish

■ A local supermarket offers a range of food products

The number of households has been increasing in Britain since World War 2, partly because households now contain fewer people. The average number of people in a household has dropped since the 1960s. In 1961 the average household size was 3.1 people. In 1993 the average household size was 2.4 people. There is a large increase in the number of people living alone.

Since 1971, the largest group of people living alone has been women over pensionable age. By 2001 nearly one in ten households will be made up of a man under pensionable age living alone, compared with one in thirty in 1971.

Trends in families

Since the 1970s there have been great changes in the way families live together. The number of traditional family households with two parents and two children is declining. The number of single parents living with their dependent children is small but growing in size. Women have delayed having children or chosen to remain childless, so there are more childless couples in their twenties.

Households classified by size					
Household size	*1961*	*1971*	*1981*	*1991*	*1993*
1 person	14	18	22	27	27
2 people	30	32	32	34	35
3 people	23	19	17	16	16
4 people	18	17	18	16	15
5 people	9	8	7	5	5
6 or more people	7	6	4	2	2
average household size	3.1	2.9	2.7	2.5	2.4

Source – 'Social Trends', CSO

The size of household varies with ethnic groups. The above chart shows the differences in the proportion of single-person households and those with dependent children.

Households

In 1994, 29 per cent of white households were single people living alone. This compares with 31 per cent of black households and seven per cent of Pakistani/ Bangladeshi households.

A high proportion of white single-person households are elderly people. The white population has a higher proportion of elderly people than other groups do.

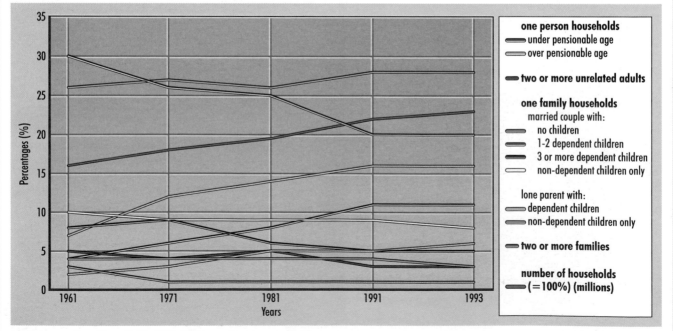

■ The composition of households, 1961–1993

Spending on food

Single-adult households have the highest average spending on food, per person.

Convenience foods are popular with households with children. Research shows that the higher the number of children in the household, the higher proportion of the food budget will be spent on convenience foods.

Household income

The chart below shows the increase in **disposable income** per head in the period from 1971 to 1993. Disposable income is the amount of money that people have to spend after taxes and contributions have been taken off. The chart shows that average incomes have risen since 1971.

Family spending on food

Research shows that the amount spent on food per head decreases as the number of people in a household increases. There are many factors which can be used to explain the results of this research. One theory is that as family size increases, less food is wasted, and the cost of providing a meal for six is little more than the cost of a meal for four. It may also be that the total income for the family is limited and the money has to be divided among more people if the family is larger.

Changing patterns in what we eat in the home

The chart below shows how our eating habits are changing. We are slowly changing to a healthier diet.

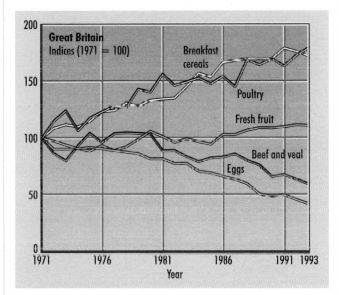

■ Changing patterns in the consumption of foods at home

Source – Ministry of Agriculture, Fisheries and Food

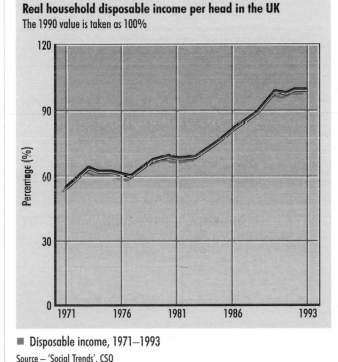

■ Disposable income, 1971–1993

Source – 'Social Trends', CSO

Questions

1 In your own words, explain what is happening to the average size of families in Britain today.

2 Shops are selling more and more ready meals for one, and small portions of food. Using the information on family trends, explain why there is a demand for this size of food product.

3 What is meant by disposable income? Do you think British people could afford to spend more on food? Give reasons for your answer.

*O*ver £600 million is spent every year on advertising food. The biggest spenders on advertising include the manufacturers of chocolate, crisps, snacks and sweets.

What is advertising?

Advertising provides information about products and services and aims to give consumers reasons to buy things. Most new products need to be advertised so that people know they are available. Advertisements should target the group most likely to buy the product and give them information they might need.

Where a product will be advertised depends upon:

- the target audience – what they read and watch or listen to
- the advertising budget available to spend on the project.

Other ways to promote a product include:

- special offers
- gifts
- competitions.

The pie chart below shows the percentage breakdown of types of advertising used in the UK.

Advertising

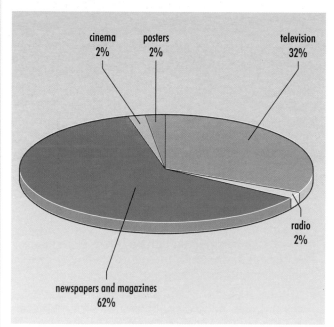

cinema 2%   posters 2%   television 32%

radio 2%

newspapers and magazines 62%

How are food products advertised and promoted?

There are different ways of advertising and promoting products, including:

- TV, radio and cinema advertisements
- newspapers and magazines
- posters by the side of the road, in shops and buildings
- displays in shops and markets
- competitions and promotions
- leaflet distribution to homes and in the streets.

'**Below the line**' advertising includes direct mail, competitions, sponsorship, in-store samplings, point-of-sale advertising, door-to-door drops.

How effective is advertising?

When Nick Kamen took off his Levi 501s in the launderette, the sales rose by 800 per cent and the advertisement had to come off the air so that the Levi manufacturers could catch up with production.

Complaints about advertising in the UK

Most complaints about misleading advertisements are a matter for either the **Trading Standards Department** or the **Advertising Standards Authority** (**ASA**).

The ASA is an independent body which oversees self-regulatory codes of practice drawn up by the advertising industry. Its sanctions include the generation of adverse publicity, the denial of advertising space, loss of trading privileges and/or discounts and ultimately, referral to the **Office of Fair Trading** for legal action. The codes require advertisements to be *legal, decent, honest and truthful* and they apply to all non-broadcast advertising.

An example of a complaint upheld against food advertisers (*summarized*)

An advertisement for a sports drink claimed, 'The unique formulation of new Isostar Long Energy delivers maximum carbohydrate loading with the speed of isotonic absorption in a great satisfying drink.'

The ASA obtained expert advice and concluded that, although the product was within the Association of Dietetic Food Industries in the EC guidelines for isotonicity, the total level of carbohydrate in the product exceeded the generally accepted maximum for isotonic drinks. The Authority considered that the evidence submitted by the advertisers did not show that the drink was absorbed as quickly as other isotonic drinks and therefore asked for the advertisement to be amended.

■ The logo of the Advertising Standards Authority

Questions

1 Why do you think marketing and advertising are important when a food manufacturer makes a new product?

2 How is advertising controlled in the UK? Why do you think controls on advertising are needed?

3 Explain where you would expect to see food products advertised.

To do

Make a collection of food advertisements from newspapers and magazines.

Choose two advertisements and complete a chart like the one below.

	Advertisement 1	Advertisement 2
Description of product		
Where is the advert from?		
What is the target group for the product?		
What is the message of the advert?		
In your opinion, why is this a good (or bad) advert?		
Would you buy the product?		

Marketing

What is marketing?

Marketing a product takes understanding and skill in appealing to a target group of people (the market), discovering what they want and then providing it. Marketing is the term for finding, serving and keeping customers.

Marketing is used to find out the demand for the goods and services and to discover how to encourage people to buy them.

People have certain needs. A **product** or a **service** should be designed to meet a need.

- **Products** include food, kitchen equipment, motor cars – goods which we buy.
- **Services** include shoe repairing, letter delivery, servicing the washing machine.

When a new product is being developed for sale, the designers need to consider:

- **what** the consumer wants to buy – the **market trends**
- **why** they will want to buy it – whether it is cheap, attractive, convenient
- **when** they buy it – a snack food could be bought by people on the move
- **where** they buy it – snack foods could be bought from garages or newsagents
- **who** will buy it – snack foods may appeal to teenagers.

Large businesses have **marketing departments** whose role is to keep track of market trends, to find out what people need and want to buy and to make sure the goods and services they are offering are meeting the demand and standard required.

Marketing a product

There are four main factors to consider when marketing a product. These are known as the **four Ps**:

- the **product** – is it what people need or want?
- the **price** – is it sold at the price that people are willing to pay?
- the **place** – is it sold in the right place, where people will go to buy it?
- the **promotion** – is it promoted effectively by advertising, special offers, displays?

Market research

Market research is used to help businesses plan how they will promote and advertise a product. It also helps find out if there is a need for a product or service. Market researchers need to think about:

- what they need to find out about the product or service
- where and how it is possible to get this information
- why this information is needed and how it can be useful.

Different ways of carrying out market research include:

- **direct research** from the public using telephone, personal and group interviews, tasting and testing sessions, questionnaires
- **secondary research** using existing information including reports such as 'Social Trends', computer databases and CD ROMs.

Research can be:

- **quantitative** – using questionnaires and interviews
- **qualitative** – asking small groups of people for their opinions on products.

A market trend is a pattern or change in the way people buy things.

■ A market researcher at work

— To do —

Invent two food products of your own – one savoury and one sweet.

1 Complete a chart like the one below to show why people might need these products, what price they will be sold at and why, where they will be sold, and what promotion you will use. One example has been completed for you.

2 For each product answer the questions What, Why, When, Where and Who? as shown on page 176. Explain why you think your products might sell well.

3 Explain what kind of research you need to carry out to see if your products will be successful with your target groups. Draw up a questionnaire to show the questions you will ask to find out if people think your products will be successful.

4 Many food products are tested by tasting panels to see if people like them. Describe the questions you will ask the tasting panel to find out what they think about your products.

	Example	Your product (savoury)	Your product (sweet)
Product	Gary's Pasta Sauce – a delicious range of high-quality sauces by a well-known chef.		
Price	£1.20 for a 500 ml jar		
Place	Supermarkets, with the other pasta sauces		
Promotion	Gary will do a series of TV adverts, there will be in-store handouts, and recipes in magazines.		

— Investigation —

Products are usually aimed at a target group – for example, teenagers, young mothers or householders. On the right is the classification one company used in their market research. They were then able to sort the data into a variety of categories. For example they could find the responses from households with four people (two of them children), social class C1, with the head of the household aged between 35 and 44 and working full-time.

Investigate how market researchers classify their target groups when they carry out market research. You may need to ask a market researcher who is conducting research in the street or in shopping precincts. The Business Studies department in your school may be able to put you in touch with organizations which conduct market research in your area. Find out why it is useful to use the classification shown on the right to carry out research into whether new food products should be developed. Write a report on your findings.

Classification

1 Occupation of head of household
2 Social class: A B C1 C2 D E
3 Size of household: 1 2 3 4 5+
4 Age: 16–24 25–34 35–44 45–54 55–64
5 Working status:
    full time (30 hours or more)
    part time (8–29 hours)
    not working (up to 8 hours).
6 Number of children under 16

Social class is a way of classifying people by job or income. These are the groups.

A   Higher managerial, administrative or professional
B   Intermediate managerial, administrative or professional
C1 Supervisory, clerical, junior administrative or professional
C2 Skilled manual workers
D   Semi-skilled and unskilled manual workers
E   State pensioners, widows, casual and lowest grade earners

Appearance

The way food looks, tastes and smells is very important. Before we eat we usually look at the food first and decide whether we want to eat it.

How do we judge the appearance of food? We might judge if it looks fresh, healthy or appetizing. The presentation of the food is important. Food should be served on clean, attractive dishes which complement the food.

Colour

We expect food to be a certain colour and may reject it if the colour is not familiar. We might reject raw apple that had gone brown, or green custard, because these are not colours that we would expect. Food manufacturers may add colours to food products to make them more attractive.

It is important to try to include a range of colours when serving a meal. An all-white meal such as rice and fish in white sauce needs livening up with extra colour, such as chopped or sprigged parsley.

Food can be decorated with a garnish to add colour to the dish. Savoury garnishes include twists of lemon or cucumber, slices of tomato, chopped parsley, and fried onion rings. Fresh, sliced fruit can be used to garnish sweet food.

Temperature matters

Hot food should be served hot, and not left to keep warm and so become dried up and tired. Cold food should be kept chilled until it is ready to serve. If food is stored for too long in the danger zone (5–63°C) it can become unsafe to eat.

Texture

We judge food by its texture. Soggy chips are not appealing, and we usually prefer a well-risen cake to one that looks flat and dry.

Again, it is important to include a range of textures in a meal. The rice with fish in white sauce may need the addition of food with a crunchy texture such as a tossed salad.

■ The appearance and presentation of food are important factors in making a meal appetizing

Smell

Smell matters. If something smells burnt we don't want to eat it. Our sense of smell is very useful in judging the safety of food, since we can smell 'off' flavours in food and reject them. Smell is part of the attraction of food – the smell of baking bread is very tempting.

Taste and flavour

Taste is detected by the taste buds in the mouth. Different areas of the tongue can detect the four basic tastes: sweet, sour, bitter and saltiness. The flavour of food is a combination of taste and smell. If we have a cold, we cannot taste food properly.

How does it sound?

We also judge food on its sound. Think of the crunch of an apple or piece of celery, the snap of a crisp biscuit or crisps, and even the 'snap, crackle and pop' of some breakfast cereals.

Sensory analysis

Tasting food during the development of a product is known as **sensory analysis**. This is used throughout food product development to make judgements about the quality of food. Sensory analysis has been defined as:

A *scientific discipline used to analyse and interpret reactions to the characteristics of food as they are perceived by the senses of sight, smell, taste and hearing.*

Source – *Institute of Food Technologists*

Everyone's perception of taste is slightly different, so when food is tasted professionally, the tasting panel needs to agree on the terminology used to describe food. The Institute of Food Technology Companies has definition lists to make sure that people on the tasting panel understand the meaning of the words they are using. For example:
- 'wet is an immediate increase in the free fluids in the mouth'
- 'juicy is a progressive increase in the free fluids in the mouth'.

Sensory descriptors

When we taste food, we are judging:
- appearance and colour
- taste and flavour
- 'mouthfeel'/texture and consistency
- smell or odour.

The words used to describe these factors are known as **sensory descriptors**. These include:
- **appearance and colour** – attractive, healthy, greasy, creamy, golden, orange, bright, dull
- **taste and flavour** – fruity, sweet, bitter, sour, salty, sharp, spicy, tangy
- **'mouthfeel'/texture, consistency** – hard, soft, rubbery, crispy, lumpy, dry, smooth,
- **smell or odour** – fragrant, burnt, herby, garlicky, fishy.

Questions

1 Create your own word bank of sensory descriptors that can be used to describe food products.	2 Describe the appearance, taste, mouthfeel and smell of the following foods. **a** an apple **b** hot bread **c** a fizzy fruit drink Add examples of your own. You could use a chart like the one below.

Food appearance and colour	Mouthfeel / texture, consistency	Taste and flavour	Smell or odour

Setting up a tasting panel

When you want to test out the foods you have made you need a tasting panel. You could use just a few people in your tasting panel or get the views of many. You need to instruct them clearly and design a tasting chart for them to complete.

Setting up a tasting area

Everyone has different perceptions of tastes, so the tasters should understand that no-one has the 'right' answer. During a tasting session, the tasters should not talk or share ideas, or look at the expressions on the faces of other tasters.

Tips on tasting food

- Set up a special, quiet, well-lit tasting area.
- Put food in identical, plain containers and serve all samples in the same way at the same temperature.
- Allow each taster to sip water or eat a plain biscuit in between each tasting to clear the palate.
- Don't give tasters too much to taste otherwise their taste buds get tired.
- Code the samples of food randomly to avoid the tasters having a preference – for example, use three random numbers or three random letters, such as 327 or DTH. Avoid using single numbers such as 1,2 or 3 as these numbers can imply that the food already has an order, for example, 1st, 2nd and 3rd. Similarly A, B and C imply there is an order to the food choices since A is often thought to be the first or highest result in a test.
- Make sure the tasters understand how to taste the food and fill in any charts.

Fair testing

Fair testing is important when tasting and comparing similar food products. Make sure that you are comparing like with like. If you are tasting apples, do not include pears in the tasting session! Food should be served in similar sized portions, on similar plates or cups, and at the same temperature.

At the foot of this page is an example of a tasting chart that can be used to test food products.

Sensory analysis

Different tests are used in sensory analysis to obtain different kinds of information.

Ranking test

This test sorts foods into an order. For example, the tasters could be asked to place five yogurts in order, starting with the one they like best. The taster should also be asked to rank the yogurts in order of sweetness.

Ranking test	Name _____	
Please taste the samples and put them in the order you like best.		
sample code	order	comments
○		
□		
△		
■		

■ A ranking test

Tick one box in each column.

Overall opinion on food	**Appearance**	**Taste**	**Smell**	**Texture**
☐ like very much	☐ like very much	☐ like very much	☐ like very much	☐ like very much
☐ like moderately	☐ like moderately	☐ like moderately	☐ like moderately	☐ like moderately
☐ neither like nor dislike	☐ neither like nor dislike	☐ neither like nor dislike	☐ neither like nor dislike	☐ neither like nor dislike
☐ dislike	☐ dislike	☐ dislike	☐ dislike	☐ dislike
☐ dislike a lot	☐ dislike a lot	☐ dislike a lot	☐ dislike a lot	☐ dislike a lot

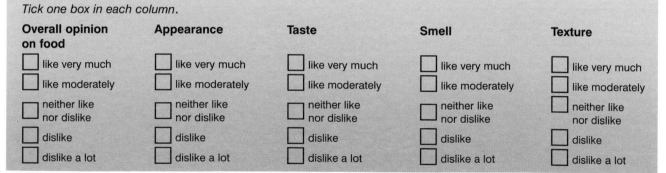

■ A food tasting chart

Rating test

In this test the foods are given a score on a scale of, say, 1 to 5. The scale could be shown graphically and the taster has to mark the point on the line which seems appropriate.

When tasting cheese the graph could range from extremely strong to extremely mild. This is an example of a five-point rating scale:

1 dislike a lot
2 dislike a little
3 neither like nor dislike
4 like a little
5 like a lot.

Rating test	○	□	△	■
1 dislike a lot	1	1	I	I
2 dislike a little	2	2	2	2
3 neither like nor dislike	3	3	3	3
4 like a little	4	4	4	4
5 like a lot	5	5	5	5

■ A rating test

Pictures can be used to help with the rating. This can be useful when working with children.

Rating Score	1 ☹	2 ☹	3 😐	4 🙂	5 😄
sample △					
sample □					
sample ○					

■ A rating test using pictures

— *Did you know?* —

Star profile

A star profile can show the sensory descriptors for the food. People on the tasting panel can rate each sensory descriptor to give the product a tasting profile. The results can be compared to see what people think about the product.

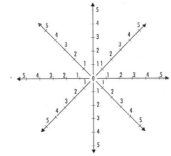

■ A star profile

Triangle tests

Triangle tests are used to see if people can tell the difference between food products. For example, can they tell the difference between one brand of crisp and another? These tests are used by food companies when they want to develop a 'me too' product – one that may be similar to another already on the market.

Triangle test
Name _____
Two of the samples are the same. One is different. Tick the odd one out.
Samples   Tick the odd one out
_____   _____
_____   _____
_____

■ A triangle test

— *Questions* —

1. Draw a star profile for each of the following foods to show the sensory descriptors you would use in a tasting session.
   a tomato and cheese pizza   **b** fruit yogurt
   c salt and vinegar crisps   **d** apple pie
2. Why do you think food companies need to carry out tasting sessions for their food product development? Think of as many reasons as you can and try to explain why they are important.

Using a computer for food work

A computer can be used in many ways to improve and speed up work on food.

The chart at the foot of this page shows the types of programs available and how they can be used in different ways. Choose the program that is appropriate for your skills and needs.

Using a computer for food work

Here are some examples to show the use of computer programs for food work.

Using a spreadsheet

The star profile on the right shows the results of tasting a tomato sauce. The tasting panel had to mark the sauce according to the eight criteria and give each of the criteria a score out of 5. These were the criteria used for tasting the tomato sauce:

1 chunky   **2** garlicky   **3** tomatoey   **4** sweet
5 spicy   **6** salty   **7** fruity   **8** rich.

A score of 0 meant that the sauce was, for example, 'not salty', a score of 3 meant that the sauce was 'quite salty' and a score of 5 meant that the sauce was 'very salty'.

The results were entered onto a spreadsheet that can draw a star profile to show the results of the tasting session as shown in the printout.

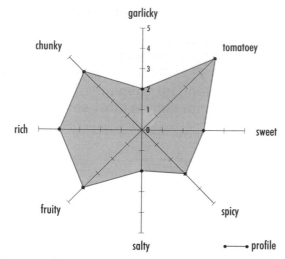

■ A printout of a star profile of the results of a tasting of tomato sauce

Using a spreadsheet

The chart at the top of page 183 shows how the same results from the same computer program using a spreadsheet can be presented using a bar chart.

A spreadsheet can also be used to keep a record of the cost of ingredients used in food preparation. The cost of basic ingredients can be stored in the spreadsheet. Then when a recipe is used, the information on the spreadsheet can be used to work out the cost of the finished dish. The

Types of programs used for work on food

Type of program	How it can be used
Word processing	Used for writing letters, creating questionnaires, writing up coursework.
Databases	
a nutritional database	Nutritional database – used to analyse recipes and modify them to make them healthier, working out daily diet, menu creation.
b recipe database	Recipe database – Used for storing recipes and identifying ingredients.
c information search	Information search – databases are available on CD ROM, encyclopaedias, up-to-date information on food issues for research.
Spreadsheets	Spreadsheets are used for calculations such as the cost of a recipe, how to increase the size of a recipe to serve larger numbers of people and costing a product for sale.
Graphics from spreadsheets	You can quickly display the information on a spreadsheet in the form of graphs, pie charts, and radar charts. This improves the presentation and accuracy of your work.
Graphics program	This can be used to produce drawings, logos and package designs and for experimental work in colour for labels. Images can be scanned in, using a scanner, and adapted on screen.
Desktop publishing	Coursework can be presented very smartly using a desktop publishing package. Text and pictures can be created on the screen and page layouts designed.
Control programs	Special programs can monitor temperature changes in food as it cooks and record the results and display them on a screen or printout.

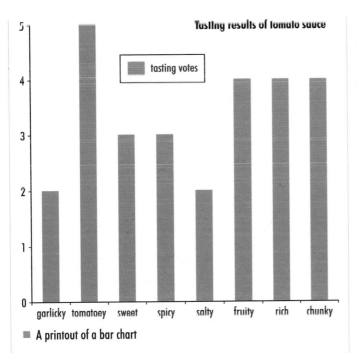

■ A printout of a bar chart

printout below shows how the spreadsheet is set up to store the cost of some items. The program has been used to calculate the cost of a gram of each food. The amount of food used in the recipe can be entered onto the spreadsheet and the cost of that weight of food calculated.

food	cost	weight in grams	cost per g	date bought
apples red	45	500	0.009	
apples cooking	39	500	0.078	
apples cox	50	500	0.1	
bacon	135	500	0.27	
baked beans	21	400	0.0525	
banana	45	500	0.09	

■ Printout of spreadsheet information

Nutritional analysis programs

Nutritional analysis programs can be used to work out the nutritional value of food products. One nutritional analysis program which is used in schools is 'Nutrients'. This program has a data bank of dietary information which contains details of the nutritional value of many foods. The dietary reference values (DRVs) for various age groups are included, so it is possible to analyse someone's diet and compare the results with the recommended amounts of each nutrient. The program also includes the facility to produce a label showing the nutritional value of the food made.

'QUICHE'

This data file contains the following foods:

Food No. 182	Flour – wholemeal	125 grams
Food No. 258	Margarine (low-fat spread)	30 grams
Food No. 232	Leeks – boiled	30 grams
Food No. 16	Bacon rashers – raw	75 grams
Food No. 109	Cheese – Parmesan	75 grams
Food No. 169	Egg white	100 grams
Food No. 269	Milk – skimmed	125 grams
Food No. 293	Onions – boiled	100 grams

■ A printout from the 'Nutrients' program

Databases

A database can be used to store a variety of information about food, including how cheese is used in a variety of recipes, and recipes suitable for gluten-free diets, low-calorie recipes and recipes suitable for young children. The example below shows how the database has been set up to keep a record of how additives are used in food products, what they are used for and examples of the food products in which they are used. This information can be used and sorted for projects and coursework which might include research on the use of additives in food products.

additive	use	food example
lactic acid	acidity regulator	soured cream dip
sodium citrate	acidity regulator	fruit pies
E304, E307	antioxidant	turkey escalopes
sodium ascorbate	antioxidant	bacon topper
butylated hydroxyanisole	antioxidant	spaghetti bolognaise
chlorophyllins	colour	soured cream dip
capsanthin	colour	turkey escalopes
annatto	colour	margarine, apple sponge

■ A printout of information from a database

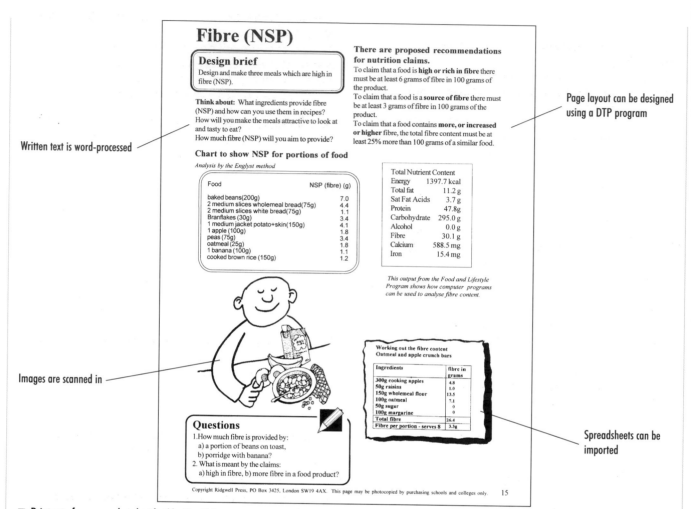

Page layout can be designed using a DTP program

Written text is word-processed

Images are scanned in

Spreadsheets can be imported

Fibre (NSP)

Design brief
Design and make three meals which are high in fibre (NSP).

Think about: What ingredients provide fibre (NSP) and how can you use them in recipes? How will you make the meals attractive to look at and tasty to eat? How much fibre (NSP) will you aim to provide?

Chart to show NSP for portions of food

Analysis by the Englyst method

Food	NSP (fibre) (g)
baked beans(200g)	7.0
2 medium slices wholemeal bread(75g)	4.4
2 medium slices white bread(75g)	1.1
Branflakes (30g)	3.4
1 medium jacket potato+skin(150g)	4.1
1 apple (100g)	1.8
peas (75g)	3.4
oatmeal (25g)	1.8
1 banana (100g)	1.1
cooked brown rice (150g)	1.2

There are proposed recommendations for nutrition claims.
To claim that a food is **high or rich in fibre** there must be at least 6 grams of fibre in 100 grams of the product.
To claim that a food is a **source of fibre** there must be at least 3 grams of fibre in 100 grams of the product.
To claim that a food contains **more, or increased or higher** fibre, the total fibre content must be at least 25% more than 100 grams of a similar food.

Total Nutrient Content	
Energy	1397.7 kcal
Total fat	11.2 g
Sat Fat Acids	3.7 g
Protein	47.8g
Carbohydrate	295.0 g
Alcohol	0.0 g
Fibre	30.1 g
Calcium	588.5 mg
Iron	15.4 mg

This output from the Food and Lifestyle Program shows how computer programs can be used to analyse fibre content.

Working out the fibre content
Oatmeal and apple crunch bars

Ingredients	fibre in grams
300g cooking apples	4.8
50g raisins	1.0
150g wholemeal flour	13.5
100g oatmeal	7.1
50g sugar	0
100g margarine	0
Total fibre	26.4
Fibre per portion - serves 8	3.3g

Questions
1. How much fibre is provided by:
   a) a portion of beans on toast,
   b) porridge with banana?
2. What is meant by the claims:
   a) high in fibre, b) more fibre in a food product?

■ Printout of page produced with *Aldus PageMaker*

Using a desktop publishing package

A desktop publishing package can be used to smarten up the presentation of coursework. You can design your page layout on the screen and manipulate text and images in the form of pictures. Entire books can be designed and laid out using desktop publishing packages. The example shows how a page from a book has been designed using Aldus PageMaker, a desktop publishing package.

Note: There are hundreds of different computer programs which can be used to create spreadsheets, databases, graphic presentations and desktop publishing like the examples given on this page. If you are using the school computer system for your work, check with your IT department and ask about the latest programs that meet your needs.

— To do —

Investigate the range of computer programs available in your school to help with a variety of work. Record your findings in a chart like the one below. Find out how each type of program can be used for food work, and try to use each program as part of a food activity. Present your results using a computer program, if possible.

Type of program	Programs available
Word processing	
Databases	
Spreadsheets	
Graphics program	
Desktop publishing	

Further information

Useful names and addresses

Berrydales Publishers, 5 Lawn Road, London NW3 2XS
Special Diet News – a regular newsletter on special diets

British Diabetic Association, 10 Queen Anne St, London W1M 0MB
Useful packs and information on diabetes

British Nutrition Foundation, High Holborn House, 52–4 High Holborn, London WC1V 6RQ
Up-to-date information on food issues

Caroline Walker Trust, 6 Aldridge Road Villas, London W11 1BP
Eating Well for Older People – and other documents available

DATA (Design and Technology Association), 16 Wellesbourne House, Walton Road, Warwicks CV35 9JB
Support information for food technology

Department of Health, PO Box 410, Wetherby LS23 7LN
Many pamphlets, especially on hygiene

Federation of Bakers, 20 Bedford Square, London WC1B 3HF
Information on bread

Food and Drink Federation, 6 Catherine St, London WC2B 5JJ
Information on food issues

Hampshire Microtechnology Centre, Connaught Lane, Portsmouth PO6 4SJ
Computer programs such as 'Nutrients'

Health Education Authority, Hamilton House, Mabledon Place, London WC1H 9TX
Useful leaflets on many issues

HMSO, PO Box 276, London SW8 5DT
Dietary Reference Values, 'Health of the Nation'

Kellogg Co Ltd, The Kellogg Building, Talbot Rd, Manchester
Nutrition information

Leatherhead Food HRA, Randalls Road, Leatherhead, Surrey KT22 7RY
Food Intolerance databank information

LoSalt, Klinge, East Kilbride, Scotland G75 0QX
LoSalt information

MAFF, National Food Survey, Room 513, Whitehall Place, London SW1A 2HH
Free publications including 'Food Sense'

Marks & Spencer plc, 47 Baker St, London W1A 1DN
Up-to-date information on food issues

Meat and Livestock Commission, Winterhill House, Snowdon Drive, Milton Keynes MK6 1AX
Information on meat

NATHE, Hamilton House, Mabledon Place, London WC1H 9TX
Information on home economics and food technology

National Dairy Council, 5–7 John Princes St, London W1M 0AP
A range of information on nutrition issues

National Heart Forum, Tavistock House South, Tavistock Square, London WC1H 9LG
SMAP (School Meals Assessment Pack)
Nutrition Information

Panasonic UK Ltd, Panasonic House, Willoughby Rd, Bracknell, Berks RG12 8SP
Microwave information

Soya Milk Information Bureau, Box 169, Banbury, Oxon OX16 9X
Information on soya milk

The Boots Co plc, Freepost, City Gate House, Nottingham NG2 3BR

Nutritional information

Whitworths Ltd, Victoria Mills, Wellingborough, Northants NN8 2DT
Information on dried foods

Women's Royal Voluntary Service, 234–44 Stockwell Road, London SW9 9SP
Information on Meals on Wheels

Examinations Boards

London Examinations (ULEAC), Stewart House, 32 Russell Square, London WC1B 5DN.

Midland Examining Group (MEG), Mill Wharf, Mill St, Birmingham B6 4BU

Northern Examinations and Assessment Board (NEAB), 12 Harter St, Manchester M1 6HL

RSA Examinations Board, Westwood Way, Coventry, CV4 8HS

Southern Examining Group (SEG), Stag Hill House, Guildford, Surrey GU2 5XJ

Welsh Joint Education Committee (WJEC), 245 Western Avenue, Cardiff CF5 2YX

Supermarkets

Asda Stores Ltd, Asda House, Great Wilson St, Leeds LS11 5AD

Co-op, CWS Ltd, Freepost MR9 473, Manchester M4 8BA

Gateway Foodmarkets Ltd, Gateway House, Hawkfield Business Park, Whitchurch Lane, Bristol BS14 0TJ

Safeway Stores plc, 6 Millington Road, Hayes, Middx UB3 4AY

J. Sainsbury plc, Stamford St, London SE1 9LI

Tesco Stores Ltd, Cheshunt, EN8 9SL

Waitrose Ltd, Bracknell, Berkshire RG12 4AY

Sample tasks and questions

Examples of an individual task and a resource task adapted from MEG Home Economics: Food and Nutrition

INDIVIDUAL TASK

Task title

You hear that the large company your friend is working for is intending to manufacture foods from raisins, nuts, flour and similar products. Your friend has been asked to design and promote a range of healthy processed foods with a traditional, wholesome theme. You intend to assist your friend with the project design.

Area of syllabus content/development

Preservation, marketing, advertising and consumer legislation.

Assessment areas

Task analysis, development and planning, execution, evaluation.

Task analysis

First, you should identify the main factors involved in designing and promoting this new range of healthy foods. Your initial research should take into account ranges already on the market. The promotion of the product range would need to be original and appealing, yet clear and honest. It should aim to give consumers accurate information, as well as to attract them to buy the products. You will need to identify the classification of preserved or convenience foods and to research successful methods of preservation. You will also need to consider suitable labelling, packaging and presentation as a shop window display.

Development and planning

You could consider a range of possible ideas before you decide upon your course of action. Record your activities, observations, results and conclusions for every product you make. This will help you to decide what modifications you need to make to the final product range. Remember to take into account value for money, profit margins and marketing/advertising the products, as well as what packaging would be suitable.

Execution

Organization

You should make your final product range, outlining and following a clear plan of action. Bear in mind the limitations of time and the importance of presentation for window displays. Take care with attention to detail, and decide how you will deal with waste. Remember also the importance of quality control.

Skills

You will need to show that you have good manipulative skills, using equipment correctly and safely. Follow hygienic working practices. Prepare suitable packaging for the products.

Outcomes

You could fill in a practical activity record sheet. Include in it details of the materials chosen, the quantity, type, and cost. Make sure there are also details of technique and sequence, the time taken to prepare the product, the cooking and the packaging, describing any finishing touches such as wrapping and containers. You should produce a range of products which fulfil the task set.

Evaluation

You will need to evaluate the effectiveness of your plan and the final outcome, and how well it meets the task specification. Comment on the general appearance, flavour, texture, shelf-life, value, nutritional content, cost, packaging and labelling. Finally, identify any changes you would make.

RESOURCE TASK
Task title

Breakfast is an important meal. Without breakfast we may well be tempted to fill up on sweets and snacks which, in excess, are not good for us. Select a suitable breakfast and:

a plan how you will prepare, cook and serve the breakfast
b carry out your plan by cooking the chosen breakfast for yourself
c evaluate your task.

Task introduction

Task analysis, development and planning, execution, evaluation.

* **Food choices** – investigate the role of breakfast. Carry out a survey to find out the nutritional value of typical breakfasts eaten in UK. Discuss suitable, healthy breakfast choices as a lead into the task set.
* **Possible resources** – books, results of class investigation, nutrition databases.

Assessment areas

Planning, execution – organization/skills, outcome, evaluation.

Exemplar assignments from NEAB Home Economics: Food and Nutrition

The assignments will involve both written and practical work. For NEAB, the assignment should include:

* a statement of the assignment
* relevant factors and priorities
* evidence of testing, observing, recording decisions with supporting reasons
* evaluation of all stages of work.

Exemplar assignments

a Eating snack food and fast food has become a way of life. Carry out an investigation to show that healthy, nutritious snack meals can be prepared in preference to commercially available ones.

b People are being encouraged to eat more non-starch polysaccharide (dietary fibre). Carry out an investigation into the importance of increasing NSP in the diet, suggesting a range of healthy, palatable NSP rich dishes.

c We are advised to eat 4–6 helpings of fruit and vegetables a day. Show how this can be achieved for a sixteen year old.

d The school canteen is losing many of its customers to outlets outside school. How can you adapt the menu and bring customers back?

e Young children do not always like the foods that they should eat for health reasons. This can be a constant battle for parents. Devise a series of dishes that parents could serve to encourage their children to eat the correct foods.

f *The food choices that we make are influenced by the multi-cultural society in which we live.* Investigate this statement and use a range of dishes to illustrate your findings.

g Providing healthy, economical meals day after day can be difficult. Carry out an investigation which would help consumers choose suitable foods and prepare a range of dishes.

h Foods can be preserved in many ways at home or by food manufacturers. Investigate the range of ways of preserving foods. Include some comparisons between home-made and commercial equivalents.

i People are being encouraged to eat more starchy foods. Investigate the way in which the use of staple foods can help in this. Show how interesting, nutritious meals can be prepared in the minimum amount of time.

j Adopting a vegetarian diet seems to be a current dietary trend. A basic knowledge of nutrition is important in order to avoid nutritional deficiencies. Carry out an investigation into the nutritional adequacy of vegetarian diets.

Food Acts

Food Safety Act 1990
A detailed booklet, 'The Food Safety Act and You', is available from Food Sense, London SE99 7TT.

Food Labelling Regulations 1984
Includes declaration on additives.

Food Composition Regulations
Regulations for specific food products such as bread.

Food Additives Labelling Regulations 1992
Defines food additives and lays down labelling requirements.

Food, Control of Irradiation Regulations 1990
Implements the control system through which applications to use the process shall be granted.

The Genetically Modified Organisms Regulations 1992
Controls the use of genetically modified organisms.

**Food Hygiene
The Food Safety (General Food Hygiene) Regulations 1995**
Places an obligation on food business proprietors to ensure their activities are carried out in a hygienic way.

The Food Safety (Temperature Control) Regulations 1995
Food business proprietors must observe certain temperature controls on the holding of food.

The Organic Products Regulations 1992
Sets rules for the production of food to be sold as organic.

The Trades Descriptions Act 1968
Makes it an offence for a person acting in the course of a trade or business to make false or misleading statements about goods.

The Weights and Measures Act 1985
Makes selling 'short weight' an offence.

The Consumer Protection Act 1987
Makes it an offence for the consumer to be given misleading statements about goods or services.

Source – The Food Safety Directorate, October 1995

Glossary

Artificial sweeteners   Products which provide an intense level of sweetness and are usually calorie-free, for example saccharin, aspartame, acesulfame-K.

Bacteria   Small microscopic organisms found all about us.

Basal metabolic rate (BMR)   The amount of energy needed to maintain the vital body functions which include breathing, keeping the heart beating and keeping the body warm.

Best-before date   Shows the consumer the period when the food product is in its best condition if kept according to the manufacturer's instructions.

Biotechnology   The industrial use of biological processes.

Blast-freeze   Freezing food quickly by blasting it with very cold air.

British Standards   Standards which set requirements for products and product performance and reliability. BS5750 (1979, 1987) relates to Quality Management Systems.

Calorie   A unit used to measure the energy value of food, usually stated in kilocalories (kcal).

Carbohydrate   Important source of the energy needed by the body, mainly found in sugars and starches.

Cholesterol   Substance made by the body, an essential part of every living cell.

Cold spots   Areas in food that is not heated properly, that occur in microwave ovens when an area cannot be reached by microwaves.

COMA   Committee on Medical Aspects of food policy – this committee provides the Government with advice on nutrition issues, published in the form of reports.

Cook-chill   A type of food production system when food is prepared, cooked and rapidly cooled then kept for a limited time under chilled storage before reheating.

Critical control points   Steps in the preparation of food which have to be carried out correctly to make sure that a hazard is removed or reduced to a safe level.

Cross-contamination   The transfer of a substance (e.g. microbes) from one area to another: one food can be contaminated with bacteria from another.

Danger zone   Temperature range within which multiplication of pathogenic bacteria is possible (5–63°C).

Dietary fibre (NSP)   The name used to describe the indigestible carbohydrates which are found in foods of plant origin, now called non-starch polysaccharide.

Dietary reference values (DRVs)   The values for healthy people which describe the range of desirable consumption levels of a particular nutrient by a population or a sub-group of a population; COMA's report on DRVs was published in 1991 – the figures are estimates of the range of requirements for nutrients in a healthy population.

Estimated average requirements (EARs)   The amounts of nutrients that most people need.

Energy measurement   Energy from food is measured in units called joules or calories;
1 kilojoule (kJ) = 1000 joules,
1 megajoule = 1 million joules,
1 kilocalorie (kcal) = 1000 calories.
(To convert between calories and joules:
1 kcal = 4.184 kJ, 1 MJ = 239 kcal.)

Energy needs   Energy needs for adults are determined by basal metabolic rates (BMR) and physical activity levels (PAL). The energy levels for adults (EARs) are worked out by multiplying the BMR by the physical activity level (PAL), i.e. EAR = BMR × PAL. (A PAL of 1.4 is used for most people in the UK as it represents a very low activity level.)

Environmental Health Officer (EHO)   The enforcement officer at local government level who covers public health such as the hygiene of food premises and food safety.

Enzyme   A protein produced by living cells that regulates the speed of the chemical reactions in the metabolism of living organisms, without itself being altered in the process; also called a biological catalyst.

Fat   A rich source of energy; fats are a mixture of different types of fatty acid: mono-unsaturated fatty acid, polyunsaturated fatty acid, saturated fatty acid.

Fibre   *see* non-starch polysaccharides (NSP).

Food poisoning   Illness caused by bacteria, chemicals or poisons in food.

Food processing   The way food is changed to turn it into something else; some food is preserved by freezing, and made safe by cooking.

Glucose   A simple sugar.

Glycogen   The form in which carbohydrate is stored in the liver.

Hazard Analysis and Critical Control Point (HACCP)   A system for caterers and food manufacturers used to control food safety procedures.

Hazard   Anything which can cause harm to a consumer: a hazard may be biological, such as salmonella in a chicken, physical, such as glass in food, or chemical, such as chemicals in food.

Hidden sugars   Sugars present in foods that cannot be easily recognized as sugars.

High biological value protein   A protein that contains all of the essential amino acids in adequate amounts.

High-risk foods   Prepared foods which are very suitable for bacterial growth. Examples include cooked meats, cooked chicken, eggs, mayonnaise and dairy products.

Hygiene   Keeping the work place clean and the workforce work in a clean way which is safe for health.

Intrinsic sugars   Sugars contained in fruit, vegetables and milk.

Macro-nutrients   The nutrients required in greater amounts by the body, i.e. carbohydrates, fats and protein.

MAFF   Ministry of Agriculture, Fisheries and Food.

Micro-organism   A microscopic organism.

Micro-nutrients   Nutrients which are needed in very small amounts, but which nonetheless are essential for health and the effective functioning of the body; vitamins and minerals are micro-nutrients.

Minerals   Elements or chemicals needed for normal growth and health, found in small quantities in foods.

Non-milk extrinsic (NME) sugars   These include table sugar, honey and found in cakes, biscuits and sweets.

Non-starch polysaccharides (NSP)   The new name for dietary fibre; includes a variety of different substances all with different properties. The two types of fibre are soluble NSP, which can help control the blood cholesterol levels as part of a low-fat, low-sugar diet and is found in oats, beans and lentils and fruit, and insoluble fibre, which is important for good health and adds bulk to faeces. It is found in fruit, vegetables, wholegrain breakfast cereals and bread.

Nutrients   The components of food which supply the body with material for energy, growth and repair, and substances which regulate vital body functions; the nutrients in food are fats, proteins, carbohydrates, vitamins and minerals.

Piping hot   Term for food that is hotter then 72°C, measured using a temperature probe.

Quality assurance   A system which aims to ensure that high quality in food is inbuilt by means of written procedures and communications.

Quality control   Operational techniques and activities that are used to fulfil requirements for quality of food (BS4778).

Quantitative Ingredient Declaration (QUID)   A system that is proposed for use on food labels, under which the amounts of certain ingredients which characterize a foodstuff will be declared, to show how much is present, for example in a chicken and ham pie.

Ranking   Placing samples of food or drink in order of preference.

Rating   Classification according to sensory analysis by people evaluating food samples under standard testing conditions.

Recommended daily amount (RDA)   The previous dietary recommendations for energy and nutrients; replaced by dietary reference values (DRVs).

Reference nutrient intake (RNI)   The amount of nutrient sufficient for most people.

Risk   The likelihood of a hazard occurring.

Salmonella   A family of bacteria which causes diseases including food poisoning.

Sensory analysis   A scientific discipline used to evoke, measure, analyse and interpret reactions to those characteristics of food and materials as they are perceived by the senses of sight, smell, taste, touch and hearing. (Institute of Food Technology.)

Sensory descriptors   A collection of adjectives which describe particular sensory properties dealing with such things as appearance, aroma, flavour, texture and after taste of a product, for example bitter, crunchy, granular, astringent.

Shelf-life   The period of time over which any particular food product can be expected to last under the recommended conditions of storage.

Special dietary needs   Some people cannot eat certain foods or drink – this may be for religious or health reasons.

Star profile   A drawing, made up of lines, which looks like a star. The characteristics of a product are plotted to show a profile of features. An apple could have characteristics of 'sweetness' and 'crispness'.

Tasting panel   A group of people who taste food and drink and give their views on characteristics like taste and texture; they may be trained or untrained.

Textured vegetable protein (TVP)   Protein made from soya beans and used as a meat substitute.

Toxin   Poison produced by a pathogen.

Trading Standards Officer   The enforcement officer at local government level who covers commercial law such as weights and measures and the correct labelling of food products.

Vitamins   Compounds needed for normal growth and health, found in small quantities in foods *see* micro-nutrients.

Index